V

# POSSIBLE

ALSO BY WILLIAM URY

*Getting to Yes*

*Beyond the Hotline*

*Getting Disputes Resolved*

*Getting Past No*

*Getting to Peace* (published in paperback as *The Third Side*)

*The Power of a Positive No*

*Getting to Yes with Yourself*

# POSS IBLE

*How We Survive (and Thrive)
in an Age of Conflict*

## WILLIAM URY

Foreword by JIM COLLINS

**HARPER
BUSINESS**

*An Imprint of HarperCollinsPublishers*

HarperCollins books may be purchased for educational, business, or sales promotional use. For information, please email the Special Markets Department at SPsales@harpercollins.com.

FIRST EDITION

*Designed by Nancy Singer*
*Illustrations by Jessica Palladino, Sillybird Design*

Library of Congress Cataloging-in-Publication Data
Names: Ury, William, author.
Title: Possible: how we survive (and thrive) in an age of conflict / William Ury.
Description: First edition. | New York, NY: HarperBusiness, [2023] |
Includes bibliographical references and index.
Identifiers: LCCN 2023020171 (print) | LCCN 2023020172 (ebook) |
  ISBN 9780063286900 (hardback) | ISBN 9780063286917 (ebook)
Subjects: LCSH: Conflict management. | Negotiation.
Classification: LCC HM1126 .U794 2023 (print) | LCC HM1126 (ebook) |
  DDC 303.6/9—dc23/eng/20230515
LC record available at https://lccn.loc.gov/2023020171
LC ebook record available at https://lccn.loc.gov/2023020172

23 24 25 26 27  LBC  5 4 3 2 1

*For Gabi*
*and all the possibilists to come*

*Hope is a passion for the possible.*

—Søren Kierkegaard (1813–1855)

# CONTENTS

THIRD VICTORY
# ENGAGE THE THIRD SIDE

# FOREWORD

On November 28, 2018, Bill Ury and I went for a hike on the Lion's Lair Trail just west of our hometown of Boulder, Colorado. It was one of those absolutely gorgeous fall afternoons, with the low light, the long shadows, and a golden glow from a late-season warm snap before the descent of winter. As we became enveloped in the bubble of our conversation, I found myself captured by the story of his behind-the-scenes efforts to defuse the growing tensions between the United States and North Korea. As with all of our walks, Bill and I got lost in discussing a wide range of topics—from the enduring lessons of the Cuban Missile Crisis to the future of the Middle East to the challenges of family businesses torn apart by squabbling heirs and even to the ultimate challenge of wrestling with the debilitating conflicts each of us carries inside.

On this walk, I was particularly struck by Bill's rare ability to bring calm and optimism to seemingly intractable conflicts and by his blend of intellectual clarity and practical wisdom. This led me to ask him a question: "If you had to boil your life's work down to just one sentence you could leave behind, what would it say?" Bill went quiet for a few uphill switchbacks, then replied, "Great question. I need to answer that." And by the time we'd descended the final switchbacks as the sun fell behind the hills, Bill had already begun thinking out loud about the sentence and how he could construct a book around it.

The only book to write is the one you cannot *not* write.

Whenever someone asks me for advice about writing a book, the first thing I tell them is that they should do everything they can *not* to write it. In response to the initial impulse to write a book, the primary response should be "No! I will not write it." And when the impulse returns to respond in kind: "I refuse to capitulate to the suffering required to write a book. I will not throw myself into the monster struggle of making ideas and words and pages and structure all come together in a coherent work. I will not do it!" But if the book idea keeps coming back at you, grabbing you around the throat and delivering the unmistakable message "You *must* write me"—if despite your most valiant and persistent efforts to banish the idea from your brain, it simply will not go away, you just might have a book worth writing. And this is especially true if you are the one best person to write the book; if you don't create it, no one else can or will.

This book meets that test. The "one-sentence" challenge lodged itself in Bill's brain and would not let go. And as he describes in these pages, he accomplished the single sentence, one born of cumulative experience and penetrating insight. With sentence in hand, he dedicated himself to the task of creating this book. In a sense, Bill had a distinctive responsibility to synthesize his life's work to date, not just for the enduring intellectual contribution but also because it arrives at a perfect moment in our divisive zeitgeist.

There are three reasons why Bill is the one best person to write this book.

First, he has deep intellectual foundations and a body of work to build upon. The big questions he circles back to in this text have roots in his seminal book *Getting to Yes*, coauthored with Roger Fisher, which has guided people through stressful, high-stakes negotiations for more than four decades. *Getting to Yes* is a true classic. Then he built on those ideas in further works, including *Getting Past No* and *Getting to Yes with Yourself* (a personal favorite). But in fact, the roots of his dedication to conflict resolution had already taken hold more than a decade before he met and worked with Roger Fisher. On one of our hikes around Boulder, I asked, "When did you first discover your interest in and instinct for what became your life's work?" Bill's answer: "Before age ten, when going to a school in Switzerland that had a bomb shelter. It was right around the time of the Cuban Missile Crisis, and that just clicked something in me." In a sense, Bill has been working toward the sentence that forms the seed architecture of this book for fully six decades.

Second, his insights are beyond the merely intellectual; they are deeply practical. I see Bill as a tactile researcher with the world as his laboratory. Instead of sharpening his intellect and insights by doing research sitting in a plush faculty office at some Ivy League institute, Bill decided early to "go to the hardest places first," throwing himself into working on political negotiations in the Middle East. Drawing upon decades of hands-on experience, he has learned *what works* in complicated and contentious negotiations. How to prepare. How to zoom out to see clearly. (I often think of Bill's "go to the balcony" metaphor when I need to calm my emotions and see a conflict from a larger and different perspective.) How to create solutions that can work for both or all parties. (I've always appreciated his metaphor of "building the golden bridge"—the notion of constructing a durable structure across the straits of contention to connect both sides.) How to activate a broader community to help both sides want to build that golden bridge. How to hold firm to the non-negotiables while finding a successful compromise. How to say no by saying yes to something even better, not only for yourself but for the entire community. How to get yourself to accept what is best—for you and others—when your emotions get in the way of your self-interest. Yet behind all his "how to" skills, Bill always has an intellectual framework, a deep understanding not just of *what* works but of *why* it works.

Third, Bill Ury is in a rare category of thought leaders who have made the journey from smart intellect to wise sage. With this book, Bill is in full-on sage mode. The world will always veer toward war and violence; the verdict of history does not support the idea that the inevitable trajectory of human society is peace and cooperation. Bill understands that a propensity for conflict is buried deep in our DNA. He begins all of his teaching, writing, and practical work with a realistic understanding of human behavior, the will to power, and realpolitik. Yet at the same time, he remains a practical idealist, dedicated to the proposition that the pursuit of peace and collaboration is *also* part of our human nature and social self-interest. He is the champion of a simple, powerful thesis: that the pursuit of peaceful resolution, even amid intractable conflicts, is a signature of strength and wisdom, not of weakness. And most of all, he shows us that it is possible.

*Jim Collins*
Boulder, Colorado
April 2023

# POSSIBLE

# CHAPTER 1

# THE PATH TO POSSIBLE

*We are continually faced with great*
*opportunities which are brilliantly disguised*
*as unsolvable problems.*
—Margaret Mead

It was a phone call that would change my life.

On a freezing Sunday night in early January 1977, the phone rang at 10:00 p.m. I was living in a little rented room in the attic of an old wooden house in Cambridge, Massachusetts, just up the street from the anthropology museum at Harvard University. I was twenty-three, writing term papers, reading the assignments of the students I was teaching, and studying hard for my graduate school exams in social anthropology.

When I picked up the phone, the voice at the other end of the line sounded strong and clear: "This is Professor Roger Fisher. Thanks for sending me your paper. I liked your anthropological lens for looking at the Middle East peace talks. I took the liberty of sending the main chart to the assistant secretary of state for the Middle East. I've been advising him, and I thought he might find your ideas useful as he plans for the negotiations."

I was speechless. Was I dreaming? I don't think I had ever been called by a professor, let alone on a weekend. And it had certainly never occurred to me that an idea that had popped into my head while writing a student paper could be of practical use to a high government official in Washington working on what was widely perceived as the world's most challenging international conflict.

Like many young people my age, I was trying to figure out what I wanted to do with my life. Anthropology—the study of human cultures and societies—was fascinating, but something was missing for me. I was longing to pour my time and energy into a project that could help people in a more direct and practical way. I wondered: Could I apply what I was learning to a major human dilemma that defied current solutions—the perennial problem of conflict and war?

Professor Fisher continued speaking:

"I would like you to come work with me. What do you say?"

"Yes," I stammered. "I'd love to."

So what was the idea in my paper that Professor Fisher liked? It arose from a simple thought experiment. Looking at the walls of my little plain attic room, I had imagined myself as an anthropologist, a fly on the wall, in an ornate room in the Palais des Nations in Geneva, Switzerland, where the Middle East peace negotiations were expected to take place. I asked myself a question: What could I observe from the way the parties were talking that would indicate whether the negotiations were going poorly or going well?

If the talks were going poorly, I posited, I would hear the nego-tiators blaming one another. They would be mired in the past. They would be focused on what was wrong.

If the talks were going well, I would hear something very different. Instead of dwelling on the *past*, the talks would be focused on the *present* and the *future*. Instead of harping on *what was wrong*, the negotiators would be discussing *what could be done*. Instead of *attacking one another*, they would be *attacking the problem* jointly.

In other words, I was simply suggesting that the *way* in which those in conflict talk with one another could either close down or open up new possibilities for agreement.

That late-night phone call from Roger Fisher was the start of my initiation into the art of opening up possibilities in seemingly intractable conflicts. Learning that art would become my life's quest.

## MY LIFELONG QUESTION

Roger Fisher's generous invitation tapped into a calling I had felt for almost as long as I can remember. I spent much of my childhood growing up in Europe, then still recovering from two world wars whose untold horrors had taken the lives of tens of millions. The suffering was still palpable in the ruined buildings and the hushed stories shared by traumatized survivors—even to a child who had not experienced it directly.

On top of that, a third world war loomed on the horizon, this time apocalyptic because of the atomic bomb. We didn't talk about it much because it was just too dreadful to think about and there didn't seem much that anyone could do about it. But there were vivid reminders. My school in Switzerland housed a mandatory nuclear bomb shelter. In the winter, it doubled as our ski storage, so I visited it often, getting an occasional chill down my spine as I paused at the massive steel blast door hinged at the entrance.

"I don't get it," I would say to my friends as I grew older. "Anytime there is a crisis between us and the Russians, the leaders can decide to launch a nuclear war that would blow the whole world to smithereens. How can this be? There's got to be a better way to deal with our issues!"

Children from many nationalities, cultures, and faiths attended my school, but we generally seemed to get along. And the disputes that did arise were interpersonal, not between groups. So, even as a boy, it wasn't hard for me to imagine a world in which we could all coexist relatively peacefully.

Conflict was present not just in the world but at home, whenever I watched my parents quarrel at the family dinner table. I found it painful to hear and tried to distract them if I could. It dawned on me that conflict affects everything in our lives—from the happiness of our families to our ultimate survival as a species.

The basic question I kept coming back to, as a curious teenager, was this: *How can we deal with our deepest differences without destroying all that we hold dear?* How can we find a way to live and work together—even with inevitable conflicts?

I studied anthropology in college to search for answers to this question, hoping to learn more about human nature and culture. Anthropologists often study small endangered communities facing external threats. The endangered community I worried about was humanity and the existential danger we pose to ourselves. Why do we so often fall into destructive conflict whenever a serious difference arises between people, between groups, or between nations?

But I didn't want to just study; I wanted to get my hands dirty. One thing I loved about anthropology was the idea that, to truly understand another culture, you need to become both a participant *and* an observer. I wanted to participate in conflicts, not merely observe them from the sidelines. I wanted to get into the thick of the action and practice the art of negotiation in the places that were the most resistant to resolution.

That one phone call led me on a journey of almost fifty years wandering the world as an anthropologist and negotiator, using real-life conflicts to stimulate answers to the basic question: What does it take to transform tough conflicts from destructive confrontation into collaborative negotiation?

I have asked this question in many traditional cultures, from the Kua community of the Kalahari to the clan warriors of New Guinea. And I have asked myself this question as I experimented with different approaches in the toughest conflicts I could find— from bitter coal strikes to US-Soviet nuclear confrontation, from boardroom battles to family feuds, and from partisan political strife to wars in the Middle East. I sought out the hardest and highest-stake conflicts, figuring that whatever methods worked on them would probably work anywhere.

I have also asked this question in conflicts with my own family and the people I love. I have learned from the setbacks as well as from the successes.

Through all these experiments, my original hunch as a boy has been confirmed: There are far better ways to handle our most serious differences. As human beings, we have a *choice*.

## WE LIVE IN AN AGE OF CONFLICT

As I look around at the conflicts we face today, I see that the simple but powerful lessons I have learned on this lifelong quest have never been more needed.

Conflict is all around us, and it is intensifying. Every day—in our homes, in our workplaces, in our country, and in the world—we are confronted by the headache and heartache of contentious disputes.

More than at any other time I can recall, destructive conflicts are *polarizing* our communities, *poisoning* our relationships, and *paralyzing* our ability to address our most critical issues. How many needs are we sacrificing, and how many opportunities are we losing, for lack of a better way of dealing with our differences?

Ironically, after many decades of working on intractable political conflicts in the wider world, I find an intractable conflict tearing apart my own country. Unthinkable as the prospect may seem, more than two in five Americans, according to recent polls, fear that the country may be sliding into a civil war. I have never seen such levels of fear, anger, and contempt for the other side. Nor have I seen such depths of resignation, numbness, and despair—so many people throwing their hands into the air and concluding that they are powerless to change the situation for the better.

The phenomenon of polarization is not limited to the United States; it is a global trend, separating families, communities, and societies around the world. "Because of political differences, my brother doesn't show up for our traditional family get-togethers. My mother is heartbroken. It's gone too far," laments a close friend in Brazil.

If anthropologists living a thousand years from now were to

look back at this moment, they might call this *the era of the human family reunion*. For the first time in human history, thanks to the communications revolution, virtually all fifteen thousand language communities are in touch with one another. Yet, as in many family reunions, it's not all peace and harmony. There is a lot of conflict.

Never before in human evolution have people faced the challenge of living with billions of others in one single community. Far from bringing a lessening of conflict, the reunion means a heightening of hostilities as people are forced to confront their differences, as resentments over inequities flare up, and as identities are threatened by different customs and beliefs. Coming together can produce more heat than light, more conflict than understanding as our differences come to the fore.

Thanks to our new ways of communicating, we are much more aware of conflicts in other parts of the world than ever before. We are inundated around the clock with news of strife and war. And, if anything, our new media for communication are designed to focus on conflict—and intensify it—if only because it captures our attention and attention brings profit.

Conflict is not going away. We live in a time of enormous accelerating changes of all kinds: new technologies like artificial intelligence, economic dislocations, environmental disruptions, demographic shifts, just to name a few big ones. The pace shows no sign of slowing down but rather seems to be speeding up. More change naturally means more conflict.

And here's the kicker: *The world needs more conflict, not less.*

I know this may sound strange, but hear me out.

What is conflict? It can be defined as *a clash between opposing positions arising from a perceived divergence of interests and perspectives.*

In my work, I often come across the common assumption that conflict is a bad thing. I used to hold that assumption myself. But as an anthropologist and mediator, I have come to appreciate that *conflict is natural.* It is part of life itself. Simply by virtue of being human, we have different perspectives and interests. Conflict arises when we express our differences—or even when we don't.

Conflict, in fact, can be perfectly healthy. The best decisions result not from a superficial consensus but from surfacing different points of view and searching for creative solutions. Conflict lies at the heart of the democratic process as well as our modern economies, where, in the form of business competition, it helps create prosperity.

Imagine for a moment a world without conflict of any kind. How would injustices be redressed? How would abuses of power be corrected? And how would constructive change come about in our families, workplaces, and communities?

Facing challenges is how we as individuals and groups learn, grow, and change. Conflict provides that challenge, stimulating us and our societies to evolve. As my friend and mediation colleague Claire Hajaj remarked to me recently, *"Constructive conflict is the foundation of human growth."*

So how can we deal with our differences constructively?

## THE WAY OUT IS THROUGH

As I was writing this book, I had the opportunity to participate in a two-week rafting expedition down the length of the Grand Canyon.

While our hardy boat captains steered us around huge rocks, plunging over steep rapids in the great Colorado River, I sought some perspective on the question of how to navigate conflicts in these turbulent times. Perspective on our human drama came more easily as I gazed up at the immense canyon walls, thousands of feet high and billions of years old. All of human history would have fit into a few inches of those towering cliffs.

Deep within the embrace of the canyon walls, far from the maddening swirl of news and social media, I asked a fellow river traveler, a seventy-year-old dairy farmer from Wisconsin named George Siemon, a question:

"George, why is our country having so much trouble agreeing on anything? What are you hearing in your conversations with farmers?"

"William," he answered, "everyone feels stuck. Instead of solving problems, people are pointing fingers. Or giving up altogether on one another. And the problems just get worse.

"What I tell young people these days is 'We've got the *solutions*. We've even got the *money*. We just can't figure out *how to work together*. That's the challenge now!"

George's challenge resonated with me. We live in a world of possibilities—possible futures for ourselves, our families, and our communities. Many are hopeful but some are positively scary. In the end, it depends on us. We have enormous opportunities to make life better for everyone—*if only* we can work together.

We are not going to eliminate conflict—nor should we.

*The real problem is not conflict but rather the destructive way we deal with it.*

*What if* we tried a different approach—a contrarian one? Instead of escalating conflict or avoiding it, what if we did the opposite? What if we turned toward it and met it with curiosity and collaboration?

This is what I learned while rafting the Grand Canyon. Once we got onto the river, there was no way out for many days. The big rapids with their giant, cold waves were coming, whether we liked it or not. We had little choice but to run them. And the best way to do so was not to resist the experience of getting cold and wet but to *lean into* the experience, meet the high waves, and paddle together like hell.

In short, *the only way out is through.*

It may feel like the last thing we want to do, but *what if* we actually *embraced* conflict? What if we wrapped our arms around it? What if we applied our full human potential to conflict—our natural capacities for curiosity, creativity, and collaboration?

In my work, I find that people naturally assume that conflict needs to be *resolved*. But is that true? I used to assume that myself. After all, I was working in the field of conflict *resolution*. But over the years, I have come to appreciate that often resolution is not possible, at least not now. In some cases, resolution is not even desirable because it deprives us of the opportunity to keep learning and growing through conflict. The truth is that we don't *always* need to agree.

Instead of trying to resolve conflict and reach agreement, can we aim for something more realistic and more sustainable than resolution? What if we were to focus on *transforming* conflict?

*To transform simply means to change the form of conflict—from destructive fighting into productive conflict and constructive negotiation.*

Instead of destroying the things we value, what if we were to create the things we value by opening up new possibilities for living with one another?

Transforming conflict is larger than reaching agreement. It means transforming the way we deal with one another and our differences. It means transforming our *relationships*. Agreements are finite and often transactional; they come and go. Transformation is relational and can continue long into the future. *Agreements are outcomes; transformation is a process.* And unlike some agreements that may take a long time to reach, transforming conflict can start right away.

When Roger Fisher, Bruce Patton, and I worked on *Getting to Yes* more than forty years ago, "yes" meant a mutually satisfying agreement. Today, I believe that the meaning of yes must be expanded. The new yes means to lean in and embrace conflicts for all they have to offer us. The new yes is a *transformative yes*.

If we can embrace and transform our conflicts, we can learn to live and work together. And if we can do that, as my friend George pointed out on the rushing river, there is no problem, large or small, that we cannot address.

## POSSIBLE IS THE NEW YES

After all these years of working on seemingly impossible conflicts, people often ask me:

"Are you an optimist or a pessimist?"

"Actually," I answer, "I am a *possibilist*."

I have a passion for the possible.

I believe in our *human potential* to get to yes—our ability to deal with our differences constructively.

I believe in our innate human capacity to cooperate even as we may disagree strongly.

I believe that no matter how challenging a conflict may be, we can learn to *work it out*.

In short, I believe that we can survive—*and thrive*—in this age of conflict.

Possible does not mean easy. There are no quick fixes. Dealing with conflicts can be *the hardest work we humans can do*. It takes patience and a lot of persistence. Hard, however, does not mean impossible. The work can be both hard *and* possible.

Possible does not mean an end to conflict. It doesn't mean "won and done." In most of the situations I have worked, tensions continue, conflict continues, but the destruction, the violence, the war can come to an end.

Possible does not mean a neat resolution. More often it means gradual improvements in relationships that over time can make a big difference. Relationships can be messy. Possible means finding ways forward where there seem to be none. It means creating little breakthroughs that can build into bigger breakthroughs over time. Possible means gradual transformation.

Possible means applying our full human potential to the conflicts surrounding us. It means using our innate capacities of curiosity, creativity, and collaboration to open up new possibilities that we had not imagined before.

In conflicts where we feel stuck, trapped, and frustrated, possible means freedom, choice, and opportunities.

*Possible is the new yes.*

Why am I a possibilist? Because I have seen with my own eyes what humans can do. I have seen the seemingly impossible become possible.

During the 1980s, I spent a decade working on averting an

accidental nuclear war, with frequent trips to Washington and Moscow. I witnessed the remarkable transformation of the US-Soviet relationship as the Berlin Wall fell and the Cold War came to an end, against all odds and expectations.

When I first visited South Africa in the late 1980s to understand the conflict firsthand and offer training on negotiation, experienced political observers believed that it would take decades and perhaps only a bloody all-out civil war to end the racist system of apartheid. Instead, in a few short years, contrary to almost all predictions, the destructive conflict was transformed and Nelson Mandela, who had been imprisoned for twenty-seven years, was elected to the presidency.

In more recent years, I had the opportunity to serve as an advisor to the president of Colombia as he sought to do what most people in his country imagined was utterly impossible: to end a civil war that had persisted for almost half a century. Hundreds of thousands of people had died, and there had been more than 8 million victims. It took six years of hard negotiation, but in the end a historic peace was forged and, to everyone's surprise, the main guerrilla force laid down their weapons.

My experience has not been limited to wars. I've watched families heal their feuds. I've witnessed bitter business rivals become friends again. I've seen leaders from all sides of the political spectrum in my own country learn to work together. I have seen human beings from all walks of life rise to the challenge of turning destructive confrontation into productive negotiation.

*If it has happened before, I believe it can happen again.*

I am not naïve about the dark side of humanity. After almost five decades, often working in what sometimes feels like the heart of darkness, I am not one to underestimate the capacity for human ignorance and cruelty. I have also witnessed the *negative* possibilities of conflict.

More than forty years ago, I had a chance to spend an afternoon, without another person around, in the remains of the Nazi death camp in Treblinka, Poland. I walked in the high grass amid rows of long raised mounds speckled with whitish bone fragments. I suspected, although I did not know for sure, that many of my extended family were buried in those mounds. I felt that every soul there was someone's family and therefore family to all of us. I experienced waves of sadness, without words to express the inhumanity we are capable of inflicting on our fellow human beings. Silently, I made a vow to myself that I would not sit still but do everything in my power to help avert the nuclear holocaust threatening us all.

Thirteen years later, while I was working on the war in Yugoslavia, I went to visit a temporary encampment of Bosnian Muslim refugees with an old childhood friend, Peter Galbraith, then the US ambassador to Croatia. The refugees were trapped in a kilometer-wide zone between a row of Serbian tanks on one side and a row of Croatian tanks on the other, all pointing their big guns at the no-man's-land in between. Escorted by Canadian UN peacekeepers equipped with flak jackets and automatic weapons, Peter and I walked past the tanks and soldiers into the ruins of a village. The houses were mostly destroyed. A stray missile was stuck in the trunk of a tree.

Thousands of women, men, and children were camped out in flimsy tents that provided little protection as the cold winter approached. They seemed utterly disoriented and had nowhere to go. Land mines surrounded them on all sides, and every few days a person would step on one by accident and lose a foot or a leg.

Poignantly, we arrived just as a woman had given birth in a make-shift hospital ward in a school gym. I could not help but reflect how these innocents symbolized the plight of humanity, caught between nuclear superpowers prepared at an instant's notice to unleash cataclysmic destruction. It was one more vivid reminder of the negative possibilities of conflict.

Most recently, while writing this book, my principal conflict work has focused on the terrible, tragic war in Ukraine. The negative possibilities are on full display as the world finds itself, three and a half decades after the fall of the Berlin Wall, in a dangerous new conflict between Russia and the West. As in the first half of the twentieth century, Europe once again is the scene of fierce battles and atrocities. The nuclear sword of Damocles hangs perilously over our heads. It almost seems as if we have come full circle.

I had originally intended to focus just on writing this past year, but I found myself unable to sit back and do nothing. As I write these words, I am seriously engaged in frequent conversations with Ukrainians and Russians, Americans and Chinese, British, French, and many others, working on practical measures that can mitigate the horrors and help bring the war to an end. I am just off a call in which our Ukrainian colleague recounted how, on one single ten-kilometer stretch of front lines in the midst of winter, a hundred soldiers were being killed each day on each side. And that is just one stretch as the days and weeks and months roll by.

To be a *possibilist* means to look negative possibilities squarely in the eye and use them as motivation to search persistently for the positive possibilities. The work is never done. Possible does not mean inevitable or even probable. Possible simply means possible.

Whether possible becomes a reality depends on us.

## WHAT IS MADE BY US CAN BE CHANGED BY US

Thirty years ago, I trekked deep into the rainforests of Malaysia to visit what many anthropologists consider the most peaceful tribe on the planet, the Semai. I wanted to understand how they deal with their conflicts.

They received me with traditional hospitality in a large bamboo house on stilts in the jungle. A dozen families shared the same space, eating and sleeping together. The next morning, after a night's sleep on a bamboo platform, I finally took the chance to ask one of their elders a question I had long wondered about:

"Why don't your people make war?"

"War?" he asked, puzzled for a moment as he reflected on the question. Then he looked directly at me and replied through a colleague of mine who was translating:

"Typhoons, earthquakes, and tsunamis are forces of nature we cannot control. But war is made by us. Therefore, it can be stopped by us."

He spoke as if the answer were obvious. For him, I suppose it was, seeing how successfully his community dealt with its toughest conflicts. As he offered this explanation, passing on the practical wisdom of his people, it resonated deeply with me. It is as close to the *possibilist* credo as I can imagine.

The challenge we face is not in the outside world but inside us. It is not a technical problem but a human one. What is *made* by us can be *changed* by us. It *is* possible.

As the Semai elder implied, we humans have the natural innate capacities to manage our differences constructively. As an anthropologist, I have long marveled at how we evolved as intensely social, highly communicative, deeply curious, and extraordinarily creative primates. Collaborative problem solving is our great human strength. That's how we have survived and thrived.

Although violence is a natural capacity of ours, so are the tools to stop it. They are the evolutionary heritage we have received as a gift from our ancestors. They are our *birthright*, ours to draw on and deploy skillfully in these challenging times. Our task is not to evolve something entirely new but rather to remember what we already know how to do and apply it to the challenges of today.

## LET'S GO FOR A WALK

Some years ago, I took a long walk in the Rocky Mountains near my home with my neighbor and friend Jim Collins, the author of leadership classics such as *Good to Great*. As we were climbing up a steep slope, Jim turned to me and asked:

"How do you retain your sense of possibility at such a dark time in the world?"

I looked out at the magnificent view of peaks and valleys stretching out before us and replied:

"Jim, it's true that we've grown far more polarized, both as a nation and around the world, and that these times may look darker than others. But in what may have seemed like better times, I was always working in the darkest, most difficult situations. It's the possibilities I see that keep me going. What better choice is there?"

"Then," said Jim, "why don't you write a book that synthesizes all that you've learned to help others realize those possibilities in these troubled times?"

That is this book.

I love to go for long walks in nature. Walking gives me clarity and perspective, inspiration and creative ideas. And it gives me the energy and sustenance I need to tackle challenging conflicts.

I would like to invite you to take an imaginary walk with me. On this journey, I hope to pass on to you the distilled lessons I have discovered about the *path to possible*, as I have sought to open windows of possibility in some of the most intractable conflicts. While this book is intended to be practical, it is not a how-to book. It is less about method and more about mindset. *The possibilist mindset is a curious, creative, and collaborative way of engaging with our differences in these divided times.*

Perhaps the most powerful way to pass on lessons, one deeply ingrained in our nature since prehistoric times, is to tell stories. Stories are what we remember most and how we learn best. So I will take the liberty of telling you my own stories—from the professional to the personal—in the hope that they will capture the essence of what I have gleaned. In my other books, I mostly shared the stories of others. In this one, I will stick mostly to my own experiences because they are the ones from which I have learned the most. I have organized these stories so that they highlight the key openings I have discovered along the path to possible.

In many of the stories, I will report conversations based either on notes taken immediately afterward and, in certain cases, on my memory alone, which I acknowledge may be fallible. In a couple of instances where the people involved were not public figures, I've changed names to protect their privacy.

Some readers may recognize a few of the stories from my other books. If I return to them, it is because they were major learning experiences for me and because, in revisiting them, I aim to uncover new insights. I have sought to tell these stories here with greater granularity and specificity, hoping you will find something new in them—just as I have.

Because the nature of my work has been to seek out the world's toughest, most impactful conflicts, I have drawn many of my stories from intense political situations—from the so-called halls of power—but let me assure you that these conflicts in their essence share many similarities with the everyday family and work conflicts we all know. The scale may be bigger, but the dynamics are similar. A conflict is a conflict; humans are humans; and the deeper lessons can be applied across the board.

I am aware that my experiences in larger-scale conflicts have involved mostly men, either as parties or even as third parties. This great imbalance is, thankfully, beginning to even out. All too often unacknowledged, women have always been influential third parties and peacemakers in the conflicts around us—at work, at home, and in the world. In many places around the planet, they are increasingly breaking through the barriers that have stood in the way of their full participation. I am very glad to see that the majority of people in the workshops I teach are now women. While there is still much work to be done, it gives me great hope for our future.

As we walk together and I describe *my path to possible*, I invite you to look at the conflicts that are challenging you—whether you are directly involved or simply concerned. What is *your path to possible*?

While I write these words, I am newly a grandfather. I had the indescribable joy of cradling my grandson, Diego, in my arms for an hour on the first day he was born. I felt the pure potential of his being, so fresh and utterly open. As I held him and looked into his innocent sleeping face, I wondered what kind of world we will leave to him and his generation. If his future self—and all his peers—could speak, what work would they be asking us to do now?

My great hope is that this book will inspire you to unleash your full human potential to transform the conflicts around you. *If we can transform our conflicts, we can transform our world.*

The choice is ours.

## CHAPTER 2

# THE THREE VICTORIES

*The Possible's slow fuse is lit*
*By the Imagination.*
—Emily Dickinson

*Wanted: a Hard Job.* That was the motto of my grandfather's company, founded more than a century ago.

In 1906, Eddie was a boy of thirteen living in Warsaw, then part of the Russian Empire, when his mother suddenly handed him his older brother's steamship passage ticket and told him he had to immediately flee to America. That day, his fifteen-year-old brother, Wolf, had been arrested and jailed by the police for talking on a street corner with two friends. His crime? Violating the restriction against congregating, imposed by the Russian imperial authorities to curb revolutionary activity.

In the courtyard of the building where Eddie and his family

lived, the security police were lining up suspected revolutionaries and executing them against a wall. I can only imagine what emotions Eddie was feeling at the time: fear and confusion, grief and anger. All I know is that whatever happened was painful enough that he never wanted to talk about his childhood.

Thirteen-year-old Eddie fled by himself the next day and joined a small group of refugees who were being smuggled across the border into Germany. The journey was not without danger; refugees had to travel by night to elude Russian border guards, and attacks by murderous highway gangs were not uncommon. From Hamburg, he boarded the ship *Pretoria*, traveling in stifling steerage quarters.

Arriving at Ellis Island the day after his fourteenth birthday, he was processed by immigration authorities under his brother's name since that was the name on the ship docket. Eddie went immediately to work in a woolen textile mill in Maine, joining his father, Max, and his eldest brother, Joe, who had preceded him.

The air in the mill was so thick with wool lint that the workers kept coughing and wheezing, easily succumbing to lung disease. Enterprising even at a young age, Eddie took up window washing instead. He and another young teenager opened up a little business in Rhode Island. There were a lot of dirty windows and buildings in those days of coal burning—and business boomed. He and his father and brother were able to send money back to Warsaw to bring over his mother and remaining siblings.

Within two decades, my grandfather wasn't just cleaning windows and buildings. He and his teams were cleaning giant steel mills near Chicago.

"I don't get it," I said to my ninety-year-old uncle Mel as I was writing this book. "How did a boy who started off washing windows and who never had a chance to get a formal education end up being hired by the biggest steel companies in the world to clean out their blast furnaces?"

My uncle, who had ended up running the company himself, looked at me and said in a well-informed tone with a touch of boyish admiration:

"It is hard to believe. At that time, the steel companies had to shut down the blast furnace for six months at great cost to clean out the heavy slag that remained as the iron was turned into steel. My father devised a way to do the job using dynamite inside the furnace. It required extreme precision, of course, to avoid blowing up the furnace. But instead of six months, it took three days!"

"What was Eddie's secret to success?" I asked.

My uncle paused for a moment to consider the question, then replied:

"It's simple. Where others saw *obstacles*, he saw *opportunities*."

My grandfather, in other words, was a *possibilist*.

## START FROM POSSIBLE

"Wanted: a Hard Job" could serve as a motto for *possibilists*.

Transforming conflict is some of the hardest work we humans can do. It calls on us to *engage* when we feel tempted to attack or to avoid. It requires us to take responsibility for conflicts around us when we may prefer to remain bystanders. It requires courage, patience, and persistence.

If *possibilists* have a core principle, it is *humble audacity*. The audacity of our goals needs to be balanced by the humility of our approach. It takes audacity to tackle seemingly impossible challenges.

It takes audacity to aim for outcomes that work not only for one party but for everyone. It takes humility to be patient and calm, and to listen in the face of provocation. It takes humility to face hard facts and keep learning and persisting.

*Possibilists* are not naïvely optimistic; they expect to encounter setbacks along the way. As a mediator in the war in Northern Ireland, a conflict widely viewed as impossible, former US senator George Mitchell reflected:

"We had 700 days of failure, and one day of success."

During those seven hundred days Mitchell humbly sat and listened to both sides. And that one day of success, which resulted in the Good Friday Agreement, led to the transformation of the conflict. Though the conflict didn't end, the war did—and that made all the difference.

At the same time as they fully acknowledge obstacles and expect setbacks, *possibilists* bring a very different *mindset* to conflicts. As I learned from my grandfather, even the hardest job can become easier with the right mindset—the lens through which we see it.

In my conflict work, I have noticed that if I simply start from the problem, it is all too easy for me to get lost in its details and difficulties. So I like to start by drawing an imaginary *circle of possibility* around the conflict. That circle contains all the potential positive ways the conflict could unfold. I find it easier to address the problem if I can situate it within the larger context of possibility.

Without discounting the difficulties, I make room for the possibility that there is a way out. I like to ask:

"What is *possible* here? Not probable but simply possible?"

We can then apply our innate capacities for curiosity, creativity, and collaboration. Using our natural *curiosity*, we can seek to understand the parties in conflict. Deploying our innate *creativity*, we can open up new possibilities. Engaging in radical *collaboration*, we can overcome tough challenges. Like good athletes—or musicians—playing together, we can tap into the surprising power of play to perform at our full collective potential.

My grandfather Eddie's *possibilist mindset* is exactly what is needed, I have found, to transform tough conflicts. *Don't ignore the obstacles, but look for the openings.*

The path *to* possible starts *from* possible.

## A SINGLE SENTENCE

"Do you think you could sum up in a *single* sentence everything you've learned about negotiating difficult conflicts that we could apply in these troubled times?" my friend Jim Collins asked me that brisk, bluebird day as we were hiking up a peak near our homes in the Rocky Mountains.

"That's a tall order, Jim."

"Darwin did it. In *The Origin of Species*, he has a single sentence that sums up his whole theory of evolution."

Jim's challenge touched a chord in me. I happen to love simplicity.

"I don't know if I can answer your question, but I'll think about it."

Over the ensuing months, I reviewed all my experiences over five decades in seeking to open up new possibilities in conflict. I thought about all the different ways I had tried to capture my lessons in concepts and metaphors. I figured if I could answer Jim's question, if I could synthesize into a single sentence what

I had learned, it might be easier to pass it on so that others could benefit—even if it took an entire book to fully unpack the meaning of the sentence.

For me, three has always been a magic number for remembering what is important. The human brain responds to patterns, and three is the smallest number we can use to create a pattern. The ancient Romans had a phrase, *Omne trium perfectum*: everything that comes in threes is perfect. There is something about three that feels both minimal and complete.

As I reflected on Jim's question on my solitary walks, my mind kept coming back to three key concepts that I have found most powerful and valuable in my conflict work. In my mind's eye, I began to visualize a path—a *path to possible*—composed of three victories to achieve along the way.

On our next walk, a few months later, I said to Jim:

"Remember you asked me what I've learned over these last decades and if I could sum it up in one sentence?"

"Yes, of course."

"I gave it some thought."

"Yes?" Jim asked.

"The problem is this: We are not going to get rid of conflict—nor should we. But we can change the way we see conflict and the way we choose to live with it. Conflict can make us *think small*. We reduce the whole thing to a win-lose battle between us and them. Often, the bigger the conflict, the smaller we think."

"So what can we do instead?"

"The secret is to do the exact opposite. Instead of thinking small, we need to *think big*. We need a wholly different approach. Instead of just starting from the problem, we need to start from the possibilities."

"Go on."

"If we want to deal with tough conflicts like the ones we face today, we have to open up new possibilities that are not at all obvious to us. Imagine that the challenging conflict is a mountain like the one we're climbing. We have to find a path—a path to possible. And that path is made up of three victories. Each victory changes our perspective on conflict."

"Yes?" asked Jim expectantly.

"The first and biggest challenge we face is not what we usually think. It is not them. It is right here," I said, pointing my finger at myself.

"In destructive conflict, we react out of fear and anger and we end up getting in our own way. We need to do the opposite. We need to get out of the bunker and go to the *balcony* instead—a place of calm and perspective where we can keep our eyes on the prize."

Motioning with my outstretched arm to the big expansive plains below us, I said:

"Right now, we're on a balcony of sorts where we can see the bigger picture, like this big view in front of us. *Balcony is the first victory to achieve—a victory with ourselves.*"

"Okay," said Jim, "what's the second?"

"In destructive conflict, we dig into our positions and build walls. Again, we need to do the opposite. Imagine I'm standing here and you're way over there," I said pointing at a peak across the valley.

"There's a big chasm between your position and mine. It's filled with all the reasons why it's hard to reach agreement, including doubt, anxiety, and fear of looking weak. If I want us to meet, I need to build a *bridge*—a golden bridge—an inviting way to cross the chasm of conflict. I need to make it easier for us to walk toward each other. *Bridge is the second victory to achieve—a victory with the other."*

"Doesn't sound easy," Jim remarked.

"It is a hard job," I replied, remembering Eddie and his company motto. "We need help."

"Where can we get that help?"

"That is the third piece of the puzzle. In destructive conflict, we see just *two sides*, us against them, battling it out for a unilateral victory. We need to break out of that trap. Because the truth is, there's always a *third side*: the side of the whole. Tangibly, the third side is the people around us who can help us—our family, friends, neighbors, colleagues. It is the surrounding community who are concerned about the conflict."

"What can they do?" Jim asked.

"They can step in and break up fights. They can help us calm down and go to the balcony. They can help us build a golden bridge. *The third side is the third victory to achieve—a victory with the whole.*

"The balcony helps us *see* new possibilities. The bridge helps us *create* new possibilities. And the third side helps us *act* on new possibilities. All three together, I believe, can enable us to transform even our most difficult conflicts."

"Okay," said Jim. "Now boil all this down for me into a single sentence."

*"The path to possible is to go to the balcony, build a golden bridge, and engage the third side—all together, all at once."*

"That's good," said Jim. "Now go write the book."

## UNLOCK YOUR FULL POTENTIAL

One of my favorite teaching stories, an ancient tale from the Middle East, illustrates the three victories on the path to possible. In the story, an old man dies and leaves his three sons an inheritance—half to the eldest son, a third to the middle son, and a ninth to the youngest son. But there's a problem. The inheritance consists of seventeen camels, a number that is not divisible by two, three, or nine.

Each of the three brothers feels that he deserves more. They get drawn into a bitter argument and are about to come to fisticuffs. The whole family is strained to the breaking point.

This ancient story brings to mind the contentious conflicts we face today. No one can agree about how to share what we have. No one is happy. There is a bitter fight. Everyone is losing, including—and perhaps especially—the community.

So what happens next in the story?

In desperation, the family turns to a wise old woman, known in the community for her calm perspective. As the brothers bicker, each complaining angrily about the others, the wise woman simply listens. She doesn't offer any advice on the spot but asks for a day to reflect on the matter.

The next day, she comes back to the tents of the three brothers, leading her own camel.

"I don't know if I can help you," she announces to the brothers. "But if you want, I have this beautiful camel. She has been very good to me and has given birth to many strong camels. I hope you will accept her as my gift to you."

The three angry brothers look surprised, taken aback by the

wise woman's generous offer. They look at each other for a moment and manage to stammer out a collective thank-you.

"You are too kind."

The wise old woman departs, leaving the three brothers with eighteen camels.

"I'll take my half," says the eldest. "That's nine."

"I'll take my third," says the middle brother. "That's six."

"I'll take my ninth," says the youngest. "That's two."

Nine plus six plus two equals seventeen. They have one camel left over—the beautiful camel given to them by the wise woman.

The three brothers return the camel to the wise woman, thanking her again for her help.

Everyone is satisfied—the three brothers, the wise old woman, and, not least, the extended family.

As old teaching stories often do, this one conveys a lot of wisdom in a few words. I have been telling this story for almost forty years but only now have realized that buried within it is the lesson of the three victories: balcony, bridge, and third side.

What does the wise old woman do? She takes a step back and goes to the *balcony*. From that place of calm and perspective, she can see the big picture—the practical value and emotional meaning of a family that can get along. She unlocks the potential that exists *within* each of us.

From the balcony, the wise woman looks for a *golden bridge*, a way out that leads to a shared victory. By offering up an eighteenth camel, she unlocks the potential for mutual gain that exists *between us*—in this case, among the three brothers.

Finally, because it can be hard in heated conflicts for the parties to go to the balcony and build that bridge, it takes the help of a *third side.* The other family members, thirdsiders who are affected by the souring of relations, urge the brothers to seek out the advice of yet another thirdsider, the wise old woman. The potential *around* us is thus unlocked.

Here is the lesson I draw from this ancient story: To succeed in transforming destructive conflicts such as we face today, we will need to unlock our *full human potential.* One victory alone is not enough. Going to the balcony unlocks the potential *within* us. Building a golden bridge unlocks the potential *between* us. Taking the third side unlocks the potential *around* us. We need all three working together synergistically.

The balcony is *first-person* work; it focuses on *I*—the self. The bridge is *second-person* work; it focuses on *You*—the other. The third side is *third-person* work; it focuses on *Us*—the community. In difficult conflicts, we tend to skip over the necessary work on the *I*—the self—to point fingers at the *You*—the other: "*You* are the problem, and *you* must change." We also often neglect to seek help from the *Us*—the community. That may be why we have so much trouble. To transform conflict successfully, we need to work skillfully on all *three* strands: *I, You,* and *Us.*

## BEGIN WITH A VICTORY SPEECH

So how do we begin our journey on the path to possible?

*The secret, I find, is to start from possible and then work backward.*

Transforming a difficult conflict is a bit like climbing a high mountain. Imagine you are at the bottom gazing up. The summit seems far away and seemingly impossible to attain. Now, in your mind's eye, imagine yourself already on top of the mountain, and from there follow the path back to where you are at the bottom. As you engage in this act of practical imagination, the summit may seem a little more reachable.

In conflicts, as in mountain climbing, it may look as though you can't get *from here to there*—where you want to go. But by using your imagination, you might just be able to get *from there to here*. And then you can turn around and find your way back.

In the face of a contentious conflict, I like to engage in a creative thought experiment that I call the *victory speech*. It is my favorite possibilist exercise.

Let me offer an example that started off at my dining room table in an informal brainstorm with my colleague Liza Hester. It was February 2017. Donald Trump had just assumed the presidency of the United States. His predecessor, Barack Obama, had warned him that his most dangerous foreign policy challenge would be North Korea.

Kim Jong Un, the thirty-three-year-old supreme leader of North Korea, was busily testing long-range ballistic missiles capable of carrying nuclear warheads. President Trump announced on Twitter his determination to stop Kim before he developed the capacity to hit the United States: "It won't happen!" Expert estimates of the risk of war varied but ranged as high as fifty-fifty.

The expected consequences were unthinkable: the US military calculated that in the opening hours of a North Korean barrage of conventional missiles, hundreds of thousands of civilians would be killed in Seoul alone. If nuclear weapons and other means of mass destruction were used, as was considered likely, the casualty estimate ran into the tens of millions. The nuclear taboo in place since

Hiroshima and Nagasaki would be breached, the global atmosphere would be poisoned with vast clouds of radiation, and our world would be set on an extremely dark course.

Liza and I knew hardly anything about the Korean conflict at the time, but we felt deeply worried by what we had learned from the news. It had been almost thirty years since I had worked on a Harvard project focused on reducing the risk of a nuclear war between the United States and the Soviet Union. It all seemed ominous and eerily familiar.

Perhaps the most common question in the media was "Who will *win*—Trump or Kim? Which leader will back down?"

But sitting at my dining room table, Liza and I were asking ourselves a very different question:

"Where is the *off-ramp* for Trump and for Kim? How can this showdown end in agreement rather than war? How can both leaders come out looking like *heroes* to themselves and the people they care most about?"

We continued the thought experiment:

"What victory speech could Donald Trump make to the American people explaining how *he* won? What victory speech could Kim Jong Un make at the very same time to his people explaining how *he* won?"

While we were not experts and knew about Trump only from reading the daily news and almost nothing about Kim other than reading a few articles, we decided to give it a try. After a short exploration on the web of Trump's tweets and comments about Korea, we scribbled on a whiteboard, set by the dining room table, three short taglines for an imaginary Trump victory speech:

- *Deal of the century.*
- *I kept America safe.*
- *I didn't spend a penny.*

We then turned to Kim Jong Un. Kim was young and relatively new in his leadership. The leader of the most isolated country in the world, he was popularly perceived as "crazy" and ruthless, having reportedly ordered the execution by firing squad of his uncle and his entire family as well as the assassination of his half-brother.

Nothing was publicly known about Kim's motivations, but from what could be gleaned from reading the observations of Korea watchers, security seemed to be the leadership's top priority. The immense trauma of the Korean War, almost forgotten in the West, was vividly recalled every day in North Korea. The casualties were staggering: almost 2 million people had perished in the northern half of the Korean Peninsula, a fifth of the entire population. Almost every town and city had been burned to the ground.

Speculating about Kim's possible victory speech, we wrote in a column next to Trump's speech:

- *Security: My rule and my country are secure.*
- *Respect: We are finally getting the respect we deserve.*
- *Prosperity: We will be the next Asian tiger.*

As we stood back for a moment and looked at the whiteboard, we experienced a dawning *aha!*: The imaginary victory speeches did not appear incompatible. It was not impossible to imagine the two leaders meeting and agreeing to de-escalate the crisis and pursue negotiations instead. Neither leader would have to back down. In fact, both could end up looking like heroes. And millions of lives would be spared.

However remote that possibility seemed at the time, the exercise had succeeded in its initial purpose for Liza and me: we had moved in our own minds from a place of impossibility to a place of possibility.

That, I find, is the magic of the victory speech exercise. It can often make the seemingly impossible seem possible. By offering a tantalizing glimpse of the destination, it encourages us to embark on the challenging journey. As it turned out, that one little informal exercise at the dining room table eventually grew into a dedicated team working for months and years on ways to help avert a nuclear war between the United States and North Korea.

As you and I embark in this book on the path to possible, let me invite you to try out the victory speech exercise on a problem of your own. It could be any situation in which you are asking someone to do something that perhaps they are reluctant to do.

Imagine for a moment that the other person has accepted your proposal. Incredible as it may seem, they have said *yes*. Now imagine they have to go in front of the people they most care about—their family, their colleagues, their board of directors, their voters—and explain why they have decided to accept your proposal. Consider it an "acceptance" speech. What would be their three main talking points—like the ones Liza and I wrote down on the whiteboard for Trump and Kim?

The victory speech is the iconic exercise of the *possibilist*. Right from the start, it can open up new possibilities where at first none seemed apparent.

## THE CIRCLE OF POSSIBILITY

Now that we've taken the bold action of imagining victory, the question becomes: How can we make the victory speech come true? This is where the hard work begins. We need to find a way to *see*, *create*, and *act* on new possibilities. That way is the *path to possible*.

Imagine a *circle of possibility* around the conflict. The path to possible takes us around the circle in a clockwise direction. The path begins with the balcony, proceeds with the bridge, and ends with the third side. The process is iterative; we keep going around the circle until the conflict in the center is transformed. While this map simplifies reality—as all maps do—it can be a valuable navigational tool.

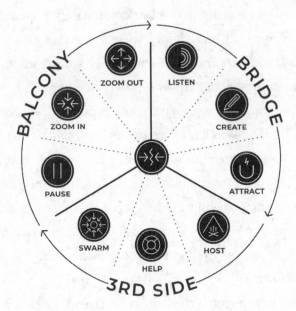

I like to think of the balcony, the bridge, and the third side as our *innate human "superpowers"*—natural capacities each of us can learn to activate and deploy. Each creates a victory on the path to possible.

Each "superpower" is, in turn, composed of three powers that we all possess. As the circle diagram suggests, we go to the balcony by exercising our powers to pause, zoom in, and zoom out. We build a golden bridge by exercising our powers to listen, create, and attract. We engage the third side by exercising our powers to host, help, and swarm.

Each power is an innate human capacity, something we already know how to do but simply need to develop further. While each power opens up new possibilities, it takes all of them working together to unlock our *full* human potential to transform difficult conflicts.

Our walk on the path to possible begins with the balcony.

# GO TO THE BALCONY

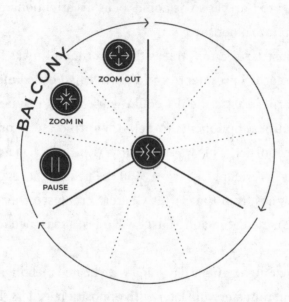

A million people were protesting vehemently in the streets of Caracas, the capital of Venezuela, demanding the immediate resignation of the embattled president, Hugo Chávez, whom they saw as an authoritarian socialist out to undermine their democratic rights and threaten their livelihoods. A million others in the streets were equally vehemently supporting Chávez, seeing him as their popular champion for social and economic justice. Fighting had broken out between the crowds and threatened to get worse. People were arming themselves.

"I am deeply worried that a bloody civil war will break out in this country like it did in mine," César Gaviria, a former president of Colombia, remarked to me over dinner at an outdoor restaurant in Caracas. I could feel the urgency and seriousness in his voice. More than 215,000 people had been killed in Colombia, and there was no end to the war in sight. Gaviria was now serving as the secretary general of the Organization of American States. He had moved his office temporarily to Caracas so he could focus his attention on stopping the descent into bloodshed.

I had just arrived in Caracas that afternoon. It was December 2003. Former US president Jimmy Carter had called me up eight months earlier to ask me if I could work with President Chávez and his political opponents to help them find a way out of their escalating conflict. This was my fourth trip, and I had an appointment to see President Chávez at 9:00 the next night together with two colleagues from the Carter Center: Francisco Diez, a skilled Argentinian mediator, and Matthew Hodes, a seasoned former UN diplomat.

The next night, after a day filled with heated meetings first with government ministers and later with opposition leaders, Francisco, Matt, and I arrived at the presidential palace and were ushered into an ornate waiting room with giant historical paintings in gold frames.

9:30 passed, then 10:00 . . . 10:30 . . . 11:00 . . . 11:30.

It was midnight when we were shown into the presidential office. We expected to meet with him alone, as we had the previous time. On that occasion, he had received Francisco and me in his private quarters with a twelve-foot-long map of Venezuela scrolled out across a conference table. Pointing at the map, he told us about his hopes and plans to combat the terrible poverty that existed across the country. As we were leaving, he showed us a painting he was working on as a gift to his daughter. It had been an informal, relaxed conversation—just the three of us.

But this time, as my colleagues and I were shown into the presidential office at midnight, we found the entire Venezuelan cabinet—about fifteen of them—sitting on a platform behind President Chávez. I wasn't prepared for this, and I felt a little unsettled.

Chávez motioned me quickly to a chair in front of him. He then turned to me and asked in a curt, clipped tone, as if he were pressed for time and I was interrupting his meeting:

"So, Ury, tell me, what are your impressions of the situation?"

I paused and looked at him and the ministers behind him.

"Well, Señor Presidente, I was speaking with some of your ministers today"—I nodded at them—"as well as to the leaders of the opposition. I believe we are making some progress."

"*Progress?* What do you mean, *progress?*" he spat back, his face reddening with anger.

He leaned in close to my face and shouted at me:

"What on earth are you talking about? Do you not *see* the dirty tricks those traitors on the other side are up to? Are you *blind*? You mediators are big *fools!*"

I froze and flashed back to a memory when I was ten years old in school in Switzerland and the French teacher had publicly humiliated me in front of the class for grammatical mistakes I had made in my essay. I felt attacked and embarrassed in front of the entire cabinet. My face flushed, and my jaw clenched.

The voice of my inner judge, which I knew so well from boyhood, piped up: "Why did you have to do that—use that word *progress*? What a mistake! Six months of work down the drain. And how dare he call me a fool!"

But in a flash, I noticed my anger rising and I remembered a subtle self-regulation technique I had learned just a few months earlier from an Ecuadorian friend when I had been describing to him my work in contentious conflicts.

"William," he had counseled me, "next time you are in a tough place, try pinching the palm of your hand."

"*Why* would I do that, Hernán?"

"Because it will give you a temporary pain sensation, and that will keep you alert."

As Chávez continued to shout at me, I pinched my left palm. It helped me focus on the challenge at hand. I took a deep breath, relaxed, and had a short internal dialogue with myself:

"What is your goal here?"

"To help calm the situation before it breaks into violence."

"So is it really going to help if you get into a shouting match with the president of Venezuela?"

In a split second, I had my answer.

I bit my tongue and pinched my palm with renewed vigor. I took another deep breath and relaxed a little more. The emotions of embarrassment, anger, and self-blame began to lift.

I focused my full attention on the angry president in front of me. Sweating heavily, his cheeks red with rage, he spat out his hot breath, flecked with spittle. He was gesticulating, waving his hands wildly to make his points. I quietly observed him as if I were on an imaginary balcony and he was a character on the stage.

I sensed that if I reacted and defended myself, he would just grow even angrier. President Chávez was famous for giving eight-hour-long impassioned speeches. We could be there all night. Or he might throw me out of his office right away.

So I chose *not* to react but to listen instead. I kept pinching my palm while nodding my head from time to time, waiting patiently for a possible opening. I grew curious about what actually lay behind his behavior. Was he genuinely upset? Was the display of theatrics designed to impress his audience? Or both?

Thirty minutes passed as the president continued his tirade. And then I noticed his tempo slowing. With nothing to react to, he seemed to be running out of steam. Studying his body language, I watched his shoulders sink slightly. He let out a weary sigh.

"So, Ury, *what* should I do?"

That, my friends, is the faint sound of a human mind opening.

Minds, as we know, do not always open easily to new possibilities, especially the mind of a forceful and opinionated personality such as Hugo Chávez. Until that moment, anything I might have said would have had the same effect as banging my head against a wall. But now he was asking me for advice. Here was my chance.

Earlier that day, Francisco and I had been driving along the streets of Caracas. We had passed protesters from both sides. We had been discussing the emotional weight of the crisis for ordinary people. It was just before Christmas, but the public mood seemed depressed. It looked as though everyone just needed a break from the strain of conflict and the uncertainty of the future.

That gave me an idea. The entire country, not just Chávez, was stewing in anger. In my experience working on stormy labor strikes, a third party would sometimes propose a *cooling-off period*, allowing heated emotions to subside. Could there be a *cooling-off period* in Venezuela now?

"Señor Presidente," I said, "it is December. As you know, last Christmas the festivities were canceled around the country because of the political protests. In your next television appearance, why don't you propose a *tregua*, a Christmas truce? Let people enjoy the holidays with their families. In January, we can resume the negotiations, and, who knows, maybe everyone will be in a better mood to listen."

I offered the idea with trepidation. I had no idea how he would receive it. Would he dismiss it as ridiculous? Would he seek to humiliate me further in front of his assembled ministers? Would he use it to fly off the handle again for another thirty minutes?

Chávez paused and looked at me with pursed lips for what felt like a long time. I looked at him closely, steeling myself for another outburst. Then his mouth opened:

"That's an *excellent* idea! I am going to propose that in my next speech!"

He took a step toward me and clapped me heartily on the back. It was as if he had utterly forgotten his half-hour tirade.

"Why don't you come see the country with me over Christmas? You will get to know the real people of Venezuela!"

He paused for a moment.

"Ah, yes, maybe you can't do that because you wouldn't be seen as neutral anymore. I understand.

"But don't worry, I can give you a disguise," he joked with a broad smile on his face.

His mood had completely shifted.

I still felt a little shocked but was greatly relieved.

It was a close call. I had been on the verge of reacting defensively to Chávez's furious attack. It could easily have ended badly, closing off possibilities. Instead, the conversation had gone in a completely different direction, *opening up* new possibilities.

By going to the balcony myself, I was able to help the president go to the balcony, and he, in turn, was able to help the country go to the balcony for a reprieve over the holidays.

What had produced this unlikely outcome?

## UNLOCK THE POTENTIAL WITHIN

It has been twenty years since that tumultuous midnight meeting, but even today, I am still learning lessons from it. It taught me that perhaps the greatest power we have in difficult situations is the power to choose *not* to react but to go to the balcony instead.

*The balcony is a place of calm and perspective where we can keep our eyes on the prize.*

Ever since co-authoring *Getting to Yes*, I had been teaching and practicing negotiation as an exercise in influencing the minds of *others*. What the experience with Chávez underscored for me was the vital importance of influencing *myself*—my own thoughts and emotions. How could I expect to influence others if I couldn't influence myself first?

The encounter with President Chávez crystallized my understanding that transforming conflict is an *inside-out process*. On the path to possible, the work *within*—the work with ourselves—precedes the work *between*—the work with others. The first-person work prepares the way for the second-person work.

Facing the challenging conflicts of today, I believe we need to take the balcony one step further than *controlling* our natural reactions. We also need to use the balcony to *expand our perspective*. As I reexamine my contentious encounter with President Chávez, I see that the balcony perspective opened up a new possibility in the form of a Christmas truce that helped me turn the situation around. The balcony opens the way to breakthroughs.

So how do we unlock the potential *within* us? How can we make sure we bring our best to the difficult conflicts we face?

As I came to appreciate during my encounter with President Chávez, we go to the balcony by exercising three natural powers. Each power is an innate human capacity, something we may already know how to do but simply need to develop and strengthen.

The first is the power to *pause*—to stop and reflect before you act. Instead of reacting, give yourself a moment to calm down so that you can see the situation more clearly. When faced with Chávez's angry outburst, I pinched the palm of my hand and remembered to breathe in order to pause and quiet my mind.

The second is the power to *zoom in*—to focus your attention on what you really want. Go deep into your interests and needs. In the heat of the moment with Chávez, zooming in gave me a chance to remember why I was there and what I wanted to achieve.

The third is the power to *zoom out*—to focus your attention on the big picture. From the balcony, you can see the larger scene unfolding on the stage. With Chávez, I zoomed out to see the exhausted protesters and imagined how families and children in Venezuela might benefit from a peaceful Christmas holiday.

These three powers have a logical sequence. Pausing interrupts our reactive mind so we can zoom in and remember *what* we want. Zooming out then helps us see *how* we can get what we want. Once we activate a power, we continue to use it. We repeatedly pause, zoom in, and zoom out as needed. The more we exercise these powers, the more habitual they become.

Eventually, the balcony becomes not just a place to visit occasionally but a *home base* from which we can continually see the bigger picture and keep our eyes on the prize. The balcony becomes a genuine "superpower" that enables us to unlock the full potential *within* us to transform conflicts.

The balcony is our *first* victory on the path to possible—a victory with ourselves.

## CHAPTER 3

# PAUSE

### From Reactive to Proactive

*Do you have the patience to wait till your mud settles*
*and the water is clear?*
—Lao Tzu

It was a pause that saved the world.

Vasili Alexandrovich Arkhipov was a senior naval officer on the Soviet submarine B-59 in the North Atlantic in October 1962. It was the height of the Cuban Missile Crisis, and the world teetered on the brink of nuclear war. A US warship tracking the sub dropped depth charges—underwater bombs—to force it to the surface to identify its exact location.

Unbeknownst to the Americans, the submarine was armed with a nuclear torpedo. Because communication might be interrupted during wartime, Moscow had entrusted the top three officers on the sub to decide independently whether to fire the nuclear torpedo if under attack. They did not need to wait for orders from the Kremlin.

As the depth charges exploded, the sub swirled around.

"It felt like you were sitting in a metal barrel which somebody is constantly blasting with a sledgehammer," Senior Lieutenant Vadim Orlov, the communications officer, remembered.

The Soviet submariners had no idea that the depth charges were just a warning and believed that they were about to die. Although no one knows exactly what was said in the sub at that moment, Orlov recalled the gist of the argument among the top three commanding officers.

"Arm the nuclear torpedo!" ordered the sub's captain, Valentin Grigorievich Savitsky. "Prepare it for firing!

"Maybe the war has already started up there while we are doing somersaults here," he screamed. "We're going to blast them now! We will die, but we will sink them all. We will not become the shame of the fleet!"

The political officer, Ivan Semenovich Maslennikov, cursed:

"Yes, let's do it, damn it!"

Only one other officer on board was needed to authorize the launch: thirty-four-year-old Vasili Alexandrovich Arkhipov, the modest, soft-spoken second captain.

As Savitsky raged, Arkhipov was quiet, then spoke up.

"I say *no*," he said firmly. "It takes all three of us to authorize a firing."

"Don't be a wimp!" shouted the captain.

"You know our orders. We are forbidden to launch the torpedo unless the hull has been breached. It's still intact," replied Arkhipov calmly.

"But the war has already started!" yelled the captain.

"We don't know that yet," Arkhipov countered.

Savitsky ultimately cooled down.

When the incident came to light forty years later in 2002, Robert McNamara, who had been the US secretary of defense during the Cuban Missile Crisis, exclaimed:

"If that torpedo had been fired, nuclear war would have started right there."

"Arkhipov stood out for being cool headed. He was in control," said his close friend and fellow submariner Ryurik Alexandrovich Ketov.

In that one fateful moment, in the midst of a fierce argument, Arkhipov exercised an innate power available to each of us: to *pause* with intention and calmly *choose* the next step.

At a time of toxic polarization in the world, in which we are so quick to react with anger and fear, we can all learn a lesson from Arkhipov—without whom hundreds of millions of us might not be alive today.

## CHOOSE TO STOP AND STOP TO CHOOSE

Where you end up depends on where you begin. If we succeed in transforming today's difficult conflicts, it will be because we began, as Arkhipov did, with a *transformative pause*.

To pause simply means *to stop to choose*. It means to reflect before you speak or act. Pausing separates stimulus and response, creating space for us to make an intentional choice. Pausing shifts our state of mind from *reactive* to *proactive*, enabling us to act purposefully in service of our interests.

When I first learned of the extraordinary story of Vasili Arkhipov and sub B-59 after it was revealed publicly in 2002, it reminded me of a conversation I had had seven years earlier in New Guinea about human aggression and our ability to control it.

In the fall of 1995, I made a field trip to a place that was famous for its warfare: the Highlands of New Guinea. The people of the Highlands were the last major population group on earth to come into contact with the modern world. Nobody in the West had known they existed until the 1920s, when pilots flying over the island saw, to their utter surprise, signs of habitation in the lush mountain valleys below. When government officials finally reached those mountain communities, they found war—lots of it.

Clan warfare was still going on when I arrived. On my very first day in the Highlands, I happened upon a "fight zone." In the midst of the brilliantly green countryside, I saw the empty shells of school buildings that had been burned to the ground. Here and there I observed orchards that had been uprooted. My local guide and I were walking down a path when suddenly we encountered a group of young warriors running in the opposite direction. With brilliantly painted bodies and feathered hairdos, they were brandishing their bows and arrows. One young warrior stopped for a moment and asked us:

"Have you seen where the fighting is?"

"No," answered my guide.

"Can you tell us what the dispute is about?" I asked as the guide translated.

"It's a fight about a land boundary," the warrior answered. "They killed one of our clansmen. So we killed one of theirs. Then they killed two of ours."

"How many men have died?"

"Eight so far."

A couple of days later, I happened to speak with a humanitarian aid worker.

"What a coincidence to meet you!" he exclaimed. "I've been giving a little course on conflict resolution for the local warriors, and I've been using one of your books, *Getting Past No*."

"Really?" I said.

"And you know what's the biggest lesson for them? It's the concept of going to the *balcony*. It didn't occur to them that when one of their clan is killed, they don't have to automatically act out their anger and go find someone of the other clan to kill. They are genuinely surprised to learn they have a choice. They can pause and let their anger cool down while they decide what they really want to do. It's positively revolutionary!"

The warriors had discovered their agency—their power to *choose to stop and stop to choose*. Although few of us are clan warriors, I suspect that each of us at times may find ourself trapped in the same reactive mindset. We tend to forget our own agency and power. But just as the warriors did, we can begin to free ourselves with this one simple realization: in every conflict, in every moment, *we have a choice*. By exercising our choice, we can start to reclaim control of our conflicts, our relationships, and our lives.

It is not easy, of course.

In virtually every dispute I have ever mediated—whether a business dispute, a family feud, or a civil war—the pattern is the same: a reaction followed by a reaction followed by another reaction.

"Why did you attack him?"

"Because he attacked me."

And on it goes.

We humans are reaction machines. When we feel threatened, as the clan warriors in New Guinea or the Soviet sub captain in the North Atlantic did, the left half of the amygdala, a little gland in the lower part of our brain, is activated. Our brain, in effect, is hijacked and taken over by our reactions. Our heart rate quickens, our blood pressure goes up, our cortisol level increases, and our sympathetic nervous system springs into action. Instantly, our bodies are primed to fight, flight, or freeze, depending on our natural proclivity and past experiences.

As I learned long ago in anthropology class, each of these reactions has an evolutionary purpose to protect us from predators and other dangers. But in the conflict situations in which we find ourselves today, these natural reactions may lead us to act in ways that are contrary to our own best interests.

Since I co-authored *Getting to Yes* more than forty years ago, perhaps the greatest lesson I have learned is this: The biggest obstacle to getting what I want is not the difficult person on the *other* side of the table; it is the person on *this* side of the table. It is me. When I react without thinking, I become my own worst enemy. I am the one who keeps getting in my own way.

We become our own worst enemies when we *attack*, hurling insults and blame at the other person or storming out of the room vowing never to return. We are only working against ourselves when we *avoid*, sitting in cold silence and ignoring an issue that will only get worse. We hurt ourselves when we *appease*, only to draw further demands. Far from being on the *balcony* in such situations, we may find ourselves hunkered down in an emotional bunker, armed with grenades we are itching to throw.

"Speak when you are angry and you will make the best speech you will ever regret," is a quote I love to repeat, coined by the nineteenth-century American Civil War veteran and writer Ambrose Bierce.

Thirty years of marriage have taught me how easy it is when I am angry and hurt to utter words of blame that I instantly regret. It is humbling to practice negotiation and self-restraint in the world and yet to come home and find myself falling into the trap I warn others against. These moments serve as a mirror, reminding me how easy it is to stumble and get in my own way. No matter what the provocation might be, I am the one responsible for my reactions. Marriage has been my great teacher, prodding me to keep learning and training me for larger-scale conflict work.

In one of my favorite Greek myths, the hero Hercules is walking down the road when a strange-looking beast suddenly rears its head. Hercules reacts instantly by attacking the beast with his great club. The beast looms larger, so Hercules strikes it again. But every time Hercules hits it with his club, the beast grows bigger.

Suddenly, Hercules' friend Athena, the goddess of wisdom, appears at his side and cries out:

"Stop, Hercules, don't you know the name of that beast?

"That beast is *Strife*. And the more you strike it, the larger it will grow! Cease hitting it, and it will grow smaller."

The timely and important lesson of this myth is that *the more we react to conflict, the bigger conflict grows*. Conflicts turn destructive because each side reacts in an escalating back-and-forth that all too often ends with everyone losing.

When I first came across this myth of Hercules, I found myself wishing that Athena would be there to whisper in my ear *"Stop . . . and choose."* Then I remembered my anthropological studies, and I realized that actually each of us has a personal Athena inside. In scientific terms, Athena is our prefrontal cortex, the region of the brain that inhibits rash, impulsive behavior. Personal agency and free will are our birthright as human beings. That, I believe, is the underlying message of the myth.

Even in the most dire of conflicts, each of us can exercise our power to stop and choose. Instead of being *reactive*, we can be *proactive*. Instead of being our own worst enemy, we can become our greatest ally.

## START BY STOPPING

It seems paradoxical, but the best way to *engage* is to *disengage*—for a moment. Start by stopping. It is counterintuitive, particularly in our world of instant communication, where quick reactions are expected. But most of the conflict situations we face call for the exact opposite. Just when you are tempted to react by attacking, avoiding, or appeasing, pause. Just because the other side may be trying to hook us like a fish, it doesn't mean we have to bite.

In May 1997, I was serving as a facilitator during a heated negotiation in The Hague between Russian president Boris Yeltsin's national security advisor, Boris Berezovsky, and the vice president of Chechnya, Vakha Arsanov.

A bloody civil war had broken out years before in the Caucasus republic of Chechnya, an autonomous region of the Russian Federation. Chechen independence fighters were battling the Russian army. The war had claimed the lives of eighty thousand civilians—including more than thirty thousand children. The two sides had agreed to a truce, but it was shaky.

The meeting got off to a rocky start. When the Chechen delegation had taken off in a private plane from their capital of Grozny, they had been forced down by Russian fighter jets. Furious, the Chechen government had ordered all Russian citizens out of the country. After the Russian authorities finally allowed the Chechen delegation to travel through their airspace, the delegates were held up at Amsterdam airport because they refused to use their Russian passports and insisted on presenting their Chechen ones. When that obstacle was finally cleared and the delegates arrived at the historic and elegant Hotel des Indes in The Hague, they were in a highly disgruntled mood. They insisted that the Russians must have been given bigger rooms than they had. Only when given a peek at their counterparts' rooms did they agree to settle into their accommodations.

We were meeting in the Peace Palace, which housed the International Court of Justice, where the Yugoslav war crimes tribunal was taking place at the same time. The Chechen delegates showed up late, accompanied by their bodyguards. They refused to shake hands with their Russian counterparts. The atmosphere was tense.

In the very first session, the Chechen vice president, Arsanov, launched an hourlong blistering attack on Russia for its oppression of the Chechen people. He began with a history lesson from two centuries earlier, when Russia had first invaded and conquered Chechnya. Speaking with barely repressed fury, he described each atrocity inflicted on the Chechen people until the present time. He ended his talk by pointing his finger dramatically at the Russian delegates across the table and shouting:

"You should stay right here in this room because you yourselves will soon be on trial for war crimes!"

As the Russians absorbed the full force of his attacks, Arsanov looked around the table, pointed at me, and declared:

"You Americans, your President Clinton is Boris Yeltsin's friend, supporting him in these crimes in Chechnya. You are all complicit. And not only are you supporting the Russian colonial oppression of Chechnya, but you are also oppressing the people of Puerto Rico! What do you have to say about that?"

All eyes in the room turned toward me. I was taken by surprise, put suddenly on the spot.

The room was hot and stuffy. As the Chechen vice president pointed accusingly at me, I felt my cheeks flush and my blood pressure go up. It had been a very long day, and I was tired. The stakes were very high, and the meeting seemed to be going nowhere, with dim prospects for success. My mind was whirling: "What do I know about Puerto Rico?"

I went blank for a moment. I was just about to answer and mumble something about Puerto Rico when I suddenly caught myself and realized that the Chechen leader was baiting me.

Thankfully, the sequential translation offered me an extra moment to pause and take several deep breaths. I noticed tightness in my chest and heaviness in my gut. As I took in some air and observed these feelings, their intensity began to subside. In the haze of all the angry words uttered that day, I tried to remember my objective—what was I trying to achieve?

Then, thanks to the short pause, a possible transformative response came to me. I looked straight at the Chechen leader and replied:

"Thank you, Mr. Vice President. I have listened with great sympathy to your account of the extremely painful history of your people. Who could not be moved? And I take your forthright criticism of my country as a sign that we are among friends and can speak frankly with one another. So let me say that we are not here to discuss the problem of Puerto Rico, however important that is, but to figure out how to stop the terrible suffering that has gone on for far too long for the people of Chechnya. Let us focus on that right now."

As my words were translated, the Chechen leader started nodding. As I gazed around the room at people's faces, I could feel the tensions begin to lower.

Surprisingly, the meeting was able to get back on track. Within a day or two, the parties were able to reach agreement on a joint declaration that, temporarily at least, stabilized the political situation.

As I was leaving, I received an invitation to meet privately with the vice president. I had no idea what he wanted. Solemnly, he greeted me and proceeded to present me with an ancient Chechen sword of rare craftsmanship with a finely worked silver scabbard, offering his thanks on behalf of the Chechen people.

I attribute that small but significant turnabout to my having paused and not taken the bait, however tempting it might have been.

Twenty-five years later, I can understand this story better through the lens of collective trauma. Many of the intractable conflicts I have mediated—from family disputes to civil wars—are rooted in deep-seated traumas from the past, episodes of pain and suffering that prove overwhelming to our nervous systems. Traumas can leave us emotionally frozen and highly reactive.

I cannot know for certain, but I can only imagine that the Chechen leader's vituperative reaction stemmed at least in part from underlying trauma. His attack on me seemed personal at that moment, but it had nothing to do with me; it was an expression of his anger and pain. Only when I paused was I able to understand that and get the conversation back on track. Only when I recovered my balance was I able to help those around me.

In high-pressure situations with opposing sides, I have learned to pause and be curious—first about my own reaction and then about theirs. *Meet animosity with curiosity.*

## BREATHE AND OBSERVE

The quickest way to pause is very simple: remember to breathe. In tense conflict situations, I notice how often, unconsciously, I forget to breathe or take rapid, shallow breaths. Taking a couple of long deep breaths—in and out—helps calm the nervous system. Breathing decreases the level of cortisol, the stress hormone, in our bodies and lowers our heart rate and blood pressure. In short, breathing can change our state of mind.

"When a person reacts to something in their environment," my friend Dr. Jill Bolte Taylor, a brain scientist, told me, "a ninety-second chemical process happens. Any further emotional response is because the person chooses to stay in that emotional loop."

She calls this the "90-second rule." In just a minute and a half, the biochemicals of fear and anger dissipate entirely, and we can find emotional equilibrium in order to consciously choose the response that best serves our interests. If we don't give our bodies the full ninety seconds to process the emotion, it could get stuck only to be released later in a reaction we may regret.

I find that taking a moment of silence, even if it might feel a little awkward, can be very powerful in tense moments. This has been confirmed by my negotiation colleague Jared Curhan, who conducted a fascinating experiment on silence at MIT. He and his colleagues observed a number of negotiations and measured how many moments of silence there were in between all the talking. They found a significant correlation between the amount of silence and the success of the negotiations in reaching mutually satisfying outcomes. The researchers called silence *the ultimate power move in negotiations.*

Within that moment of silence, I notice what is going on. I observe my sensations, feelings, and thoughts. I recognize the old familiar faces of fear, anxiety, anger, and self-judgment. If I take a moment to recognize them and even name them to myself, I begin to diminish their power over me.

Before a challenging meeting, I try to take a few minutes of silence to center myself. Even a single minute with my eyes closed helps me tune in to my thoughts, feelings, and sensations. When I quiet my mind, I can better focus on the conversation. My busy mind is like a glass of water filled from the faucet. At first, it's fizzy and opaque. But if I wait a minute and let the water settle, the bubbles slowly dissipate, and the water turns crystal clear. A moment or more of silence helps my mind settle so I can begin to see more clearly what is happening within.

Benjamin Franklin, a highly practical and scientific man, once advised, "Observe all men, thyself most."

It takes work to observe oneself. I think of it as cultivating my *inner scientist*. I become an investigator and study my own sensations, emotions, and thoughts. I ask myself, what is that sour taste in my mouth? What is the queasy feeling in my gut? What is the shaky sensation in my chest? Asking questions activates the prefrontal cortex, the area of the brain that gives us choice.

By recognizing my feelings and thoughts, I can put a little distance between them and me. I am no longer the feeling itself but the one *experiencing* the feeling. With curiosity and empathy, I have learned to befriend uncomfortable feelings that at first I tried to suppress. As I pay friendly attention, the feelings and thoughts begin to subside—and I grow more attentive and present.

Learning to observe yourself is not easy in conflict situations, but with practice, we can get better at it. These turbulent times offer us opportunities to practice every day.

## RESOURCE YOURSELF

In contentious conflicts such as the polarizing political battles we face today, it is easy to get burned out. Outraged by the provocations of others, we get angry. Perceiving the stakes as high, even existential, we feel anxious. Our nervous systems go into a state of high arousal.

But it is hard to sustain such high levels of anger and anxiety for long. We become overwhelmed. We may drop into the opposite extreme—an emotional state of depression, resignation, and despair. We throw our hands up in the air and disengage altogether. It's easy to oscillate between the two extremes until we are weary and thoroughly worn out.

After working in high-stakes existential conflicts for decades, I understand this emotional cycle all too well.

What's the alternative?

In between the state of *hyper*-arousal of our nervous system—marked by anger, rage, fear, and anxiety—and the state of *hypo*-arousal—marked by despair, resignation, depression, and numbness—lies an *optimal emotional zone*, described by the psychiatrist Daniel Siegel as the *Window of Tolerance*.

In this optimal zone, we feel more calm, more grounded, more relaxed and in control. We continue to have the same fluctuating emotions, but they are not as exaggerated. Instead of being controlled by our emotions, we can begin to regulate them. We can function more effectively and manage the stresses of conflict more competently.

What helps me stay in the optimal zone is to *resource* myself. By that, I simply mean to engage in regular activities that help me pause and relax my nervous system. Conflict work can be draining for third parties and much more so for the parties in conflict. Resourcing helps build resilience so that we can remain in the optimal zone and recover more quickly when we drop out of it.

There are many ways to resource ourselves to handle the emotional stress and strain of conflict—from doing physical exercise to listening to music to practicing mindfulness, meditation, and prayer. It helps to spend time with close friends or family members—or with a coach or counselor. I have tried all of these myself and found them all useful at different times. Through trial and error, you will discover what works best for you.

My favorite way to resource myself is to take a long daily walk around the lake near my home and up into the nearby foothills. I do my best thinking when walking. It helps clear my mind, making space for creativity and insight. Walking balances my moods and builds emotional resilience. When I "fall off" the balcony, walking helps me return to it.

Where possible, I love to walk in nature. The sheer beauty of nature in all its magnificence is the best antidote, I find, to the stress of conflict. Beauty—and the awe it inspires—is my balm. As my reactive mind becomes present, I can see the conflict situation more clearly and notice new possibilities.

My favorite place to walk is the mountains, which I have loved ever since I was a small boy growing up in Switzerland. The mountains where I live now in Colorado remind me that they have been here and will be here for eons, placing all of our human dramas in perspective. And the dancing clouds, ever changing around the tops of mountains, never cease to delight. The mountains help me cultivate a larger perspective on the conflicts I face. They serve as a giant balcony.

Before any difficult negotiation, I try to take a walk in order to listen for openings. Once, ten years ago, I traveled to Paris for a negotiation seeking an end to a highly acrimonious dispute between two estranged business partners. I was representing one of the parties, who had become a friend. The long-running dispute had taken a heavy financial and emotional toll not only on the principal parties but also on their families and the employees in the business. I was feeling the weight of the conflict. I had flown across the ocean the night before and my mind was feeling a little foggy from jet lag, so I decided to spend the morning wandering through the streets of Paris.

It was a beautiful September day. The sun was shining, and the bright blue sky was dotted with white, puffy clouds. As I walked the streets of this magnificent city, my thoughts turned toward the upcoming negotiation. I felt relaxed, newly energized, and clear.

Toward the end of my walk, I passed by a temporary outdoor sculpture exhibit from China in a plaza. Giant silver and golden Buddhas were suspended on wires in the air. In the brilliant sunlight, the figures were flying, dancing, and laughing, clearly enjoying the beauty of life.

I had been unsure about how to start off the talks and frame the issue, but suddenly, here in these unexpected pieces of art, I had my answer. Why, I wondered, do we get so lost in fighting when life is so precious and fleeting?

An hour later, I was seated at lunch with a distinguished French banker, a cultivated and dignified gentleman in his early seventies, who was a mentor for the other party in the bitter business dispute. As I introduced myself, I could see a quizzical look on his face. He had followed the story of the conflict from the beginning and had his reasons to be deeply suspicious of any approaches.

After some initial pleasantries, he turned to me and asked:

"So tell me, *why* are you here?"

I thought for just a moment—and the answer came quickly as I remembered those laughing Buddhas.

*"Parce que la vie est trop courte,"* I answered in French. "Because life is too short for this kind of conflict where everyone suffers— your friend and my friend, their families, their employees."

The banker looked a bit surprised. That was not exactly what he had been expecting to hear.

That simple phrase—"Life is too short"—set a very different tone for the negotiation. It reframed a highly adversarial conflict as a collaborative negotiating effort by two friends of the parties to help resolve an unfortunate and costly dispute.

And from that one phrase, born out of the sheer emptiness of a morning stroll and inspired by a glimpse of beauty and wonder, came all the other phrases that led four days later to the two former estranged business partners sitting down at a table in a law office to sign an agreement and wishing each other well.

The lesson for me was the extraordinary value in tense conflict situations of taking a transformative pause.

Resourcing ourselves can sometimes be very simple. Many years ago, I had the opportunity to participate in a conference in Trento, Italy, about the future of humanity with the Dalai Lama. In a question-and-answer session, one of the participants asked a lengthy and complex question about the difficulties he was experiencing in dealing with his reactive mind during his meditation practice. The question was translated into Tibetan at great length. The Dalai Lama listened carefully and reflected for a moment, then offered a brief answer in his Tibetan-accented English:

*"Get more sleep."*

## BUILD A BALCONY

Given just how hard it is to remember to pause in the heat of conflict, I have learned over the years to compensate by *building* a balcony. In every way I can, I seek to create intentional places and times to pause. Advance planning helps.

Building a balcony may simply mean designing a planned break—or series of breaks—in what may be a contentious meeting. Or it may mean deciding in advance that the first meeting will be just for mutual understanding and that thorny decisions will be made only at the second meeting after a good night's sleep. Or it may mean incorporating a walk into a tense work session where people can get out in nature, stretch their legs, and walk side by side. A planned pause can serve as a safety net for a difficult meeting.

Building a balcony can also take the form of recruiting a trusted person whom we can call on for help whenever we feel as though we're becoming reactive. The professional hostage negotiators I know never negotiate alone, because they know how easily they can become emotionally overstretched when people's lives are on the line. For the same reason, I prefer to work with partners on any sensitive or protracted conflict. They serve as my balcony, and I serve as theirs.

Perhaps most tangibly, building a balcony means choosing and designing a physical environment in which the parties can pause. I came to appreciate the power of the right environment at a highly polarized meeting of twenty American civic leaders in October 2005.

Worried about the growing political polarization in our country, a group of colleagues and I invited the leaders of major national organizations, equally drawn from the right and the left, the conservative and progressive sectors of society. Each of these leaders regarded those on the other side as political enemies. Their mass fundraising messages to their constituents habitually vilified each other's organizations.

"I really don't know how this is going to work," one of the potential participants said to me before the meeting. "We have nothing in common. Isn't this meeting just going to blow up in our faces?"

The leaders had never met in person except on television talk shows to debate and attack one another. It took real courage for many of them to even come, as they naturally faced criticism from their own side for associating with the enemy. Though they differed greatly in their political views, they did share one thing in common: a deep concern about where the country was headed.

They were extremely busy people, used to packed days advocating, organizing, and lobbying. We designed the meeting to last three days—to allow enough time and psychological space to give the participants a chance to get to know one another as human beings, not just as political targets.

We wanted to put as much distance as we could from the tense atmosphere of Washington, DC, where most of them worked. We picked an old Girl Scout lodge, transformed into a rustic inn, in the Rocky Mountains near Denver. It was a beautiful spot on the shore of a shimmering mountain lake.

*Place has power.*

We often associate relaxation with hanging out with friends and family, but I have found it to be almost an essential precondition if we are to engage our differences constructively. We may not be aware of it, but when we walk into a contentious situation, our nervous systems are on alert, constantly vigilant for threats. A welcoming environment helps us relax and feel safe.

One of the wisest pieces of advice I've ever heard is *"If you have something hard to do, begin by relaxing."* It may seem paradoxical, but it makes sense. When we are overstressed, we are not at our best. Relaxing is how we come into our highest potential, exactly what we need when facing difficult conflicts.

When the civic leaders arrived at the inn, an early-autumn snow was beginning to fall. It had been a long trip. They were tired, hungry, and not a little anxious at the prospect of spending time with their political adversaries. They were welcomed with warmth and care, placed in comfortable cabins, and provided with delicious fresh meals. Surrounded by beauty, nourished, and sheltered, the leaders began to relax.

We began our discussion the next morning in the barn, sitting in a big circle. My colleague said:

"We'd like each of you to tell a story from your younger days about what first inspired you to go into a political life. As you think of that story, see if you can name a core political value that the story evokes for you. Like freedom or justice or dignity, for example."

We divided the participants into groups of four to share their stories with one another. Then we all gathered again to glean the essence of the stories. Though each story was different, the core values revealed a great deal of overlap. The exercise was eye-opening for all of us. However sharp the participants' political differences were, their underlying commonalities were clear.

"Now we'd like to hear about your hopes and fears for this country. What kind of country would you like your children and grand-children to grow up in?"

As the leaders spoke about themselves and what they cared about most, they began to relax. They remembered that they were all citizens of a country they loved. They stopped seeing one another as one-dimensional caricatures and began to connect with one another as human beings. Little gestures of kindness—asking about someone's altitude headache or bringing someone a cup of coffee—started to multiply.

In those three days, we found ourselves on the balcony—literally, at 8,000 feet in the mountains. The prolonged pause in beautiful surroundings had a calming effect on everyone. When we did talk about charged political issues, people seemed less reactive. The quality of listening improved.

On the third day, one participant remarked to the entire group:

"Let me confess that when I arrived and saw who actually was here and from what organizations, I felt like immediately turning around and going back to the airport to catch the next flight home. Now I feel differently."

Another participant piped up:

"It's a good thing there was a snowstorm that locked us in here so we actually had to be with each other."

Everyone laughed.

In the end, the group made tangible progress exploring common ground. And they formed unlikely relationships across political lines. Small but significant transformations began to occur. The most immediate concrete result emerged from two participants, both women, one very progressive and one very conservative. They spent so much time talking and getting to know each other that they decided to do some work together, with their organizations, on issues on which they could both agree.

They did not have to wait long. Three weeks after the retreat, there was a hearing in the US Senate on the issue of a privatized internet. The senators were astonished to see the unlikely partnership of the two organizations, normally political enemies, testifying together against the proposed measure. The senators backed down quickly, figuring that if the issue had succeeded in uniting these two organizations, it was a certain political loser.

That meeting in the mountains vividly demonstrated for me the power and benefit of designing a conducive environment in which parties in conflict can pause together. Building a strong and robust balcony in advance can help us contain people's natural reactions and open up new possibilities we had not imagined.

## A BIG WAVE STARTS SMALL

Even the biggest wave in the ocean starts off very small, almost undetectable. The same is true of the process of transforming conflict. It starts off quiet and still, with a *pause*.

If I had to pick one person who exemplifies reaching our full human potential for transforming seemingly impossible conflict, that person would be Nelson Mandela. Mandela was the very archetype of a *possibilist*.

Arrested by the apartheid government of South Africa for his activities as the leader of the resistance movement, Mandela spent twenty-seven years in prison, most of it confined to a tiny cell on Robben Island. On February 1, 1975, he wrote from his prison cell to his young wife, Winnie, in her prison cell in Kroonstad:

> The cell is an ideal place to learn to know yourself, to search realistically and regularly the process of your own mind and feelings.... At least, if for nothing else, the cell gives you the opportunity to look daily into your entire conduct, to overcome the bad and develop whatever is good in you. Regular meditation, say of about fifteen minutes a day before you turn in, can be very fruitful in this regard.... Never forget that a saint is a sinner who keeps on trying.

As a young man, Mandela was known for his fiery hot temper; he was a boxer, quick to strike out. In that little cell, as he recounted in his autobiography, *Long Walk to Freedom*, he learned a lot about himself and what matters most in life. He could have raged and agonized but, in a supremely challenging situation of enormous injustice, he courageously made the choice to use his time behind bars as a pause on the balcony. He learned to pause his reactive mind with a regular practice of meditation. He exercised the essential power each of us has, even in the worst of situations, to pause and choose our response.

By learning to influence his own mind and heart, he was later able to become an extraordinary influencer of the minds and hearts of millions of others around him. It was there, in his solitary jail cell, that he helped lay the foundations for transforming the conflict in South Africa—through the core practice of pausing.

Pausing is the first essential step on the *path to possible*. It is how and when we make the fundamental *choice* of whether to deal with conflict destructively or constructively.

*Pausing is the key that enables us to escape the prison of destructive conflict.*

# CHAPTER 4

# ZOOM IN

## From Positions to Needs

*Who looks inside, awakes.*
—Carl Jung

T his is a five-month-old female scheduled for surgery on her tethered spinal cord in Chicago later this week," the doctor announced in a cold clinical tone to the medical students surrounding him. "I've seen many surgical cases just like this where the patient came out paraplegic."

The doctor making his rounds was referring to my precious infant daughter, Gabi, who was being cradled in her mother's arms as we were waiting for our appointment at the Children's Hospital. The doctor seemed utterly unaware of the impact of his words on my wife, Lizanne, and me. It was as if we were not there.

In shock, I froze for a moment and felt my blood curdle with fear, disbelief, and anger. I was about to burst out with indignation, but before I could muster up words, the doctor had moved on with his students.

A month or two later, we were back in the clinic at Children's Hospital. The highly delicate and risky surgery in Chicago had thankfully been successful. Gabi needed a pediatric surgeon for further surgery on her organs.

"Perhaps the most important doctor Gabi is going to need to accompany her in her childhood is a pediatric surgeon. The best surgeon in town for her is Tom Tanner," said my friend Dr. Ed Goldson.

"Dr. Tanner?" I repeated, faintly recognizing the name.

It turned out to be the very same doctor who had been so oblivious and insensitive in his commentary making the rounds with his students.

"Never!" said Lizanne to me when I reported Ed's recommendation.

"I agree. No way. Not someone so insensitive. He can't take care of Gabi!" I echoed.

But even as the matter seemed completely resolved, I had a doubt in the back of my mind.

I went for my favorite walk in a nearby canyon to reflect on what was truly important. What did we *really* want? It didn't take long for the answer to come. I could feel it in my gut. It was clear: we wanted the best care available for our daughter. Her life and well-being were at stake.

I came back and decided to do a little more investigation. I called the nurse in the surgery clinic and asked her about Dr. Tanner and what he was like.

"I find him to be a very caring doctor," she told me. "He really is dedicated to his patients."

I decided to approach Lizanne on the issue again—a bit gingerly, given her feelings. I told her about my walk as well as my conversation with the nurse:

"I was really surprised to hear this from the nurse, but she sounded sincere. We obviously want to do what's best for Gabi long term. I think we should meet with Dr. Tanner, just you and me, to see what he's really like. What do you think?"

Lizanne agreed.

We went to see Dr. Tanner in his office. We made no mention of our first encounter. I am not even sure he remembered it. We talked with him at length about Gabi's condition and prognosis. He spent more than an hour with us to answer our many questions in detail. He seemed competent and kind. Lizanne and I left with a very different impression from our first one.

We decided to give him a try. In the end, Dr. Tanner became Gabi's doctor for more than ten years. He followed her case closely and performed four complex and risky surgeries on her, one lasting nine hours. Before and after each of them, he met with us and answered all our questions. He became close, a familiar and trusted ally in our daughter's harrowing medical journey.

Two years later, as life would have it, he and his wife suffered their own heartbreaking tragedy when their six-year-old daughter was diagnosed with life-threatening cancer; she died a year later. Dr. Tanner's heart opened, and he grew even more empathetic and caring. Our relationship with Dr. Tanner, which had started off so brusquely, opened up possibilities far beyond what we ever could have imagined.

None of that would have happened, of course, if my wife and I had followed our initial impulses. During our daughter's medical saga, Lizanne and I encountered many difficulties with overwhelmed doctors and nurses; we learned how easy it is to be distracted by our initial reactions and forget what matters most in conflict situations. In this case, our deepest interest was ensuring that we found the very best, most expert care for our daughter.

## FOCUS ON WHAT MATTERS

"What do I *really* want?"

It sounds like a simple question. But in my experience, the answer is often unclear, especially when we are trapped in conflict. We may believe we know what we want, but do we really?

As a result of not knowing what we really want, it is all too easy for us to act in ways that are contrary to our deepest interests. That's why we often experience outcomes where everyone loses.

Our first natural power—to *pause*—opens up the time and space for us to exercise our second natural power—to *zoom in*. By zoom in, I simply mean to focus your attention on what you really want.

In the language of negotiation, to zoom in means to focus on the *interests* that lie underneath our *positions*. Positions are the things we say we want. Interests are our underlying motivations—our desires, aspirations, concerns, fears, and needs. Whereas positions are *what* we say we want, interests are *why* we want what we want.

My favorite teaching story for illustrating this distinction is one my co-authors and I used in *Getting to Yes* more than forty years ago. Two students are quarreling in a library. One wants the window open. The other wants it closed. The first student opens the window; the second goes and slams it shut. An argument breaks out, and the librarian comes over to find out what's the matter.

"*Why* do you want the window open?" she asks the first student.

"To get some fresh air."

"*Why* do you want the window closed?" she asks the second student.

"Because the wind is blowing my papers around."

The librarian then goes to the room next door and opens a window, thereby providing fresh air for the first student without a draft for the second.

So what happens in this simple story? The two sides' positions are clear. One student wants the window open, while the other wants the window closed. But the conflict is transformed when the librarian asks the magical question *"Why?"* She seeks to get at what each student really wants. One wants fresh air, while the other wants to avoid a draft. Uncovering the underlying interests leads to opening up a new possibility—an open window in the next room.

Note that it is not just a compromise, splitting the difference between the two opposed positions. In that case, a half-open window might have left both students unsatisfied, with not enough fresh air for one and too much draft for the other. An open window in the next room is an integrative solution that satisfies the interests of both sides.

This story was inspired by a short passage I found in a groundbreaking paper, "Constructive Conflict," written nearly a century ago in 1925, by a brilliant teacher and author from Boston named Mary Parker Follett. Aptly called the "prophet of management" by the eminent business thinker Peter Drucker, Follett was way ahead of her time.

I like to use the library story to illustrate the vital distinction between our positions and our interests. Even when positions are directly opposed, as in the case of a closed versus open window, the interests may not be opposed. They may simply be different, as in the example of fresh air and no draft. As the story illustrates, positions close off possibilities, whereas interests open up new possibilities.

For many decades, I have taught the importance of focusing on the interests behind positions to tens of thousands of people from all walks of life, from law students to diplomats, from business managers to UN peacekeepers, from first graders to seniors in retirement communities. I never cease to be impressed at how consistently this simple distinction produces an *aha!* for people, even for those who know it already.

But as I've learned over the years while dealing with contentious conflicts since writing *Getting to Yes*, we may need to go even deeper into our interests than we might normally go.

Imagine an iceberg where positions are the visible part of the iceberg above the ocean surface and interests lie beneath the surface. What we don't see is much bigger than what we do see. Now imagine that the interests we are able to identify are the middle part of the iceberg below the surface. If we are to succeed in opening up new possibilities in seemingly impossible conflicts, we may have to dive even deeper to the lowest part of the iceberg, where our core needs and values reside. In those depths, we can find the secret to transforming difficult conflicts.

To reach these deeper motivations, we must *zoom in* and focus our attention on what lies underneath our positions.

## FOCUS ON WHAT'S UNDERNEATH

In January 2000, I was in Geneva working with the Centre for Humanitarian Dialogue to mediate a peace agreement between the government of Indonesia and a guerrilla movement known as the GAM—the Free Aceh Movement. For twenty-five years, the GAM had been fighting a war for the independence of Aceh, a region on the island of Sumatra.

My colleague Martin Griffiths, the director of the Centre, had succeeded in persuading both sides to come to the table. The leaders of the guerrilla movement were the first to arrive. The plan was for my colleagues and me to spend a day alone with them to prepare them for their meeting with the foreign minister of Indonesia.

We had dinner the night before at a lovely Geneva restaurant. The GAM delegation was headed by the founder of the movement, Hasan di Tiro, an Acehnese nobleman descended from the sultans of Aceh, who had for centuries ruled a powerful kingdom. Di Tiro was a man of proud bearing, very conscious of the long and distinguished history of Aceh. Sadly, he had suffered a stroke and thus was quiet most of the time, although paying keen attention. He was represented by the GAM's prime minister, Malik Mahmud, an intelligent, earnest engineer.

The next day, we met in the manor house that served as the headquarters of the Centre. The house stood in a beautiful park on the shores of the stunningly blue Lake Geneva, with a view on the other side of the towering, snowcapped Mont Blanc.

The GAM leadership were seated at a table, formally dressed in suits.

I stood facing them, a flip chart at my side.

"Let me ask you a question to start us out. I understand your *position*. You want independence from Indonesia. Now please tell me your *interests*. In other words, *why* do you want independence?"

I stood, colored marker in hand, poised to record their answer.

They looked at me blankly. There was an awkward silence. They seemed to be struggling with the question. Their position of independence was so self-evident and so unanimously shared that they seemed to feel no need to probe more deeply.

At that moment, a sobering thought dawned on me. They had been fighting a war for twenty-five years. Many thousands had died—men, women, and children. The leaders in that room knew their *position*, but did they really know their *interests*? Had they thought through, articulated, and prioritized their underlying aspirations and deepest concerns?

*Why* were they really fighting for independence?

On reflection, I realized that those leaders were not unlike so many of the other parties I've worked with in conflict. They were stuck in their positions, ignoring their interests, and thereby missing a real opportunity to open up new possibilities.

After the awkward silence, I followed up with other questions to help them zoom in on what they really wanted:

"Can you explain to me what independence will provide for you?

"Do you want independence for *political* reasons? In order to give you self-rule? To have your own parliament and your own elected leaders? Is that it?"

"Yes, we want those things, of course," the prime minister replied. "But we want more than that."

"We want to have control over the natural energy resources that lie off the coast of Aceh," one of the Acehnese leaders added.

"And we want our children to be able to go to school in their own language," another said.

"We want to practice our religion the way we want to practice it."

I noticed the participants coming alive as they got engaged with their deeper motivations. They were *zooming in* behind their positions to focus on their underlying interests. I asked them to rank the various interests in terms of importance to them. They thus began to develop a strategic agenda for the talks the next day.

"Tell me something," I continued. "Without giving up your aspiration for independence, is there some way you can advance these interests you listed in the talks tomorrow with the Indonesian government?"

"Are you saying we can keep our goal of independence and at the same time negotiate our political, economic, and cultural interests?" asked the prime minister.

"Exactly. Negotiating doesn't mean you have to abandon altogether your dreams of independence sometime in the future. It means improving the lives of your people now."

It was a big realization for the leaders, reframing their understanding of negotiation and what it could achieve for them.

The subsequent talks in Geneva resulted in a temporary cease-fire for humanitarian purposes. The bigger result was that it initiated a deep strategic review within the independence movement about their underlying interests and the best way to pursue them.

Five years later, in the wake of a devastating tsunami in their region, with the mediation of former Finnish president Martti Ahtisaari, the GAM negotiated an agreement with the Indonesian government. They received a large measure of autonomy, which satisfied many of the political, economic, and cultural interests that they had specified. Elections were held in Aceh, and, strikingly, the winning candidates for governor and vice governor turned out to be leaders of the GAM.

This experience highlighted for me the real power of *zooming in*. Asking the magical *why?* question invites people to go deeper into their motivations. As the GAM leadership learned, even if you cannot obtain your *position*, you may be able to find ways to advance your underlying *interests*. But that is possible only if you have done the hard work of uncovering those interests. Zooming into your underlying motivations opens up the real possibility of reaching a mutually satisfying agreement that addresses the interests of all.

## KEEP ASKING WHY

It is often not enough to ask ourselves *why?* just once. To get to the deepest level of the iceberg, we may need to keep asking *why?*—two, three, four, even five times in succession.

"I have a question for you," announced the sales director of a software firm where I was giving a workshop on negotiation some years ago. His voice had a tone of frustration and desperation.

"Our biggest customers are constantly demanding changes to the software. They want us to tailor it to their needs, but it is very costly and time consuming. They don't want to pay for it, and it's cutting very seriously into our revenues. The situation is untenable. I need to say no, but I just can't. They are our most important customers, after all."

I recognized that he was avoiding a conflict that needed to happen—in a constructive way—if the business was going to succeed. In an effort to help, I asked him a series of *why?* questions:

"*Why* do you want to say no? What are you trying to protect?"

"Maintain revenues," he replied.

"Okay, fine, but *why* do you want to maintain revenues?" I asked.

"Because we need to make a profit," he said with a tone of finality.

"Of course you do. But tell me *why* you need to make a profit," I said.

"So our company can survive!" he exclaimed.

"I got it. Now humor me and tell me *why* exactly you want your company to survive," I persisted.

"So we can all have jobs!" he said with a tone of exasperation as he motioned to his colleagues in the room.

"But *why* do you want a job?" I asked.

He paused and looked at me, quizzically.

"Well, so I can put *food* on my family's table!"

There was real emotion in his voice. I sensed from his tone that we had reached bedrock. Feeding his family was his most basic underlying need.

It was an uncomfortable process for him. With each answer, he thought he had concluded the matter. But as he continued, more and more resolve came into his voice. The discomfort paid off.

I said to him:

"So, going back to the question you asked me, next time you find yourself in the situation of having to say no to a really important customer, imagine that saying no is allowing you to put food on your family table. You are not just maintaining revenues; you are protecting your family. That will give you the strength you need to say no when you need to."

Asking yourself why—repeatedly—can bring you strategic clarity, and with that clarity comes resolve and power. It's like the roots of a tree: the deeper the roots go, the stronger the tree will stand even in the midst of stormy weather. Putting food on the family table had a much deeper meaning and strength for the sales director than an interest in maintaining revenues or generating profit did.

## UNCOVER BASIC HUMAN NEEDS

"It looks like I'm going to be fighting this man until my last day. Maybe it's my destiny and I should just accept it," my friend Abilio Diniz sighed to me. I could hear the tremendous frustration and anger in his voice.

Abilio, one of Brazil's best-known business leaders, was then over two years deep into a bitter dispute with his French business partner. The conflict had taken over his life. It was poisoning him with rage, keeping him from his family, and unsettling the lives of the company's many thousands of employees.

By the time I got involved, the board meetings had grown highly explosive, with at least a dozen law firms and multiple PR firms engaged, countless lawsuits, character assassination in the press, and suspicions of corporate espionage. Even the presidents of France and Brazil had gotten onto the phone with each other to discuss its impact. The *Financial Times* called the dispute "perhaps the biggest cross-continental boardroom showdown in recent history."

The clash centered on a dispute between the business partners over control of Brazil's leading supermarket retailer, Pão de Açúcar. The supermarket had begun as a local neighborhood bakery that belonged to Abilio's father. When Abilio was a boy, he had worked behind the counter. He had helped his father build the bakery into a huge supermarket chain. Pão de Açúcar was his identity and his lineage.

Many years later, needing funds to expand the business further, he had brought in a leading French businessman, Jean-Charles Naouri, as his partner. Abilio had taken the much younger man under his wing and had taken pleasure in mentoring him.

"We were close," Abilio reflected to me. "He would come to our home and bring gifts. I visited him at his home, too, in Paris."

Abilio loved to make business deals—it was one of the secrets of his success. However, in 2011, when he sought to merge the business with another big retailer, Jean-Charles objected and filed a lawsuit. Each partner felt betrayed by the other, and a hotly contested battle began.

Emotions run high, positions become entrenched, and destructive fighting breaks out. Attack leads to counterattack. This dispute was like so many others we face today.

"All the doors to negotiation are closed," Abilio's daughter Ana Maria had first written to me, asking for help. While the email was polite and measured, it bore many of the hallmarks of angst and heartache that are common in difficult disputes. It was clear that she and the family were at their wit's end. They wanted their father and husband back.

Unsure of whether I could help, I offered to listen at least. On my next trip to Brazil, Abilio invited me to his home for lunch with his entire family. It was a beautiful morning. Sunlight poured in through the windows as I was graciously welcomed by his wife, Geyze. I could feel the love and concern for him from his family, but he wasn't able to relax into their warm embrace.

Abilio's youngest child, a lively boy of three, ran around the room. But his father was too preoccupied with his dispute to appreciate his young son's energy and enjoyment. I looked at the boy and his spirited six-year-old sister, then back at Abilio. He was seventy-six at the time. His time was precious. I remember thinking to myself, "What kind of life do these children have when their father is engulfed by a fight that is draining his life force?"

I also sensed the terrific anger inside him. He was known for having a volcanic temper. I could sense that the first opponent he needed to face was himself. If I was going to be of any help, I would need to help him get to the balcony.

He and I sat down in his living room surrounded by glass looking out on the garden and the pool. I had just finished up a couple of long days of teaching, and my voice was strained. I wanted to be sure he could hear me so I could connect with him. Each time before I spoke, I sprayed a bit of honey into my mouth. Though my voice was weary from overuse, his voice carried a weariness that reflected the emotional weight of the situation.

So I began my conversation by asking him my go-to question:

"Abilio, what do you *really* want from this negotiation?"

Like any good, intelligent businessperson, he knew the answer to the question. He immediately rattled off the list of his demands.

"I want all my stock to be convertible so I can sell it. I want the elimination of the three-year non-compete clause. I want the company headquarters. I want the company's athletic team."

"I understand that all those things are important to you. But what do you *really* want?" I persisted.

He paused and looked at me.

"What do you mean?"

"Well, you are a man who seems to have everything. You can do anything you want. You have these beautiful young children here. What do you *really* want at this moment in your life?"

He took a few moments to grapple with the question.

Finally, he took a deep breath.

"*Liberdade*," he said with a sigh. "Freedom. I want my freedom."

That was it. When I heard the tone and deep emotional resonance with which he pronounced the word *freedom*, I knew he had reached his bedrock need. It touched him. And it touched me. Who, after all, does not want to be free?

Before our meeting that day, I'd read about Abilio—the boy and the man—in his memoir. Freedom is important to all of us, but it had special resonance for Abilio. One morning in December 1989, as he was leaving his home, he was kidnapped by a group of urban guerrillas. He was pushed at gunpoint into a car and held hostage in a coffinlike box with only pinholes for air. He was constantly assaulted by loud music. He was sure he would die until suddenly he was rescued a week later during a surprise police raid.

Now, years later, he found himself held hostage again, this time to a conflict that utterly consumed him. He needed to understand himself, yes, but, if I was to help, I, too, needed to understand him.

Up to that moment, I wasn't sure whether I was the right person to help him get the material items he demanded. But when he said he wanted his *freedom*, I began to think that perhaps I could help him after all.

I realized that it wasn't just an ordinary business conflict but an all-too-human conflict with all its psychological complexities and possibilities. It was the kind of conflict we all face today in our families, our workplaces, and the larger world.

"And what does *freedom* mean to you, Abilio?" I asked.

"Time with my family," he said as he pointed to his children, "which is the most important thing in my life.

"And the freedom to make the business deals I love to make."

He could have replied, "*Freedom from* my enemy" or "*Freedom from* this nightmare." That would have been negative freedom. Instead, he focused on positive freedom, *freedom for*. He focused not on what he wanted to escape from but on what he wanted to move toward.

In conflicts, we often get so caught up in taking positions that we lose sight of our basic human needs. Yet in my work, I have found that the conflicts that truly trouble us, big and small, are usually not just about surface interests but are driven by deeper motivations. In the opening example about my daughter, Gabi, the basic needs my wife and I cared most about were Gabi's safety and well-being. For the Acehnese leaders, the basic needs included political autonomy and cultural identity. My friend Abilio's basic needs were freedom and dignity. Other basic needs include security, economic sustenance, belonging, and respect. Needs go deeper than wants and desires.

Here's the secret: At this deeper level, you will discover less conflict and more possibility than at the surface level of positions or even at the middle level of interests. In Abilio's dispute, the positions could not have been more opposed. At the level of interests, there was less conflict but still considerable tension: a better financial deal for Abilio generally meant a less favorable one for Jean-Charles. But at the level of needs, *more* freedom for one did not mean *less* freedom for the other. Nor did *more* dignity for one mean *less* dignity for the other. On the contrary, the agreement we reached offered both men dignity and the freedom to pursue their big dreams.

Here's what I have learned from conflicts such as this: *the deeper we go into motivations, the more possibilities we find for transforming conflict.* So don't just stop at positions or even interests. Keep zooming in until you reach basic human needs.

## PAY ATTENTION TO EMOTIONS AND SENSATIONS

Emotions and sensations offer perhaps the surest indicator that we have uncovered basic needs. There was something in Abilio's tone when he pronounced the word *liberdade*—freedom—that gave me a sense that I had hit gold. It is like the ring of a bell when you hit it just right.

Tone of voice can be revealing, often more than words, precisely because tone conveys emotions. The way Abilio pronounced the word *freedom* sounded sad, wistful—almost as if freedom were an elusive dream to him. If his first answer to my question about what he *really* wanted had come from his *head,* clear cut and logical, his second answer sounded as though it came from his *heart* and *gut.*

In negotiations, it is common for us to think of emotions as getting in the way. But emotions—and the physical sensations that accompany them—carry vital information about the deeper motivations that drive us. Fear, anger, and frustration can be signs that some basic need of ours is not being met. If we can pause and listen to our emotions and sensations, we will find that they are saying to us:

"Pay close attention. Something important may be at stake."

In conflict situations, I find it very helpful to *zoom in* and notice what emotions and sensations I'm feeling. When I feel angry, it tells me that an important boundary may have been crossed.

"What is that boundary?" I ask myself.

When I get a queasy feeling in my stomach or feel a slight pang in my chest, I get curious. I have come to understand these sensations and feelings as possible *signposts* pointing me in the direction of my basic human needs.

"What needs of mine are not being met?"

Taking a pause allows me to zoom into myself and notice my emotions and sensations. Because I have paused, I don't need to *react* to the emotions that arise but can simply *observe* them. Pausing provides me the emotional distance necessary to digest valuable information about my needs without getting reactive.

*Isn't that interesting?* I can say to myself.

When I reach the deepest need inside myself, I often feel a sense of emotional relief and a spaciousness opening up in my chest. I feel my shoulders relax. I feel a yes coming from my gut, which some scientists now call our second brain. These emotions and sensations tell me that I'm on the right track.

Over the years, I have come to appreciate how our emotions and sensations can be good friends and allies, providing vital clues for understanding ourselves—and others around us.

On the path to possible, emotions and sensations are signposts pointing to the underlying basic human needs—such as safety, freedom, and dignity—needs that we must satisfy if we are to transform conflicts and relationships in these turbulent times.

## EYES ON THE PRIZE

That one revelatory insight about freedom took Abilio—and me—on a journey of possibility that transformed a bitter conflict with his business partner, Jean-Charles, into a friendly relationship once again. It seemed utterly impossible, yet that was what eventually happened.

*Zooming in* on what Abilio *really* wanted proved to be the key breakthrough that led to everything else. From that moment on, freedom became the touchstone that governed my conversations with him and my negotiations with the other side. Freedom became our guiding light. Whenever Abilio fell back into rage and despair, taking refuge in rigid and extreme positions, I would remind him of his realization of what was *most* important. It helped him let go, bit by bit.

Freedom was what he wanted, and freedom was what he got.

As Abilio said to me the day he signed the agreement together with Jean-Charles:

"I got *everything* I wanted. But *the most important thing is that I got my life back*."

Those who felt the greatest relief, of course, were Abilio's family members.

"I arrived in Brazil this morning from New York," wrote his daughter Ana María to me the day after the agreement. "I flew directly to meet my father. I couldn't wait one more minute to see how he was. I found him very serene and enthusiastic about the future and his new life after Jean-Charles. I was very happy to see him like that."

But perhaps the most poignant expression of the change came from Geyze and Abilio's three-year-old son, Miguel.

"Papai isn't on the phone all the time anymore," he told his mother.

I was moved by how Abilio and his family chose to celebrate the dramatic transformation of the conflict that had burdened their lives for so long. Together they traveled across the ocean to Cascia, Italy, where they gave thanks to Santa Rita, the Patroness of Impossible Causes. Santa Rita had become a nun while successfully ending a violent family vendetta that had claimed the life of her husband and many others. Her story, like Abilio's, reminds us that we all have the capability, even when conflicts seem utterly impossible, to find creative ways forward.

As I was writing this book, I visited Abilio, who had become a good friend along with his whole family, for his eighty-fifth birthday celebration. There, in front of his wife and children, his family and friends, he talked movingly about his life and recounted the story of how he had transformed his conflict with Jean-Charles. He declared that the past nine years had been the happiest time of his life. He had been able to truly enjoy his hard-won freedom. He talked about time spent with his family, driving his children to school every morning, and picking them up in the afternoon. And he spoke about the rewarding new business deals he had made in the intervening years.

It left me wondering.

Would Abilio have enjoyed his freedom without the learning and growth stimulated by the conflict? Could this be the *hidden gift of conflict*—that by putting us in touch with our deepest needs, it gives us a chance to satisfy those needs in a way we might not have done without the conflict?

So my questions for you, as you consider your own conflicts, are:

What do you *really* want? What is your equivalent of freedom and dignity? What matters most to you? Keep asking yourself the magical *why?* question until you hit bedrock. Listen to your emotions and sensations as cues. Focus on your basic human needs. Be curious. You may uncover new possibilities you have not yet imagined. That is the great power of *zooming in*—a power available to each of us at any time.

Keep your eyes on the prize.

**CHAPTER 5**

# ZOOM OUT

## From Blinders to Big Picture

*The garden of the world has no limits,*
*except in your mind.*
—Jalāl al-Dīn Rūmī

I t was my first big failure as a mediator.

It started with a dream invitation. "I have a juicy proposition for you," Stephen Goldberg, a visiting professor at Harvard Law School, said to me one evening over dinner at the Faculty Club. "I just got off the phone with a high-level officer at the national mine workers union and an executive from the coal employers association. They have a really tough conflict on their hands at a coal mine in eastern Kentucky."

"What's it about?" I asked, my curiosity piqued.

"Well, all I know is that the miners keep going out on wildcat strikes. Management reacted by firing a third of the workforce," Steve replied. "It has gotten really ugly. Both officials are afraid that the strike will spread to other coal mines. They're worried it might even trigger a nationwide coal strike that could shut down the whole economy."

"What do they want you to do?"

"They're asking me to *mediate*," said Steve. "Here's the rub: I'm an arbitrator. I listen to the facts, and I make the decision. I haven't had any experience facilitating an agreement between the parties. Would you like to join me and help me figure out what to do?"

I was a graduate student looking for any chance to get out of the library and into the field to practice mediation. I had been saying to friends, "I need to get my hands dirty." Little did I imagine that I would be offered a chance to literally get my hands dirty in a coal mine.

"Sign me up," I told Steve.

Steve and I flew down to Kentucky the next week. At the local airport, he hired a helicopter to take us directly to the mine. I felt excited, not just because it was my first helicopter ride but because I was finally involved in a real-life major mediation.

As we flew over the bucolic green rolling hills of Appalachia, I looked down and saw the landscape with gashes in the hills and huge piles of slag, evidence of coal mining.

When we arrived at the mine, we went straight to the office, where we met the mine manager and his foreman.

"We run this mine by the contract—firmly and fairly. The troublemaker is the union president," said Mike Johnson, the mine manager, a bright, earnest engineer in his mid-thirties. "If we can just get rid of him and a couple other bad apples, the problem will go away. I guarantee you!"

Next we met with the union leader, Bill Blount, and his fellow union officers.

"The bosses treat us like dogs. They spy on us and try to scare us. I'll tell you what: fire the mine foreman and a couple others, and the situation will get much better, I promise you that!" said Bill, an ambitious, intelligent miner in his forties, new in his leadership job.

The other union officers nodded their heads vigorously.

"How about we all sit down together?" Steve asked. Steve had the bearing of a former Marine and radiated authority.

"No way we're going to sit down with them. There's no use talking with them. The only thing they understand is power," replied the union leader.

The problem, we learned, was this: when a miner felt he had been treated unfairly, he would take his water canteen and turn it upside down, emptying out the water. That was a sign to the other miners that he was going home. To protect the disgruntled miner from getting fired, the other miners would empty their canteens and go home, too, figuring that management wouldn't fire all of them.

It was called a *wildcat* strike because it violated the contract. As the incidents multiplied, management took the local union to court for an injunction against striking. When the miners paid no notice and continued to strike, the judge, in his infinite wisdom, decided to jail the whole workforce for a night.

Predictably, the move enraged the miners and their families. They began taking their guns to work. The mine's phone operator started receiving anonymous bomb threats. A bomb in a coal mine filled with methane gas could set the whole mine on fire. Even the threat of it meant that the mine needed to be closed while a search was carefully undertaken.

Steve and I had our work cut out for us. Over the next six weeks, we shuttled back and forth between the eight union leaders and the mine's management. We met with each side numerous times and got to know them a little better. We listened carefully, trying to understand what exactly was triggering the wildcat strikes and what could help bring them to an end. I was fascinated, both as a fledgling mediator and as a budding anthropologist.

Drawing on the suggestions we heard, Steve and I drafted a set of proposed changes to the contract. We focused on improving the procedure for handling grievances. We figured that if miners saw a good way to *talk out* their gripes, they wouldn't *walk out*.

On that basis, both sides finally agreed to sit down for a two-day meeting to iron out the details. There were eight representatives each from the union and from management. Steve chaired the meeting. To everyone's surprise, they reached agreement. The leaders were exhilarated. Each negotiator walked up to the head of the table and signed their name on the document solemnly, as if they were signing a peace treaty between warring nations.

"Wow," Steve said to me. "We did it!" I felt giddy with the first big success of my mediation career, even more because the odds had seemed so stacked against us.

We received congratulatory calls from the national union and the employers' association, including the two officials who had first called Steve for his help. Everyone was relieved by the outcome and impressed by the unlikely success of our mediation effort.

There was just one little procedure to complete: the miners needed to ratify the agreement. Everyone expected it to be a mere formality, given the support of the union leadership.

And indeed, the vote was nearly unanimous—in resoundingly *rejecting* the very agreement their leadership had just painstakingly negotiated.

My first major mediation was a complete bust. I felt the wind knocked out of me. All my initial excitement turned into a queasy feeling of disappointment.

What had happened?

As we learned, the miners had rejected the agreement simply because they believed that anything management had signed on to must be a trick. They didn't *trust* it. Even if the proposed agreement on paper addressed many of their grievances, it felt safer—and far more satisfying—to deliver a deafening *no*.

Steve and I—and the negotiators on both sides—had failed to foresee this problem because we had assumed that the conflict was between two monolithic parties, union and management. We had assumed that the union leadership spoke for their constituents—the rank-and-file miners. We had assumed that whatever the leadership agreed to would be supported. We were dead wrong.

It was as if we had *blinders* on, preventing us from seeing the *bigger picture*. We didn't see the messy complexity of the situation. There were many parties, not just two, and the leadership was diffuse, not just concentrated at the top. We had left out of the process the most critical stakeholders of all: the coal miners themselves. *They*, not the leadership, were deciding to go out on strike almost every week. If they weren't listening to their leaders in striking, *why* would they listen to their leaders in negotiating?

As I reflect on this failure, perhaps the biggest lesson I take away is the vital importance in any conflict of *zooming out* to a place of perspective where you can see the larger context and understand what is really going on.

## FOCUS ON THE BIGGER PICTURE

We each have the power to zoom out. By *zoom out*, I simply mean to *expand your focus to see the bigger picture*. Widen the lens on your camera. From the balcony, you can see the whole play unfolding in front of you with all the characters. Zooming out enables you to see new possibilities you hadn't seen before.

I have a distinct memory of an early experience of zooming out. It was a week before my sixth birthday. My family and I were staying in a little Swiss village on the lower slope of a high mountain. It was a Saturday morning, and I was up very early. My parents liked to sleep in late on the weekend. I felt an impulse to go out for a walk to explore the world.

I put on my clothes and headed out the door onto a lane that led up the mountain and past the wooden chalets with their brightly painted shutters and flower boxes filled with red geraniums. Soon the lane ended, and I continued onto a dirt walking path that led up the green grassy slopes to the rough wooden barns and cow pastures. The cows grazed, and their bells tolled slowly and sonorously. The fresh air was lightly scented with manure.

The higher I got, the smaller the village became. From the high mountain slopes, I turned around, looked down, and took in the big, sweeping view of the valley and the surrounding high mountains with their craggy peaks. I could see the entire village below me: the houses, the streets, and the river flowing through. I suddenly felt breathless—very small but exhilarated. I turned around and walked home, only to find everyone still asleep.

In the conflicts I have worked in over the last five decades, I've noticed how constricted our perspective can get. Our view can be limited to just one room in a single house in the village instead of taking in the big view, where we can see all the houses and the entire valley.

What limits our perspective, I find, are assumptions commonly made about negotiating conflict: There are *two parties* sitting at the table. The aim is to reach *agreement*. The time frame is *short term*. And the issue is *zero sum*: more for one means less for the other.

The possibilities for moving forward are thus highly constricted.

But if we are able to see the bigger picture, new possibilities start to open up. We may see *many parties* we may have missed. We may see *alternatives to agreement* that we hadn't considered. We may see *longer-term* scenarios we hadn't thought of. And we may see that the issue is not zero sum after all but rather *positive sum*: there can be more for everyone.

That is the great power of *zooming out*, a natural ability available to each of us.

## SEE THE THREE TABLES

From my failure at the coal mine, I learned a lesson that has served me well in the forty years since. That is to begin by zooming out and asking which stakeholders are *missing* from the table. Who am

I leaving out? Who else can influence the outcome? Who can block a possible agreement? Whose voice is not being heard?

I have often seen family conflicts escalate because a family member was left out of the decision-making process. I have seen companies that are in a rush to build a new plant forget to consult the local community, only to find that the community organizes itself and files a lawsuit that delays the project and sometimes blocks it permanently. As I learned at the coal mine, we sometimes leave out key players who surprise us later by sabotaging the agreement.

In a conflict negotiation, our attention naturally goes to the table, literal or metaphorical, at which the parties sit. That may be the *main* table, but it is not the *only* table. Zooming out from the balcony enables us to see at least *three* tables, depending on how many parties there are. In addition to the main table, there are at least two tables of internal stakeholders. For the union leadership, their constituents were the coal miners. For management, the stakeholders were the board and the employers' association.

As I have learned over the years, the real difficulty in getting to yes is not just in the *external* negotiation between the two parties but also in the *internal* negotiation within each party.

In my workshops, I like to ask:

"If there are two types of negotiation, the *external* ones with people outside your organization or family and the *internal* ones inside your organization or family, which type do you personally find more challenging?

"How many would say *external*—the outside negotiations are more difficult?"

Some hands go up.

"Okay, how many would say *internal*?"

The great majority of hands go up.

People look around, surprised at the uneven showing.

"Isn't that interesting?" I ask. "Both types can obviously be challenging, but the ones most of us seem to find hardest are the ones closest to us, with people in our family, with our colleagues with whom we are supposed to be on the same team."

An external negotiation can be hard, make no mistake, but an internal negotiation can often be even trickier. One reason is that we don't treat internal negotiation with the same care and preparation that we bring to external negotiation. We tend to wing it, assuming that the people on our team are with us, as the union leaders did in the case of the coal miners. To overlook internal stakeholders is to invite failure.

When dealing with a conflict, I have learned to begin by making a map of all the stakeholders, starting with the three tables. I ask myself and others:

"Who is sitting at the main table of negotiations? Who is sitting at the two internal tables? If there are more than two parties to the dispute, who is sitting at the other internal tables?

"What other stakeholders are there? Who is affected by the conflict? Who can block agreement—and needs to be consulted? And who can influence the parties to behave constructively—and needs to be recruited?"

The map starts to fill up with many stakeholders. Understanding the complexities may seem daunting at first, but in my experience, it can often reveal unexpected obstacles and can open up new possibilities for transforming a difficult conflict. That is the great benefit of zooming out from the balcony and seeing the whole stage with all the characters in the play.

## IDENTIFY YOUR BATNA

Zooming out can help us in another very important way in conflict situations: it can show us how to meet our needs even if we *can't* reach agreement with the other side.

I like to ask a simple question in my workshops:

"What's the *purpose* of negotiation? *Why* negotiate?"

"To reach agreement," participants typically respond.

"That is our *assumption*. But is it true?" I query.

The purpose of negotiation, I would suggest, is *not necessarily* to reach agreement. The real purpose is to *explore* with the other side whether you can meet your needs through negotiation better than you could by *not* negotiating—in other words, better than by using your *BATNA*.

*BATNA* is the acronym for Best Alternative To a Negotiated Agreement. It is a term my co-authors and I coined more than forty years ago in *Getting to Yes*. BATNA means your best alternative course of action for satisfying your interests if you *cannot* reach agreement.

Imagine a fork in the road. One fork leads to agreement. The other leads to your best alternative. Think of your BATNA as your "walk-away" alternative. It is your Plan B.

Developing your BATNA gives you the confidence that, no matter what happens in the negotiation, you have a good alternative. It makes you less dependent on the other side to satisfy your needs.

I think back to my friend Abilio, the Brazilian business leader who was immersed in a bitter dispute over control of the supermarket chain that he had built with his father. When Abilio told me that what he *really* wanted was his freedom, I asked him:

"Is there anything you can do, *independent* of whatever happens with Jean-Charles, to give yourself the freedom that you want so badly?"

That is the BATNA question.

Abilio looked at me blankly for a moment. So I clarified my question:

"When I asked what freedom means to you, you said it means freedom to spend time with your family and to pursue new business deals. My question to you is: Do you really have to wait for the dispute to end to do those things? Or can you start *now*?"

I looked into his eyes and could see a light beginning to dawn.

"The deeper question is *who* can truly give you the freedom you seek? Is it Jean-Charles? Or, in the end, is it only *you* who can give yourself that freedom?"

That turned out to be a big realization for Abilio—and for me. He realized that the power to fulfill his deepest need was in his own hands. It was not *dependent* on any other person or any particular outcome. He didn't need to wait for the resolution of his dispute.

Within days, he planned a sailing holiday with his family. Within weeks, he became the board chair of another company he was interested in. He also found a new office space, separate from company headquarters, where he could conduct business deals on his own. In short, he reclaimed his agency, his power, his choice.

Tellingly, those actions freed him from his psychological dependence on his opponent and the need to get him to behave a certain way. The sense of freedom Abilio won for himself created the emotional space for him to let go. Paradoxically, his letting go made it a lot easier for us to negotiate an agreement, one that ended up dramatically enhancing his ability to live his life as he truly wanted.

We may resist thinking about our BATNA because it seems like *negative* thinking. But as Abilio discovered, BATNA gives you freedom and confidence. It can make agreement more likely, not less. BATNA is best understood as *alternative positive* thinking. It opens up new possibilities.

I learned this lesson in the aftermath of the coal mine debacle. After the initial shock of the rejection of the agreement by the coal miners, my colleague Steve and I regrouped and tried to figure out what to do next. Could we do anything to recover from the blow of the failed ratification?

"Can we try to re-negotiate the agreement?" Steve asked.

"I asked Bill, the union leader," I answered. "He doesn't think there's a chance in hell that could work. I think he and the other union leaders are feeling really deflated."

"Any other ideas?" Steve asked. "Or are we at the end of the line?"

I paused for a moment. I wondered if we had a BATNA—a course of action independent of agreement.

"Here's a crazy question for you. Do we really *need* the agreement to be ratified by the miners?"

"What do you mean?"

"Well, we've been assuming that everyone needs to get on board before we even get started implementing the new process. But given the complete absence of trust, why not just try things out bit by bit and see if they work?"

"But don't we need the miners' approval? Wasn't that the problem in the first place?" Steve countered.

"You're right. But, as far as I can tell, the miners aren't objecting to the substance of the agreement, which is pretty much in their favor. I doubt many of them even read it. The problem seems to be more emotional. They're feeling angry and resentful. And they don't trust management one whit. Why would they?"

"So what are you suggesting instead?"

"My suggestion is to take the proposals in the agreement for how to handle grievances and try to implement them *informally*. Just ask management to do its part, and let's see if the miners respond favorably to the changes."

"That's not going to be easy. *How* exactly would you go about doing that?" Steve asked skeptically.

"Well, you and I would have to spend more time down at the mine, listening to the miners and uncovering their grievances before they go out on strike. Then we'd have to get management to pay attention and deal with the grievances satisfactorily so there wouldn't be a reason for a walkout."

Steve looked a bit doubtful. And it wasn't just him. Management and union both felt burned by the failure of the ratification vote. But they didn't object to my trying. After all, nothing else had worked. And the higher-ups in the national union and the employers association remained deeply worried about the dispute escalating into a national crisis.

"Be my guest," said Steve. "I'm off to France next week with my family for the summer."

And that was how I came to spend the summer of 1980 at a coal mine in Kentucky.

I will recount my hair-raising adventures working with the coal miners later, but the point is this: I had remembered to *zoom out*, which enabled me to question basic assumptions such as the necessity of getting agreement before trying to implement a new process.

Zooming out enabled me to see a new alternative—a BATNA—that was not evident to others.

In any conflict I find it vital to keep asking the key BATNA question:

"How can I meet my needs *if I cannot* reach agreement with the other side? What is my Plan B? How can I improve it?"

## FACE YOUR WATNA

"I like to look not only at my BATNA but also at my *WATNA*—my Worst Alternative To a Negotiated Agreement," a business leader once told me. "At moments in a deal when it looks like it might all fall through, I like to remind myself of what is the worst thing that could happen to me. I tell myself that if the other side is not actually going to *kill* me, then I will *probably* survive. Believe it or not, that helps reassure me and settle down."

He had a good point. Often, we get so wrapped up in a situation that it seems like a matter of life or death. Zooming out to the worst-case scenario can paradoxically help bring us much-needed perspective.

Sometimes, however, the negative scenario *is* a matter of life and death.

I spent the better part of the 1980s working on the problem of how to avert an accidental nuclear war. Based at the Program on Negotiation at Harvard Law School, my colleague Richard Smoke and I wrote a report at the request of the US government about how to reduce the risk of an accidental nuclear war between the United States and the Soviet Union.

In just one of many interviews we conducted, Benjamin Read,

a former high-level diplomat, told us about one close call, unknown to the world, that had haunted him for years:

"One Saturday morning, I was on duty at the State Department and received an urgent phone call from the National Military Command Center informing me that an American nuclear missile had misfired and was headed toward Cuba. I ran into the office of Dean Rusk, the secretary of state, to tell him the news."

"Is it armed?" Rusk asked anxiously.

"I'm sorry, we don't know, sir."

Rusk stared at Read.

"Well, call the Soviet ambassador immediately and let him know."

Read called the Soviet Embassy but was informed that the ambassador was out to lunch and could not be contacted. He told Rusk the news.

Rusk stared at Read again.

"Then call the Swiss in Havana. They pass messages for us," he said. "Tell them to let the Cubans know."

Read called the Swiss, but the connection was bad and the person at the other end of the phone could not understand the message.

The attempt at crisis communication failed dismally. Thankfully, the nuclear missile, which turned out to be unarmed, overshot Cuba and landed in the sea. What might have become a humanitarian disaster and superpower nuclear crisis—or worse—was averted by sheer luck.

"Did the government ever investigate this incident and figure out how to prevent it from happening again?" I asked Read.

"No," he replied. "I think everyone just moved on and forgot about it."

The misfire of a nuclear missile was just one of many close calls Richard and I included in our report to the US government, which served as the basis of a later book, *Beyond the Hotline: How Crisis Control Can Prevent Nuclear War.*

Far from making me throw up my hands in despair, I found that facing the grim negative possibilities of superpower conflict—the WATNA, in this case—motivated me to dive deeper and look for possible ways to prevent them. I saw it as an opportunity.

It was a good lesson for me. Ever since I was a child growing up in the shadow of the atomic bomb, I had worried about the nuclear threat. Taking concrete action offered me a welcome dose of immunity. Not only did action dispel anxiety, but it went even further and brought a sense of adventure and joy in fighting the good fight.

It was only by zooming out and looking at the negative scenarios that we could uncover positive possibilities: What could be done practically to reduce the risk of accidental nuclear war?

Richard and I came across one novel idea that seemed promising: What about establishing nuclear risk reduction centers, staffed around the clock, in which US and Soviet specialists would stand ready to communicate and de-escalate if, for example, a missile accidentally went astray?

I went on to help organize exchanges between US and Soviet policy experts on the question of how to avert nuclear war between our countries. I made many trips to Washington as well as to Moscow, traveling with my friend Bruce Allyn, a talented young scholar who spoke fluent Russian.

Tensions were high between the United States and the Soviet Union. In March 1983, President Ronald Reagan publicly branded the Soviet Union the "evil empire" and "the focus of evil in the modern world." Six months later, a Soviet missile shot down a Korean Air Lines plane on a flight from New York to Seoul that had accidentally strayed over the Soviet Union. All 269 passengers were killed.

On our first three-week trip to Moscow, Bruce and I were tailed by the KGB but still succeeded in having meetings with policy experts and government officials. We encountered a lot of skepticism about the idea of nuclear risk reduction centers. Wouldn't they just be used by the other side for the purposes of spying? What if they were misused to spread disinformation? Wouldn't their existence just make leaders more reckless in crisis situations?

My colleagues and I encountered many of the same questions in DC, but we persisted, working with two senators who were advocates of the idea: Senator Sam Nunn, a Democrat from Georgia, and Senator John Warner, a Republican from Virginia.

In addition to working the inside channels, we decided to try to build public support for the idea. *Parade* magazine invited me to write a piece about the nuclear risk reduction centers, and an artist drew a vivid, dramatized picture of US and Soviet officers working side by side to help avert an accidental nuclear war. The drawing went onto the cover of the magazine sent out to its 40 million readers.

Thankfully, the negative possibilities helped motivate the political leaders, too. At the start of his presidency, Ronald Reagan had signed a presidential directive calling for the United States to develop the ability to "win" a nuclear war. It was an option not to be ruled out. But almost three years into his term, he had a change of mind. He watched a prerelease version of *The Day After*, a fictionalized television drama about a nuclear war in all its gut-wrenching terror, depicted through the lives of ordinary people going about their day in a town in Kansas.

The film, watched by a hundred million Americans in its initial broadcast, brought home in a real way the utter senselessness of nuclear war. After screening the film, Reagan wrote in his diary, "It's very effective & left me greatly depressed," adding that there must "never [be] a nuclear war."

In November 1985, Reagan met for the first time with Soviet leader Mikhail Gorbachev in Geneva. Together the two leaders issued a short but memorable declaration that lives to this day in international agreements:

"A nuclear war cannot be won and must never be fought."

At the summit, Reagan and Gorbachev agreed, as one of several practical measures, to explore the possibility of creating nuclear risk reduction centers in Washington and Moscow. Having both recognized the negative possibilities of nuclear war, the two leaders discussed one positive possibility to avoid it. A few months later, I was invited to serve as an advisor to the White House Crisis Center. My job was to write a detailed proposal for the creation of the centers.

A year later, I stood in the Rose Garden behind the White House on a beautiful sunny day, the air sweet with the scent of the roses. As I watched President Reagan announce the agreement to create nuclear risk reduction centers, together with Soviet foreign minister Eduard Shevardnadze, I wanted to pinch myself. Here was evidence of what was possible.

It was a small but concrete step in the process that led to the end of the Cold War, which dramatically reduced nuclear risk.

The lesson I drew was: Face the *negative* possibilities and use the impetus to create *positive* possibilities that prevent the worst alternative from happening.

## BECOME AN ARCHAEOLOGIST OF THE FUTURE

"Imagine it's twenty years out. If peace were to come, what would you see? If you were an archaeologist from the future, and you were digging around, what artifacts would you find?"

The instruction came from my friend Rob Evans, a highly skilled facilitator of collective creativity. The occasion was a weeklong workshop in Colorado my colleagues and I had organized on the ever-challenging Israeli-Palestinian conflict.

In conflicts where a solution may seem impossible in the near term, we can *zoom out* to see a positive future. We can thus free our minds from the assumptions that constrain our imaginations. We can open up new possibilities for the longer term.

The participants from Israel, Palestine, and Egypt went to work in small mixed teams, recording their ideas on flip charts. An hour and a half later, they proudly displayed their work. One easel depicted a train ticket for a high-speed train between Tel Aviv and Gaza. Another showed a badge from the high-tech Gaza Google campus.

One of our Palestinian colleagues walked in the next morning and saw the walls covered with these ideas for the future. He smelled the rich, delicious aroma of a Middle Eastern dish called *shakshuka* being jointly prepared by a Palestinian and an Israeli and joyously announced:

"This is a museum of hope!"

The creative conversations in the ensuing days activated a sense of possibility in the participants that, they report, continues to motivate them to this day.

It makes me wonder what an *archaeologist of the future* exercise could reveal to us about the many other seemingly impossible challenges facing us today—from defusing political polarization to averting catastrophic war to making the transition to clean energy. Just imagine, for instance, that we as humanity succeed in greatly reducing the risks of extreme weather events and other disruptive climate change. What artifacts would archaeologists from the future find in their excavations?

Would they find, for instance, ubiquitous remains of solar and wind power stations? Would they find the remnants of high-voltage direct current (HVDC) grids linking the entire planet, creating enormous energy efficiencies? In other words, would they find widespread evidence that we were deriving our energy from limitless resources such as the sun and the wind? Working backward, would they conclude that we had faced the full magnitude of the problem, courageously worked through our differences, and deployed our innate creativity and collaboration to realize the positive possibilities of abundant clean energy?

Thought experiments like these, I have found, can create genuine hope and inspire practical action.

## CHANGE THE GAME

Finally, zooming out to see the bigger picture allows us to step back and consider perhaps the most important question of all. If conflict can be understood as a kind of game with players, rules, and goals, then we can ask ourselves:

"Are we playing the right game?"

In these divided times, we tend to reduce conflict to a win-lose, zero-sum struggle between "us" and "them." But is this the most useful way to achieve what we really want?

To shed light on this question, I like to offer participants in my seminars a challenge:

"Find a partner and prepare to arm wrestle."

Each person puts their arm up on a table and clasps their partner's hand tightly, ready to press it down onto the table.

"The objective of this game is to win by maximizing your points. Every time you get the other person's arm down, you get a thousand points.

"Everyone ready? Get set. *Go!*"

I look out at the room and see people everywhere struggling to pin their partner's hand down. After a minute or so, I say:

"Okay, you can stop. As I was looking at you, I saw a lot of stalemates. Zero points for one and zero points for the other. In some cases, I saw one person succeed in forcing the other's hand down. They get a thousand points.

"But then I saw a few others trying a totally different approach. Both your arms were going up and down like windshield wipers. Who would like to explain?"

One participant pipes up:

"Well, after trying unsuccessfully to force each other's arm down, we realized that the best way to win was to cooperate instead. So I relaxed my arm, and they got a thousand points. Then they relaxed their arm, and I got a thousand points. And then we looked at each other and realized we didn't have to stop there. We could just keep going and rack up points."

"How many points did you get in the minute I gave you?"

"Tens of thousands."

Everyone laughs—the laugh of recognition.

That's the secret. That's the zoom-out moment when we realize that *the greatest power we have in conflict is the power to change the game.*

How often in life do we approach conflicts as if they were like an arm-wrestling contest where the basic question is who wins and who loses? Instead, as this exercise makes clear, we can *choose* to play a much better game in which we can all benefit, often much more than we could even by winning a win-lose game.

Winning and losing can be fun in sports or card games. But when it comes to human relationships of interdependence—whether in the family, at work, or in the larger community—that question all too often produces an outcome in which everyone loses. If you're asking "Who's winning this marriage?" your marriage is probably in serious difficulty.

In contentious conflicts, we tend to frame the issue as essentially *zero sum*—more for one means less for the other. But in just about every real-world conflict that I have ever worked on, the issue is *not* zero sum. With a little bit of creativity, as in the arm-wrestling game, the results can often be *positive sum*—with more for everyone. And as in family feuds, business battles, and wars, the results can be negative sum—with less for everyone. Even if both sides can't always win, it's always possible for both sides to lose, along with everyone around them.

The opportunity to change the game was never more dramatically illustrated for me than in the struggle against apartheid in

South Africa. In early 1995, I had the opportunity to listen to the newly elected president, Nelson Mandela, and his old political adversary, former president F. W. de Klerk, describe their journey from war to peace.

Mandela talked about how he believed that his side would prevail in the long term but asked himself what kind of country they would inherit after decades of civil war and economic ruin. De Klerk spoke about how he had come to realize that, yes, his side could hold on to power for another generation, perhaps, but eventually they would have to give in to the demographic reality along with the increasing financial and political pressure from the outside world.

In other words, both leaders zoomed out to the long term and realized that the struggle they were trying to win by defeating the other would eventually result in a giant loss for both sides. That was their first insight—that the conflict was strategically stalemated.

Then came a second insight: If both sides could lose through a spiral of violence, perhaps both sides could benefit through a reverse spiral of dialogue and negotiation. They could find a compromise.

Finally, there came a third insight: the possibility of *transformation*. As Roelf Meyer, a negotiator for the National Party government, explained to me at the time, both sides gradually came to believe in the possibility of a third outcome, not a lopsided victory for one side nor even a split-the-difference compromise.

As Mandela declared:

I never sought to undermine Mr. de Klerk, for the practical reason that the weaker he was, the weaker the negotiations process. To make peace with an enemy, one must work with that enemy, and the enemy must become one's partner.

The new outcome the leaders on both sides envisioned was a genuine transformative victory for both sides—a peaceful, democratic, multiracial, inclusive, and prosperous South Africa where there was room for everyone.

The negotiations were difficult and marred by bouts of political violence, but in the end, South Africans made history by going to the polls for their first-ever inclusive democratic election. Perhaps the most telling sign of the transformation was that Mandela invited his former enemy, ex-president de Klerk, to serve as executive deputy president and de Klerk accepted. Now both leaders could reassure the people of South Africa and show the world that a new relationship was possible. When I heard them speak on that day in January 1995, they were both serving in their new roles.

As Mandela declared:

> We were expected to destroy one another and ourselves collectively in the worst racial conflagration. Instead we as a people chose the path of negotiation, compromise and peaceful settlement. Instead of hatred and revenge we chose reconciliation and nation-building.

Zooming out to see the bigger picture enables us to identify and thus to change the fundamental game of conflict. We don't have to stay trapped in a win-lose game in which everyone loses. We can *choose* instead to play a game in which everyone ultimately benefits. That is what *possibilists* do.

## SEE THE POSSIBILITIES

In this deeply divided world, there is perhaps no more important power for us to activate than to zoom out to see the bigger picture. If we are to tackle today's challenges with the curiosity, creativity, and collaboration they require, we need to free ourselves from our limiting assumptions about what *is* and *is not* possible.

When I look up at the night sky in a city, I see very few stars because of the ambient light. In the mountains, where I am currently writing, far away from city lights, I marvel at the dark sky, thick with twinkling stars. Like the stars, the possibilities in conflict are there. The question is: Can we *see* them?

Let me invite you to consider a conflict from your life. For a moment, zoom out and identify the various stakeholders, both the people directly involved and those indirectly affected. Ask yourself: Whom am I missing? Whom am I leaving out? Whom should I include? Who can block me—and how? And who can help me—and how?

Zoom out and ask yourself: What is my BATNA? How can I meet my needs if I cannot reach an agreement? How can I develop my BATNA to make it even better? What is my WATNA—my worst alternative to a negotiated agreement? How can I avert the worst and aim for the best?

Zoom out to the future—twenty or fifty or even a hundred years. If *possibilists* had been hard at work and you were an archaeologist of the future, what artifacts would you find? As you imagine such a future, what next steps could take you in that direction?

Finally, zoom out and consider the game you are playing. This is perhaps the biggest opportunity of all. What could you do to change the game from a win-lose battle to a game of constructive conflict and cooperation?

If you zoom out and consider all these questions, you will likely uncover new possibilities that you had not imagined before.

Zooming out is the culminating move of going to the balcony, our first victory on the path to possible. From the balcony, we begin to see the outline of the golden bridge. This is our next victory to achieve—a victory with the other.

# BUILD A GOLDEN BRIDGE

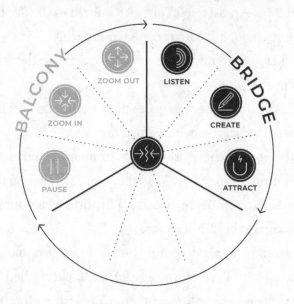

"My right eye will fall out, my right hand will fall off, before I ever agree to the dismantling of a single Jewish settlement."

Israeli prime minister Menachem Begin wasn't leaving much room for negotiation.

It was September 1978. President Jimmy Carter had invited Begin to meet with Egyptian president Anwar Sadat at Camp David, the presidential retreat set in the beautiful wooded hills of Maryland, an hour and a half's drive from Washington, DC.

Carter had hoped that in this relaxed, informal setting, the two leaders could come to terms on an agreement to end the state of hostilities between their two countries that had led to four devastating wars in thirty years. But after three days of contentious conversation, the parties were deadlocked.

Begin insisted on retaining the Jewish settlements on the Sinai Peninsula, the Egyptian lands that Israel had occupied in 1967 during the third Arab-Israeli War, also known as the Six-Day War.

To Begin's demand, Sadat replied immovably:

"Never! If you do not agree to evacuate the settlements, there will be no peace."

Both leaders told their teams to pack their bags. All hope for a Middle East peace agreement seemed lost.

Like the rest of the world, I was immensely surprised when President Jimmy Carter showed up thirteen days later on television, flanked by Sadat and Begin, signing a historic peace agreement in the East Room of the White House.

At the time, I was a doctoral student in anthropology at Harvard, working with Professor Roger Fisher. I had studied the Arab-Israeli conflict and had only recently returned from a long trip to the region. I was painfully aware of the decades-old conflict over land and identity that, in the world's eyes, had become the very symbol of impossibility.

What was the story behind this astonishing breakthrough? I wondered. How had the leaders managed to build a bridge across the chasm of deep-seated conflict? How, in other words, had they reached agreement to end an interminable war? And what lessons did it have for all of us in transforming seemingly intractable conflicts? If Arabs and Israelis could learn to transform their conflict, perhaps there was hope for the rest of us.

I had been paying close attention to the summit. A few weeks earlier, Roger Fisher had called me into his law school office after he had returned from his summer holiday on the island of Martha's Vineyard. He had a big smile on his face and sounded excited, as if he had gone fishing and caught a big fish:

"This past weekend, I played tennis with Cy Vance, who happened to be my neighbor's houseguest. After the game, Cy asked me if I had any negotiation ideas for Camp David. So I brought him over to the house and gave him a copy of our little book. I drew his attention to the part that describes the one-text process and told him he should think about using the process to reach an agreement with Sadat and Begin next week. Can you arrange a meeting right away with Louis Sohn and others to discuss the idea so we can write an advice memo for Vance by Friday?"

Cyrus, or "Cy," Vance was the US secretary of state. The "little book," *International Mediation: A Working Guide*, was a book of practical ideas for negotiators that I had spent the previous year working on with Roger. Never formally published, it was the predecessor and inspiration for *Getting to Yes*. In the guide, Roger and I had written about the *one-text process*, a negotiating procedure used with success during the UN multilateral conference on the Law of the Sea. We had first learned about it from Harvard Law School professor Louis Sohn, who had served on the US negotiating delegation.

The one-text, as we called it, is an ingeniously simple alternative to the usual haggling over opposed positions. Instead of pressing for concessions, a third party drafts a possible agreement and asks the parties to give their comments. The third party then continually revises the text to address the concerns until a consensus is reached. The one-text is a way to build a golden bridge.

I set up a dinner at the Harvard Faculty Club the following night for a meeting of the Devising Seminar. The seminar was a series of meetings organized by Roger, to which he would invite professors and visiting diplomats to discuss a particular world conflict in order to "devise" creative solutions. It was an experiment, a lab of sorts. Could we engage in a different kind of conversation that would help create new possibilities in conflicts that seemed impossibly stuck?

*Devise* was a word Roger liked because it implied practical creativity. The dictionary definition of "devise" is "to form in the mind by new combinations or applications of ideas or principles." That is a pretty good description of what we were trying to do.

"What is the best advice we could offer Cyrus Vance?"

Roger posed that question to the half-dozen people gathered around the dinner table. I recorded their ideas on a flip chart. Drawing on the ideas, Roger and I then wrote up a three-page memo, focusing on the *one-text process*, and sent it off to Vance.

In the first three days of the summit, that memo lay unused in Vance's briefcase. Then, just as the parties were preparing to leave Camp David in failure, President Carter decided to give the talks one last try. He called Vance into his cabin and asked him for advice. Vance remembered the memo and proposed using the one-text process. Carter agreed and asked him to prepare a proposal.

In a conventional process, a third party proposes a line somewhere in the middle between the two positions. Each party often objects vehemently, rejecting the proposal. Since concessions are politically painful, nobody wants to make the first one, fearing that it will signal weakness and open the door to even more concessions.

But the one-text process takes a very different approach. No one is asked to make a concession, at least up front. The focus is not on the concrete positions but rather on how to create options that can satisfy the underlying interests.

So the US mediators went to the Israelis and Egyptians and told them:

"We're not asking you to change your *position*. Just tell us more about your *interests* and *needs*. What do you *really* want? And what are you *most* worried about?"

The Americans listened intently to each side as both shared their aspirations and fears.

The Egyptians emphasized their vital interest in sovereignty. The land had been theirs since the time of the pharaohs, and they wanted it back. The Israelis focused on their vital interest in security. Egyptian tanks had rolled across the Sinai Peninsula three times to attack them, and the Israelis wanted to make certain that would never happen again.

The Egyptians had floated a creative proposal to demilitarize parts of the Sinai. The Americans decided to incorporate the idea into their first draft of the one-text, demilitarizing the Sinai and creating a security buffer for Israel. Basically, the Egyptian flag could fly everywhere but Egyptian tanks could go nowhere. It was an ingenious idea, addressing the Israelis' concern for security while retaining Egyptian sovereignty.

But in conflict negotiation, it is not enough to have a good idea; you have to get buy-in from the parties. People usually don't trust ideas that are not theirs.

The one-text process keeps the draft proposal highly informal so it can easily be revised to incorporate ideas and suggestions from the parties. There is no letterhead on the draft, no attribution, no status. It is a non-paper. It might even have coffee stains on it.

"This is not an American proposal," said the Americans to the parties. "It's just an idea. We are not asking you for a decision. Actually, we don't want a decision at this point. We just want you to let us know what you think of it. Feel free to criticize it. The more criticism, the better. Where does the draft not address your core interests? Where is it unfair?"

In heated conflicts, I have found, *nobody wants to make a painful decision, but everybody loves to criticize.*

The Israelis criticized the US text heavily. So did the Egyptians. The Americans then went back to their cabin and redrafted the text, trying to improve it for one side without making it worse for the other.

To address Israeli security concerns about an Egyptian surprise attack, President Carter added to the text the offer that US military and contractors could participate in the monitoring of the demilitarization. The latest technology could track even a goat crossing the solitary desert.

Then the US mediators brought the draft back.

"We've worked on it some more to take into account what you said. Again, we don't want a decision at this point, just more criticism and suggestions so we can make it better."

Each time the one-text improved, the parties saw not only their needs addressed but their ideas and language incorporated into it. They began to buy in.

The mediators repeated the same process again—and again—

revising the draft and consulting the parties. In a very long week, they produced *twenty-three* separate drafts.

As everyone's patience began to wear thin and the parties grumbled that they were being held prisoner, President Carter presented the final draft to President Sadat and Prime Minister Begin separately and said:

"I know it is not everything you want, but here is the best we have been able to do. At this point, I am asking you to decide what is best for you."

Now the two antagonists were faced with a much simpler and more attractive decision than in the conventional negotiation process of haggling over positions. Instead of having to make multiple painful concessions up front without knowing exactly where the process would end, they had to make only *one decision* and only *at the very end*, when they could see exactly what they would get in return.

President Sadat could see that he would get the entire Sinai Peninsula back for Egypt.

Prime Minister Begin could see that he would get an unprecedented historic peace.

Separately, each leader said yes. Carter and his colleagues were euphoric. Everyone prepared to go to Washington for the formal signing at the White House.

Then, as so often happens in difficult conflicts, there was a last-minute blowup. A bridge had been built, but the parties were nervous about stepping on it with their full weight.

Begin flew into a rage, triggered by a proposed side letter Carter had promised to Sadat. In that letter, Carter had reconfirmed the long-standing US posture of neutrality on the status of Jerusalem, a raw nerve for the Israelis. Begin broke off the talks and ordered his delegation to withdraw.

Bitterly disappointed, Carter walked over to Begin's cabin to say goodbye. He brought with him signed photos of the three leaders together—Begin, Sadat, and himself. Earlier in the week, Begin had requested one photo for each of his eight grandchildren. Carter had signed each photo, but instead of writing his usual "Best wishes," he had written "With love" and added the name of each grandchild. He had paid careful attention and knew how much Begin's grandchildren meant to him.

"Mr. Prime Minister, I brought you the photographs you asked for."

"Thank you, Mr. President."

Begin looked coolly at Carter, but when he glanced down and saw written on the top photo, "To Ayelet," he froze for a moment. When he looked at the next one, "To Osnat," his lip trembled and his eyes filled with tears. He read each of the eight names aloud— "Orit," "Meirav," "Michal"—and he began to weep openly.

Carter spoke up, his voice breaking.

"I wanted to be able to say, 'This is when your grandfather and I brought peace to the Middle East.'"

The two men began to talk, this time in a new tone. Begin was quiet, even friendly, but still firm about his decision. He asked Carter to withdraw the side letter, but Carter gently yet firmly explained that he was willing to let the talks fail rather than break the personal promise he had made to Sadat.

But as Carter prepared to leave, he quietly mentioned to Begin that he had rewritten the letter, merely citing the US position "as stated by Ambassador Goldberg in the United Nations General

Assembly on July 14, 1967." He had left out what that position was. He asked Begin to read it again with an open mind.

Pensive, with a heavy heart, Carter walked back to his cabin, where he met Sadat and told him the bad news. Within hours the whole world would know of the failure at Camp David with all its likely consequences for new wars. Then the phone rang. It was Begin.

"I will accept the letter you have drafted on Jerusalem."

I can remember vividly hearing this story directly from Jimmy Carter a few years later, as I was accompanying him on a mission to help stop the civil wars then ravaging Sudan and Ethiopia. It touched me and gave me a real sense of how even complex high-level negotiations like this can come down to human beings grappling with human feelings and seeing the humanity in one another.

The historic signing of the Camp David Accords proceeded to take place, surprising the entire world.

It was just a beginning, of course. The Arab-Israeli conflict was far from resolved. The agreement failed to address the legitimate needs of the Palestinian people. Sadat himself fell victim to an assassin's bullets just a few years later. But the peace forged during those thirteen days has now endured more than forty years through revolution, coup d'état, and other wars in the region. Against all odds, the talks at Camp David succeeded in *transforming* destructive confrontation into peaceful coexistence.

*The conflict did not end, but the war did.* And that made all the difference.

The dramatic story of Camp David deeply influenced me at the very outset of my life's work in negotiation. By so clearly demonstrating that even the most seemingly impossible of conflicts could yield a transformative outcome, the accords confirmed my belief in our human potential and cemented my commitment to becoming a practicing *possibilist*.

## BUILD A *GOLDEN* BRIDGE

When I was six years old, my family and I traveled to San Francisco from Europe by ship. Passing under the Golden Gate Bridge made an enormous impression on me, as we floated between its tremendous towers and under its huge span and sweeping cables. We moved into a house not far from the bridge on the other side from the city. I crossed the bridge countless times as a boy in a car and sometimes on foot and bicycle. I came to love that bridge, and it is the image that comes to mind often in my work.

Building a bridge may be the most common metaphor for the process of trying to reach agreement and foster a relationship between adversaries. In intractable conflicts such as the Egyptian-Israeli conflict, a giant chasm separates the two sides, filled with dissatisfactions and distrust, unmet needs and insecurities. How can we possibly *bridge* such a gap?

In conflict, our tendency is to push for our position. After all, our position may seem utterly reasonable to us. But what does the other side usually do when we push? Naturally, they push back. We end up in an impasse, as happened in the first three days at Camp David.

How can we get out of this trap? Successful negotiators, I have long observed, do the exact opposite: Instead of pushing, *attract*. Instead of making it harder for the other side, make it as easy and as attractive as possible for them to say yes to the decision you would like them to make.

In *The Art of War*, a brilliant treatise on military strategy written twenty-five hundred years ago, the Chinese general and philosopher Sun Tzu emphasized the importance of leaving your enemy a way out. This phrase has often been translated as "Build your opponent a golden bridge to retreat across." In my book *Getting Past No*, written decades ago, I reframed this principle as building a golden bridge for the other party to *advance* across. I have been teaching this precept ever since.

*A golden bridge is an inviting way for the parties to cross the chasm of conflict.*

I believe that the story of Camp David holds an important lesson for us as we face the seemingly impossible conflicts of today. Though the context is different, the similarities are telling. Today as then, fear, anger, and pride have taken over. So many parties are entrenched in rigid ideological positions, refusing to budge like Begin when he declared that he would rather lose his right eye and right hand than change his position. There seems to be no way out other than to resort to destructive fighting.

In the face of such challenges, it would be easy to lower our sights. But in transforming difficult conflicts, the lesson I have learned is to be *audacious*. If we are missing our target, it is not because we have been aiming too high but rather because we have been aiming too low. We need to up our game. We need to build not only a bridge but a *golden* bridge.

If we are to succeed, we need to unlock the *full* potential that exists *between* the parties. A golden bridge is far more than a mere compromise. At Camp David, a compromise US proposal might have divided the difference between the initial Israeli and Egyptian positions, leaving both sides deeply dissatisfied. A golden bridge is an integral outcome that meets the essential needs of all parties. Because each side was satisfied, the agreement proved to be far more sustainable than a weak compromise would have been.

Counterintuitive as it may seem, my experience has shown me that a *golden* bridge is often more achievable and more robust than an ordinary bridge.

A golden bridge goes well beyond a classic win-win agreement. It aims to *transform the relationship*. The Camp David Accords were not just an agreement to resolve an outstanding dispute; they brought about a remarkable transformation of the relationship between Egypt and Israel. The two adversaries did not become close friends, far from it, but they ceased to be mortal enemies. They became peaceful neighbors, cooperating to assure their mutual security.

If our goal is more audacious, so, too, must be our means. This brings me to a key lesson of this book. When I think back to passing under the Golden Gate Bridge as a boy, I have an unforgettable memory of the two huge towers supporting it on each side of the wide entrance to the bay. Similarly, *a golden bridge needs to be supported by two giant pillars: the balcony and the third side*. All three structural elements are needed to bridge the enormous gap that often exists between the parties.

In the story of Egyptian-Israeli peace, the *balcony* was the natural retreat of Camp David, about as far away from the Middle East as one could possibly imagine. The setting was Rosalynn Carter's inspired idea. A month earlier, she and her husband had spent a relaxing weekend alone at Camp David. She shared her husband's dream of making peace in the Middle East and knew of his frustration. She proposed to him that he give it one last try. She suggested that perhaps a simple, rustic, and bucolic place such as Camp David, isolated from the world's limelight, could help provide the right atmosphere within which the parties might achieve a breakthrough. And she was right.

Just as important as the balcony was the *third side*. Without a determined, skilled, and influential third party such as Jimmy Carter, the two leaders, Sadat and Begin, would almost certainly never have been able to come to terms.

Here is the paradoxical lesson I have learned about how to build a bridge across a great chasm: *If you want to make it easier, start by making it harder.* Aim for an audacious outcome, and use equally audacious means. We are often capable of achieving far more than we think possible. Don't just build a bridge; build a *golden* bridge. Support the bridge with the balcony and the third side. It is the synergy of all three that makes the seemingly impossible possible.

## UNLOCK THE POTENTIAL BETWEEN

We build a golden bridge by deploying three natural powers. Each power is an innate human capacity, something we may already know how to do but simply need to develop and strengthen.

The first is the power to *listen* deeply: to hear what those on the other side really want. Leave where *your* mind is and start the conversation where *their* minds are. Seek to understand their needs. At Camp David, Carter and his team listened carefully for thirteen days to understand the deeper needs of the parties for sovereignty and security. Listening conveys respect and builds trust.

The second is the power to *create*: to invent options for mutual gain. Once you understand the other's perceptions and needs, begin to craft creative ways to bridge the gap. At Camp David, Carter and his team developed the creative, mutually satisfying solution of a demilitarized Sinai.

The third is the power to *attract*: to make it easy for them to say yes. Creating good options is usually not enough to persuade people. Obstacles often stand in the way. At Camp David, the parties hit a hard impasse and were about to leave. Carter used the one-text process to break the impasse by simplifying the decision-making process and increasing the parties' buy-in.

The three powers have a logical sequence. *Listening* focuses on the *people*; it produces a propitious psychological atmosphere for *creating* options, which focuses on the *problem*. *Attracting* then makes it easier for the parties to accept the options; it focuses on the *process*. Once we activate a power, we continue to use it. We continually listen, create, and attract as needed.

All three powers combine to transform inflexible opposed positions into creative possibilities. Deployed together, they enable us to build a golden bridge that unlocks the full potential *between* the parties.

The bridge is our *second* victory on the path to possible.

## CHAPTER 6

# LISTEN

## From Your Shoes to Theirs

*If we could read the secret history of our enemies, we should find in each one's life sorrow and suffering enough to disarm all hostility.*
—Henry Wadsworth Longfellow

Bad day, man. Bad day!" Dennis Rodman growled into the phone at me.

"I'd like to ask you about Kim Jong Un," I told him. "You're the only American who seems to know him."

"What do you want, anyway?"

"I'm really worried about the situation with North Korea. I believe your insights could help prevent a catastrophic war."

"I got it handled."

He sounded irritated and hung up.

I sighed. It had been a long day, and I began to feel as though I were on a fool's errand. A friend of Rodman's had arranged to introduce us over dinner at his house in Los Angeles, where Rodman was a guest. I had flown in for the dinner, but Rodman hadn't shown up. Hence the phone call.

It was May 2017. As I previously recounted, the United States and North Korea were on a collision course. The North Korean leader, Kim Jong Un, was testing nuclear missiles with the capacity to reach the United States, and President Donald Trump was determined to stop him. No one knew how the crisis would end. The question in the air was: Who will back down? Experts estimated the chances of war as high as fifty-fifty.

Much was known about Trump but almost nothing about Kim, who had been portrayed in the American press as "irrational," "ruthless," and "paranoid." Surfing the web for clues a few weeks earlier, I had found one tantalizing detail. There was one person who had gotten to know Kim: the retired basketball player Dennis Rodman.

A star of the world champion Chicago Bulls team in the mid-1990s, Rodman had traveled to North Korea four times and had struck up an unlikely friendship with Kim, who had turned out to be a passionate basketball fan, with a boyhood admiration for the Bulls. Despite heavy criticism and ridicule in the press, Rodman had seemingly defended his connection with Kim.

What were Kim's intentions? I wondered. What did he really

want? What would it take for him to stop the extremely dangerous course he was on? I thought that if I had a chance to meet with Rodman and *listen* to his stories about Kim, maybe I could peer into Kim's mind and get a clue for how that nuclear crisis might be defused.

The first step in building a bridge across the chasm of conflict is to *listen*.

## THE COURAGE TO LISTEN

Listening is the most basic act of human connection. We associate negotiation with talking. We tend to think of an effective negotiator as a persuasive talker. In my experience, however, effective negotiation is far more about listening than talking. Effective negotiators are persuasive listeners. They listen more than they talk.

If I had to pick one human ability essential to building a golden bridge, it would be *empathy*—the ability to leave *our shoes* for a moment and put ourselves in *their shoes*. Listening enables us to empathize and understand the other side—their wants and needs, dreams and fears. What does the world look like through their eyes? What does it feel like to be them? If we had lived their life, how would we act and react? Of course, we may never wholly understand them, but it never ceases to surprise me just how powerful this exercise can be if we simply deploy our innate capacity for empathy.

Empathy is often confused with sympathy, but it is different. Sympathy means to "feel *with*." It means to feel sorry for a person's predicament but without necessarily understanding it. Empathy, in contrast, means to "feel *into*." It means to understand what it is like to be in that situation.

If empathy seems like a lot to swallow in an adversarial situation, you can choose to think of it as *strategic empathy*: understanding the other so that you can better advance your own interests.

In today's polarized times, listening may be the last thing we feel like doing. It means listening to people we may not like and listening to things we may not want to hear. It requires patience and self-restraint to control our natural reactions.

Other people on your side may criticize you just for listening to the other side.

"Why should we listen to them?" you may hear. "They don't listen to us!"

But how can we expect *them* to listen to us if *we* do not listen to them? Someone needs to start.

Listening may not be easy, but in my experience, it can make all the difference. We are trying to change the minds of others, but how can we change their minds—and hearts—if we don't know where they are? Even if you consider the other to be your mortal enemy, remember that the first rule of warfare is to know your enemy.

When Nelson Mandela was in prison, one of the first subjects he studied was Afrikaans, the language of his enemy. It was surprising, even shocking, to his comrades in prison, but he studied the language intensively—and he encouraged others to do the same.

He then proceeded to delve into the history of the Afrikaner people and their traumas during the Boer War, when thousands of their children, women, and elders had been imprisoned in British concentration camps. In the process, he developed a deep respect for their spirit of independence, their religious devotion, and their courage in battle. That understanding proved to be of enormous help later when it came to persuading his political adversaries to agree to end the cruel and unjust system of apartheid.

What we need today is precisely the kind of *courageous listening* that Mandela modeled. As he showed, listening has immense power to change hearts and minds. There is no more important practice if we are to transform the destructive conflicts that threaten our families, our workplaces, our communities, and our world.

Listening is the golden key that opens the door to human relationship, available to us at any time. Yet in our daily lives, we often forget to use this precious faculty. I recall how humbling it was to practice listening at work, only to come home sometimes and hear my daughter say, "Papi, you are not *listening* to me!" It was an incredibly valuable reminder that listening is a lifelong practice.

Listening is what I set out to do with Dennis Rodman. Through listening to him, I hoped to listen to the mind of Kim Jong Un.

## LISTEN FOR THEIR DREAM

It wasn't easy to reach Rodman. When I realized that he was the only American who knew Kim, I asked around among my friends to see if anyone had any ideas. One friend knew someone who had met Phil Jackson, the former coach of the Chicago Bulls. But that attempt went nowhere.

Then one day, while I was taking a walk in the mountains, I suddenly remembered that my ninety-year-old uncle Burt in Chicago had an old business association with the Bulls. I called Burt, and he suggested that I speak with my cousin Karen, who, it turned out, had once met one of Rodman's friends, a coin collector in Los Angeles named Dwight, at a party. With an introduction from Karen, I called

Dwight and explained my request and the urgency of the situation. He generously agreed to help:

"Dennis sometimes visits LA and stays with me. He will be coming next month. Why don't you come have dinner with us?"

I quickly agreed and made arrangements to fly to LA for the appointed evening.

When I arrived at Dwight's house, a Hollywood-style mansion in the hills with iron gates, I was buzzed in by Blanca, a kind housekeeper. Neither Dwight nor Dennis was there. Dwight's collection of movie posters from the silent movie era occupied almost every chair and sofa, leaving little room to sit. Fox News was blaring on the enormous TV screen.

Dwight showed up a half hour later, bearing pizzas.

"Dennis not here? Well, he's not the most reliable person. He goes out to the bars and often doesn't come back until late."

Dwight called Rodman to remind him that he had a guest.

"Maybe he'll come back, let's see," Dwight said with a note of uncertainty.

He disappeared. After a while, Blanca asked me:

"Why don't you eat some pizza?"

"It's okay. I'll wait for Dwight."

"Oh, he prefers to eat alone upstairs."

"Oh."

After a while, Blanca decided to call Dennis to remind him of his visitor. She put me on the line. That was when I spoke to him, and he hung up on me.

I was beginning to feel I had reached a dead end. I was thinking about returning to the airport hotel to catch an early flight back home when Dwight suddenly reappeared. I briefed him about my phone conversation—or non-conversation—with Rodman. He said:

"Well, why don't you stay the night? I can give you the room right above him. Sometimes he comes back at three or four in the morning. Maybe you could catch him and speak to him then?"

It didn't seem very promising, but the stakes were high. I sighed and accepted Dwight's kind offer, called the hotel, changed my flight, and canceled my appointments back home for the next day.

I had trouble sleeping. I kept an ear out to hear if Rodman had returned but heard nothing. I finally fell asleep, only to wake up around six to the sound of a car leaving.

"Drat, I missed my chance."

But when I entered the main house, Blanca said:

"That was Dwight leaving. You're in luck. Dennis must have come in last night because his car is here. The problem is, he often sleeps in for two or three days."

As that piece of information settled in, she saw the look of disappointment on my face and asked:

"Would you like me to wake him up?"

I hesitated, remembered the previous evening's irritable conversation, but reminded myself again of the stakes.

"I guess so. Yes. Thank you."

She disappeared and came back a few minutes later.

"He says he will come out."

Then she went off to a doctor's appointment, leaving me alone to wait.

Forty-five minutes later, the front door swung open. In lumbered

Dennis Rodman, six feet seven inches tall, his arms and legs covered with tattoos, rings in his ears and nose, repeating his phrase from the previous night:

"Bad day, man."

"I know. Listen, sorry to bother you like this, but there's a lot at stake. If we're going to avoid a nuclear war, it's critical we understand Kim's psychology. You are the only one who seems to know him. I'd love to hear your insights."

Rodman grabbed a bottle of water from the refrigerator, and we sat outside by the pool.

He began to describe his first visit to North Korea. He told me how surprised he had been to find Kim suddenly sitting by his side at a basketball game and how they had gone out to dinner that night and then drinking. That was how they had first gotten close.

"Kim took me home one time, and I held his baby," Rodman said with emotion in his voice.

Rodman promised Kim that he would come back to Korea for Kim's birthday and bring some basketball stars with him. When Rodman fulfilled his promise, Kim told him:

"You're the only person who has ever kept his promise to me. You're a friend for life."

"No one else may believe this," Rodman said, "but Kim told me he doesn't want war. I believe he is serious when he says he wants peace."

I was impressed by Rodman's conviction as he spoke. He continued:

"Kim once told me his dream. His dream is to walk down Fifth Avenue, go to Madison Square Garden, and watch the Bulls play the Knicks, sitting on the floor with me. Can you believe it?"

That little gold nugget about Kim's dream was worth the entire trip. A tiny bell went off for me, like the one I heard when my Brazilian friend Abilio, whose story I recounted earlier, told me about *his* dream of freedom. I got a little glimpse into the human being behind the caricature, the avid boyhood fan of the Bulls. In a wild flight of imagination, I wondered what it might take to make Kim's dream come true.

Why not find out? With the negative possibilities so dark, we needed to look for any thread of positive possibility. Rodman's conversations with Kim raised the faint chance that Kim just might be open to engaging with the United States and the West. If he and Trump could meet—which seemed highly improbable at the time— maybe, just maybe, the immediate crisis could be de-escalated and nuclear war averted.

While I was listening to Rodman, it occurred to me that one possible reason he had developed such personal chemistry with Kim was that they appeared to share the same feeling of "me against the world." They both seemed to feel misunderstood, underestimated, stigmatized, and treated like outsiders. They were rebels out to prove their detractors wrong.

From what I knew about Donald Trump, he shared some of the same personality characteristics. Like both Kim and Rodman, he took great pleasure in proving the world wrong. In a psychological sense, the three of them were akin.

Listening to Dennis Rodman and his insights that day encouraged me to devote the next two years to working on the North Korea conflict. Months later, in a meeting with a top expert in the White House, I asked if anyone in the government had ever talked to Rodman, the only American who had gotten to know Kim. The answer was no. He had been written off as unserious. Yet I found my conversation with him psychologically revealing and highly insightful.

Donald Trump and Kim Jong Un insulted each other heartily in the summer and fall of 2017. Trump labeled Kim "Little Rocket Man" and threatened North Korea with "fire and fury like the world has never seen." In return, Kim declared, "I will surely and definitely tame the mentally deranged U.S. dotard with fire." But to the surprise of almost everyone—except perhaps Dennis Rodman—the two adversaries became friends a year later at their first, historic meeting in Singapore.

While the three summits between the two leaders did not yield a peace agreement, they did change the psychology of the conflict. Although the conflict was far from *resolved*, it was *transformed*. The risk of nuclear war decreased dramatically, from as high as 50 percent, according to expert opinion, to less than 1 percent. I found myself sleeping more peacefully at night.

My experience with Dennis Rodman reminded me of the value of persistence in seeking to understand the other's needs and dreams. Who could have foreseen the unlikely friendship that later developed between Trump and Kim? Trump was ridiculed when he talked about the "love letters" he had received from his new friend Kim. But they made a certain psychological sense to me, thanks to my conversation with Rodman.

This kind of listening is a bit like detective work. We are trying to get to the bottom of the story. Keep digging and listening until you hit gold—their dreams and fears. That is how you can begin to build a *golden* bridge.

## LISTEN TO CONNECT

In conflict, we naturally start with where *our* mind is, what *our* position is, what *we* think is right. Deep listening means leaving where *our* mind is and starting the conversation where *their* mind is. It means listening from within *their* frame of reference, not just ours.

In deep listening, we listen not just for what's being said but for what's *not* being said. We listen not just to the words but to what's *behind* the words. We listen for the other person's feelings and perceptions. We listen for their wants and needs, fears and dreams. We are genuinely curious about them. We *listen to connect*.

I learned this lesson of listening to connect perhaps most vividly during my first meeting with Venezuelan president Hugo Chávez, eight months before the tumultuous midnight encounter I described earlier.

It was March 2003. In Venezuela, there was widespread fear of a civil war. Former president Jimmy Carter had asked me to meet with Chávez to explore ways to avert violence. I was anxious not to lose that precious opportunity to influence the country's leader. I told myself that I might have only one chance and likely I would be granted only a few minutes of his time. What was the best advice I could offer? I began to think hard and started rehearsing what I would say.

A week before the meeting, I was visiting family in Brazil and, in the rainforest, heard someone sing an old song with a line that struck me like a flash:

*"Do not offer advice to those who do not want to listen."*

The more I reflected on that little piece of indigenous wisdom, the more it resonated: Offer advice only if invited. Drop whatever agenda I had and just go into the meeting ready to listen. Be present and listen for where Chávez's mind and heart were. Listen for the possibilities that might show up only in the moment. Accept the risk of losing the one chance I would have to get my prepared ideas across.

Dropping my agenda did not mean *not* preparing. If anything, it meant the opposite. To be attentive to all possibilities in the moment, I needed to research the man. I read up on Chávez, delved deeply into his speeches, trying to learn from his life story, listening for his drivers and dreams. Understanding Chávez as much as possible would help me meet him where his mind was.

The morning of the appointment, I took a moment to sit in the garden in front of the guesthouse where I was staying. The natural beauty helped calm my anxious mind and its rapid chatter.

An hour later, as my taxi approached the gates of the presidential palace, protesters blocked the way and pounded loudly on the hood. It startled me. Emotions of anger and fear were running high in the crowd, but eventually the taxi was let through.

Upon entering the palace with my friend and colleague from the Carter Center, Francisco Diez, we found a long line of petitioners in the corridor, citizens waiting for a moment with *el presidente*. It seemed as though our meeting might be just a quick courtesy call, over before it began. As Francisco and I waited for our turn, I took another moment to pause and clear my mind. I wanted to be ready to listen as deeply as I could and focus my full attention—to be able to meet the moment.

After waiting for an hour or so, Francisco and I were ushered into a vast ornate living room where the president was receiving visitors. He greeted us with a big smile and a firm handshake and motioned us to sofa chairs next to him. He looked at me expectantly.

"President Carter sends his warm regards," I said.

"Gracias. Please convey mine to him."

"I will, with pleasure."

I paused and looked at him. "I understand we both have daughters who are five."

"Ah, yes, Rosinés." He smiled as he said her name. "And your daughter?"

"Gabriela. We call her Gabi. Aren't they a joy at that age?"

"Si," he agreed. "A big joy."

"As I came in," I continued, "I saw many paintings of Simón Bolívar. I've been reading an excellent biography about him. What a visionary and courageous leader!"

Chávez perked up. As I knew from my readings about him, the great nineteenth-century liberator of the Spanish colonies in Latin America was his idol, the leader he mentioned most with fervent admiration. Chávez's dream, I sensed, was to be a modern-day Bolívar.

"My favorite painting of him is right here," he exclaimed animatedly as he pointed to the giant portrait of Bolívar looking down at us.

"Do you know that is *why* I'm here?" he asked. "Back in 1992, when I was a colonel, I received orders to crush with force the people's protests at rising food prices. Simón Bolívar warned, 'Never open fire on your own people.' So I organized an uprising and ended up in prison. And when I was released by popular demand, I started running for president."

Chávez proceeded to tell me stories from his life in the military, the reprimands he received in the barracks for reading books on economics and politics, his time in jail, and his political campaign for the presidency. Almost an hour went by.

When he finished his story, he finally turned to me and asked me with curiosity:

"So, Professor Ury, what are your thoughts about our conflict here in Venezuela?"

That was my cue. I would offer advice *only* if asked.

"Señor Presidente, I have worked as a third party in many civil wars. Once the bloodshed starts, it can be extremely difficult to end. I believe that you, as leader of this country, have a great opportunity. Perhaps *only you* can prevent a civil war before it happens."

"How would I do that?" he asked.

"What about starting a dialogue with the opposition?" I suggested.

"*Talk* with them?"

His face flushed, his eyes flashed with visible anger, and his tone of voice grew sharp and loud.

"They are traitors who tried to mount a coup against me and kill me less than a year ago right here in this room!"

He motioned with his hands to the very spot in the corner of the room where he had been detained. I paused and took a breath, not knowing quite how to respond. Rather than try to convince him, I simply reflected back what I had heard.

"I understand you perfectly. Since you can't trust them at all, what possible use could there be in talking with them?"

"Exactly!" he replied.

Then an idea began to form in my mind.

"Since you don't trust them one bit, let me ask you: Is there any action they could possibly take right now that would send you a credible signal that they were ready to change?"

"*Señales?* [Signals?]" he asked as he paused to consider the unexpected question.

"Sí." I nodded my head.

"Well, for one thing, they could stop calling me a *mono* [monkey] on their TV stations."

He gave a bitter laugh, contorting his face into a grimace as he pronounced the word *mono*. Clearly, he took it as a racist allusion to his part-indigenous ancestry.

My ears perked up. I had observed elsewhere how feelings of humiliation significantly increase the chances of escalation into violence.

"That's utterly unacceptable," I said. "It needs to stop, of course. Is there another signal like that they could send?"

"Well, they could stop putting uniformed generals on television calling for the overthrow of the government. That's treason!"

Chávez began to warm to the idea of signals. As our conversation drew to a close, he designated the minister of the interior, sitting off to the side, to work with Francisco and me to develop a list of practical actions that each party could take to build trust and de-escalate the crisis. He asked us to return the next day to report on our progress.

A window of possibility had just unexpectedly opened up.

As I said goodbye to the president, I glanced at my watch. Two and a half hours had passed. I am convinced that had I followed my first idea to begin the meeting by offering my recommendations, he would have cut the meeting short after a brief hearing. Instead, because I had listened to *connect* with him, the meeting had gone on to be productive and became the first of many. A relationship developed. The gamble had paid off.

President Carter called me later to report that he had heard back from Chávez that he had really enjoyed our meeting. Carter seemed surprised—as was I. After all, I was a *yanqui*, and Chávez was known to be suspicious of Americans. I was an academic without any power, and he was a powerful political leader. It was an unlikely human connection.

It was a big lesson for me. Before the meeting, I had made the all-too-common mistake of focusing on what I could *say* to him, not on how I could *listen* to him. That is the conflict trap we all too often fall into, particularly in today's times.

The wisdom of that song from Brazil reminded me of the futility of offering advice to those who don't want to listen. It did not mean taking a passive stance—on the contrary, it meant that I would have to work to prepare the other person to *want* to receive my advice. If I wanted Chávez to listen to me, naturally I needed to begin by listening to him.

This experience, perhaps more than any other, taught me to take a risk and let go of my prepared agenda, as hard as that might be. Only then, I learned, could I hope for a breakthrough.

## DROP YOUR PRECONCEPTIONS

One of the biggest barriers to our understanding the other side is our preconceptions. In situations of conflict, we feel threatened and naturally go into a defensive posture. Our thinking becomes limited, and we easily descend into stereotypes. We judge the other.

Putting ourselves in another's shoes calls on us to suspend our judgment and drop our preconceptions. It is a lesson that, even as an experienced mediator, I find myself having to learn again and again.

In 2012, I began working on the Syrian civil war with my colleague David Lesch, a distinguished American historian specializing in the politics of the Middle East. He had written an insightful biography of Syrian president Bashar al-Assad. The war had been raging for a year, and David was lamenting to me about the utter absence of dialogue between the warring parties. They had almost no understanding about how the others perceived the situation and what they really wanted. David had tried to organize an informal confidential dialogue, but fear, suspicion, and animosity had gotten in the way.

So I proposed to him an exercise in *indirect* listening. He and I—and other colleagues—would listen to knowledgeable and well-connected leaders on all sides of the conflict. We would ask them the same set of a dozen or more questions: Why had the conflict started? What were their concerns and fears? What were their dreams and aspirations for the future? We would collect all the answers and then convey back to the leaders what we had learned. While the exercise would not replace direct dialogue among the parties, we hoped it might help increase mutual understanding as a prelude to future negotiations.

As part of the exercise, David, his colleagues, and I came together for a week just before Christmas 2012 outside the Turkish city of Gaziantep, a few miles from the Syrian border. The war was raging, with thousands of people dying and millions of refugees fleeing in every direction.

We had arranged to interview a dozen Syrian rebel commanders and opposition political leaders. They would literally step out of the battle to be interviewed, only to return afterward to a living hell. The atmosphere was heavy with the daily loss of lives. One rebel commander we spoke with had just lost his wife and children in the fighting. I felt a heaviness in my chest and my gut roiling as I listened to the accounts of bloodshed and violence.

On the last day, our interviewee was a young man in his late twenties, heavyset, with a beard. A commander of more than three thousand men, he had been introduced to us as a Salafist jihadist.

I observed my own stereotypes coming into play, remembering the tragedy and trauma of the 9/11 attacks. As I looked at him, I decided to deviate from the standard questions and try a more personal approach to delve beneath the surface:

"What was your occupation before the war?"

"I was in university."

"Oh. What were you studying?"

"Poetry."

"Poetry?" I was surprised.

"Yes, I was studying poetry. I come from a family of poets. In fact, I won first prize in a national poetry contest."

He recited, half singing, a couple of lines of poetry in Classical Arabic. It sounded beautiful, and I found myself moved.

"So how did you end up as a fighter?"

"When I was sixteen, I wrote a poem that made an allusive reference to the political situation here. The authorities found out and took me in for interrogation. In prison, I was tortured."

"Tortured?" I repeated, feeling shocked.

"Yes. I was tortured three times. Last year, when the revolution started off, it was peaceful. But then the security forces opened fire, and I saw my friends and fellow protesters being slaughtered in front of my eyes. I had no choice but to join the rebels."

I could not help but feel a wave of instinctive empathy.

"I understand. If I may, I'd like to ask you another question. I am curious about your personal dream. After the war, what would you like to do?"

"Well, I am not likely to survive. But if I do, I met a young woman in Egypt, and I'd like to marry her and have a family. That's my dream."

He had a gleam in his eye as he spoke. We then turned to his fears and hopes:

"What are you most worried about when you think about the future of your country?"

I was imagining he would name his political enemies—inside and outside the country. Instead he said:

"What I worry most about are the extremists."

I was startled. I had classified him as one of them in my mind.

"Why is that?" I asked.

"I'm in favor of sharia law, of course. But I don't believe in imposing it by force. I'm worried about those who are fighting with us who want to impose it by force. That would really divide our country."

Finally, I asked him:

"Tell me, is there any personal message you would like us to bring back to people in the West?"

He paused for a moment.

"Yes, when they watch the news about Syria, they see us as numbers. Just ask them to imagine that your child, your wife, is one of those numbers. Every single one of us has a life and a soul. We all have souls. Just tell them that."

I found myself speechless for a moment, humbled. The negative preconceptions I had brought to the conversation dissolved. Through listening with curiosity and empathy, I was able to get out of my shoes and place myself in his. It didn't mean agreeing with his views; it meant understanding him as a human being.

Who knows? If I had been born in his shoes, in that same gut-wrenching situation, would I have followed the course he had? Who could honestly say?

As we said goodbye, the young commander said something telling: "You know, other Westerners—journalists and diplomats—have come to speak with us. But you are the first ones who really *listened.*"

It was an important lesson for me, underscoring that if I wanted to truly listen, I would have to drop my preconceptions. It is hard to do in conflict situations, but an attitude of open-minded curiosity helps. In that unlikely conversation, with each successive question and answer, my understanding and empathy deepened.

I was reminded of an old saying: the longest distance in the world is the distance between the head and the heart. It doesn't mean giving up our rational faculties. It means using both our heads and our hearts to tap into our full potential.

## TO LISTEN IS TO RESPECT

I sometimes ask people in conflict this question:

"Can you recall a moment when someone important to you didn't *listen?* How did it feel to be unheard?"

I hear answers such as:

"Disrespected."

"Unseen."

"Angry."

"Diminished."

"Lack of trust."

"Excluded."

"Now recall a moment when you felt truly listened to. How did it feel to be heard?"

People answer:

"Valued."

"Like I belonged."

"Included."

*"Respected."*

In my conflict experience, I have long noticed that the cheapest concession you can make, the one that costs you the least and yields the most, is to listen and thereby offer a little respect.

In contentious conflicts, respect may be the last thing we feel like giving. We might feel that those on the other side don't deserve our respect. But remember, *basic human respect doesn't mean approving of their behavior—or even liking them.*

Respect, in the sense that I am using it here, is not something that needs to be earned by virtue of good behavior. Every human being deserves it simply by virtue of being human. Even enemy warriors in extreme circumstances are often able to show this kind of basic human respect.

Showing respect does not come from weakness or insecurity but rather from strength and confidence. Respect for the other person flows directly from respect for yourself. You give respect to the other not so much because of who *they* are but because of who *you* are.

To respect simply means to give value to the other as a human being and pay positive attention to them. The word *respect* comes from the Latin roots *re*, meaning "again" (as in "*re*-do") and *spectare*, meaning "to look" (as in *spectacles*). It means *to look again*—to recognize the human being behind the aggravating behavior.

To respect means to treat the other with the same dignity with which you would like to be treated. Dignity is every human being's birthright. When we respect others, we honor the same humanity that exists inside of us. Dignity, in this sense, is indivisible.

Once when I was facilitating a conference at a heated moment in the Venezuelan conflict, the rector of the Andrés Bello Catholic University, Father Luís Ugalde, stepped in to make a clear and powerful statement:

"Let's start by getting three things straight. *First, the other exists. Second, the other has interests. Third, the other has power.*"

His intervention was right on target because the lack of respect of the other was a central obstacle to making progress in that conflict. The rector's three points are a good reminder for us in these days of polarized conflicts.

The simplest way to show basic human respect is to listen.

## BEGIN BY LISTENING TO YOURSELF

It is not always easy to listen.

In heated conflicts, our minds naturally whirl with thoughts and emotions such as fear and anger. We have little mental or emotional space to listen and understand what the other is saying. Confronted with attacks and threats, we naturally react and start defending ourselves and blaming the other side. Even if we want to listen, we may not be able to.

The secret to listening well to *others*, I have found, is to listen to *myself* first. It is to begin by going to the balcony. If I can't find a way to *pause* and resource myself, how can I find the capacity to listen? If I don't *zoom in* to what *I* really want, how can I zoom in to listen to what *they* really want? If I don't *zoom out* and see the bigger picture, what incentive do I have to listen? *Balcony is a prerequisite for bridge.*

As I was beginning to write this chapter, as life would have it, a serious difference arose between my daughter, Gabi, and me. The immediate issue was the promise of a trip that had been postponed several times owing to the Covid pandemic. When the trip was finally rescheduled, I realized I couldn't go and tried to explain why. But what I saw as an understandable reason, she saw as a broken promise. She felt extremely hurt and broke off all communication with me.

I felt hurt as well; it felt as if there was a hole in my heart. She was living far away, so I wrote to her several times to apologize and try to repair the relationship but she rejected my initiatives as insufficient. The professional advice I received was just to give it time, but with time, the emotional distance between us only seemed to grow. I was deeply sad and felt stuck.

Looking back at this painful episode, I can now see that I failed to truly listen to Gabi—to her feelings and perceptions. I *thought* I was listening, but I now realize that it was more with my head than with my heart. I was protecting my own feelings rather than listening deeply to hers.

Before I could listen to my daughter, I needed to listen to myself first and see where I was not fully present. I needed to pause and go to the balcony. If I wanted to be more aware of her feelings, I needed to be more aware of my own psychological patterns. Rather than blaming the problem on her, I needed to take full responsibility. I had to let go of any impulse to be in the right. I had to demonstrate more humility and vulnerability.

Listening to myself helped me listen to my daughter. I thought I had understood her, but it turned out, as I reread her messages to me, that my understanding had been incomplete and superficial. I had to take off my shoes and put myself in hers. Even if my point of view seemed valid to me, I needed to start on her side.

In an audio message I sent her—so she could hear my voice—I began validating carefully point by point what she had been saying to me. I took full responsibility for the breakdown, apologized humbly, and asked her forgiveness. And when I did, she responded. We met the following week and spent it together. We took an entire day, just the two of us, to listen to each other and answer any questions the other had. Our relationship started to heal.

Humbling as it was, it was a big lesson for me. It showed me, once again, just how difficult it can be to listen well. No matter how difficult my work with wars and political battles can be, I find no conflicts more challenging than those within the family. Listening is never more gratifying than in healing a rift with someone you love.

The simple power of listening—deep, open-hearted, curious, empathetic, and respectful listening—is the key to escaping the conflict trap and opening up new creative possibilities.

**CHAPTER 7**

# CREATE

## From Either-Or to Both-And

*We should never allow ourselves to be bullied by an
either-or. There is often the possibility of something
better than either of these two alternatives.*
—Mary Parker Follett

What will it take to persuade these Marxist guerrillas who have been fighting for fifty years to lay down their weapons?"

That was the formidable challenge Colombian president Juan Manuel Santos put to the small team of peace negotiators and advisors he had selected to open up secret exploratory talks with the

FARC—the Revolutionary Armed Forces of Colombia—in February 2012.

To help him and his negotiating team, Santos had assembled an unusual group of international advisors.

Jonathan Powell had served as chief of staff for fourteen years to British prime minister Tony Blair. Jonathan had been chief negotiator for Northern Ireland, helping to bring the thirty-year war there to an end.

Shlomo Ben-Ami had been foreign minister of Israel, negotiating with the Palestinians during the Oslo peace process, which had shown so much early promise only to fall tragically short.

Joaquín Villalobos had served as a commander of FMLN, a Marxist guerrilla group in El Salvador, for twenty years. He had been a principal negotiator of the peace agreement that had ended a lengthy civil war that had torn the country apart.

Dudley Ankerson was a former British official and expert in Latin American politics and security affairs.

In all my years, I had never worked on a team like this. Each person brought different strengths and world-class practical experience to a "mission impossible" such as the Colombian civil war. I felt honored and humbled to work with them. To be honest, it felt a little bit like being invited to join the Avengers, the team of Marvel comic book heroes.

There was no conflict in the world that seemed more intractable than the civil war that had gripped Colombia for almost half a century. Few people there could remember what it was like to live in peace. In those fifty years, the war had claimed 450,000 lives and produced 8 million victims.

The largest guerrilla group, the FARC, was fortified by an

endless supply of funds from the drug trade and kidnappings. The fighters and their leaders had taken refuge in the jungle in the 1960s, and their mentality had hardly changed. In the fifty years that had followed, there had been many failed attempts at negotiation. The most recent one had come a decade earlier, but it had collapsed disastrously, with the government and the president humiliated in the public's eyes.

Since then, the guerrillas had been officially branded as a terrorist group. Negotiating with such a group seemed like a fool's errand and likely political suicide for any leader who might attempt it.

But Santos, the new president and a former defense minister, wanted to attempt the seemingly impossible. What greater legacy to leave his country than peace, as elusive as it seemed? Two decades earlier, he had spent a year at Harvard, where he had been a teaching assistant in Roger Fisher's negotiation workshop. He had learned about the creative possibilities that negotiation might offer.

I flew down to Bogotá in June 2011 at the request of President Santos. The plan was for a single meeting to offer some negotiating ideas. As we talked in the presidential palace, I was impressed by his deep commitment. From my work elsewhere, I had a strong sense of just how hard it would be to transform such a complex and deep-rooted conflict. But he seemed willing to invest the political goodwill he enjoyed—and the credibility he had built as defense minister—and risk it all on giving peace a chance. The senseless suffering moved me, and I was inspired by the possibility, however slim, of bringing it to an end. When he asked me to help, I felt an instinctive yes.

Little did I know that I would travel to Colombia twenty-five times over the next seven years. From my prior experiences with thorny intractable conflicts such as this one, I did know this: any sustainable outcome could not be *either-or*. Either-or meant *either* a unilateral victory for one side *or* a unilateral victory for the other. We had to seek a way out that was *both-and*: an outcome that *both* sides could tout as an advance, if not an actual victory. It needed to be a shared victory for all Colombians. And to meet this challenge, we would need to unleash our natural power to *create*.

## TO CREATE IS HUMAN

Creativity is an innate human capacity. Every child is born with it. We owe virtually all our human achievements—from science to art to music—to the practical deployment of our creative intelligence, both individual and collective.

To create means to *generate concrete options that meet the parties' interests*. The act of creativity turns an *either-or* dilemma into a *both-and* outcome. In my teaching, I like to offer participants a simple challenge:

"Imagine this everyday scenario: An employee comes into your office one morning and asks for a raise. You tell them that you are sorry, but there is no money in the budget. They leave your office clearly disappointed. You start worrying as the person does very good work and may get demoralized—and start looking for another job.

"Here's the challenge," I tell the participants. "I want you to imagine what possible *interests* the employee might have for wanting that raise, other than just money. If the raise is their position, what are the possible motivations behind it?"

The ideas come flying in:

"Recognition."

"Wanting to move forward with their career."

"Self-worth."

"Inequity with others doing the same job."

"More responsibility."

"Rising cost of living."

"Tuition for kids' education."

"Supporting elderly parents."

"Getting married."

"Getting divorced."

"That's great," I tell the participants. "Now I want you to use your creativity to generate a list of at least ten concrete *options*. A raise is just one option. Given there is no money in the budget, what are other specific things you could offer to your employee that might satisfy one or more of their interests?"

The ideas come flooding in:

"A new title."

"A promotion without a raise."

"Travel to represent the organization."

"Flextime to help take care of elderly parents."

"Ability to work from home."

"An award."

"Invite them to make a presentation to the board."

"A career plan."

"A high-visibility project."

"Explain the fairness of the salary scale."

"A tuition loan."

"A promise of a raise next year."

"Ask them."

I am amazed at how easily our creativity flows when we are given license to brainstorm freely. The ideas pop up rapidly like popcorn. Each person easily comes up with a few ideas, but together, the group comes up with far more.

"That only took five minutes," I tell the participants. "While most of the interests may not apply and most of the options may not be workable, all it takes is *one* interest and *one* option and you may have a more satisfied employee. For a tiny investment of time, you may get a very large payoff."

By delving deep into what people really want, we may discover that although the parties' *positions* may be rigidly opposed, their *interests* may not be. That gives us a chance to *expand the pie before dividing it up*. Through the application of creativity, there can be more for all.

This exercise is a simple demonstration of the power of human creativity when it is unleashed to solve a difficult problem. We see applied creativity on display all around us in the marvelous new technologies at our disposal. The question is: Can we apply the same individual and collective creativity to transforming today's no-win conflicts?

## APPLY COLLECTIVE CREATIVITY

The day before I was to fly to Colombia to meet with the other international advisors for the first time, Sergio Jaramillo, the high commissioner for peace, called me to ask:

"What do you need to facilitate our negotiating strategy session?"

"Two flip charts and some colored markers," I replied.

The exploratory talks with the FARC were about to begin. President Santos had asked us to prepare a negotiating strategy. Since he was taking a big political risk and the talks, if exposed, could easily be torpedoed, the meetings were to be kept secret to see if an initial agreement in principle could be reached. The involvement of international advisors was also to be kept confidential. We were whisked into and out of the country by the president's security detail—and secluded while we were there.

Sergio found a quiet, private place for us all to meet, a villa deep in the tropical forest, four hours' drive down the mountains from Bogotá. Enrique Santos, the president's elder brother, drove me there. Santos had asked his brother to join the delegation for the exploratory talks as a signal of seriousness to the other side.

Together with the celebrated author Gabriel García Márquez, Enrique had founded a leftist journal, *Alternativa*, in his youth— and had gotten to know many of the FARC leaders who had later gone underground to fight.

Upon arriving at the villa, I found the flip charts set up outside near a swimming pool. The heat was sweltering.

The president's challenge seemed like a real stretch. How could we persuade the guerrillas to disarm?

The Colombian military was applying plenty of military pressure on the guerrillas every day. But where was the bridge—the golden bridge—that the guerrillas could be invited to cross? For that, we would need a lot of creativity.

As the ten of us—five advisors and five peace negotiators— gathered, I decided to stimulate our imaginations by starting off with my favorite *possibilist* exercise: writing the other side's victory speech. As I described earlier, the victory speech is a creative thought experiment that invites us to picture success and work backward from it.

"Imagine for a moment," I asked the group, "that the FARC have accepted the government proposal. Incredible as it may seem, they have agreed, in principle, to disarm and demobilize in the context of a peace agreement. This will be the first time in fifty years of war they have agreed to even *talk* about this issue. Now imagine their leader, Timochenko, has to stand in front of the fighters and explain why the FARC leadership has decided to accept the government's proposal. What could he possibly say?

"Enrique, I know it's not easy, but imagine that all of us are the guerrilla forces and you are speaking to us as Timochenko—what would you say?"

Enrique tried to demur, but everyone encouraged him to give it a try. So he stood up and faced us. I asked him to speak in the first person as if he were the FARC leader.

"Compañeros!" he declaimed. "We have fought bravely now for almost fifty years for the sacred cause of social justice. Many have fallen, and we remember them in our hearts. Now we have a chance to continue our struggle for the rights of the people in a different way—through a struggle at the negotiating table and at the ballot box . . ."

Enrique went on for a few minutes. He ended with:

"And we will never surrender! The struggle will go on until we achieve our aims!"

Everyone rose to their feet spontaneously and gave him a standing ovation.

Once we were seated again, I asked if there were any questions for Timochenko, alias Enrique. The first came from Joaquín, the former guerrilla commander from El Salvador:

"How do we know this is not a trick?"

"We are prepared," replied Enrique as the FARC leader, "and we will not put down our guard. Meanwhile, we will continue fighting, of course."

The questions were tough, but Enrique answered them well.

The participants were now smiling and laughing. Our creative juices were flowing. We were tapping into the innate human capacity for play. The possibility of peace seemed alive.

So I turned to the flip chart and asked the group:

"As you listened to 'Timochenko,' what were the principal interests he touched on? What is most important to the FARC?"

"Social justice and land reform," called out Sergio. "After all, that was the original cause that led them to take up arms back in the 1960s."

"Political power," said Frank Pearl, a former peace commissioner. "They want to govern the country one day so they can carry out their political program."

"Personal security," Enrique reminded the group. "Remember all the killings in the decade of the eighties?"

Thirty years earlier, there had been an agreement that the FARC could come out of the jungle and run for office. But during the elections and their aftermath, dozens of their leaders had been assassinated and more than four thousand of their followers had been killed.

I recorded the group's answers on one of the flip charts.

The previous attempt at negotiations, ten years earlier, had developed an agenda that included more than a hundred issues. It had been hopelessly complicated. This time, we were determined to keep it as simple as possible to give peace its best chance.

So I asked the group:

"What four or five points can we put on the negotiating agenda that would address the FARC's interests and make it possible for Timochenko to make this speech?"

I was asking them what the heart of the agreement would be. What *formula*—to use a term from my negotiation colleague William Zartman—would contain the essence of the deal? What could the FARC receive in return for demobilizing and disarming?

I turned to the second flip chart and began to record the participants' responses. We all agreed that it made sense to begin with agrarian reform: facilitating access to land for those who didn't have it, reducing rural poverty, and extending public services to the countryside.

"It will allow the FARC leadership to show their supporters and fighters that they got something for their long fight," Enrique pointed out. "It will help them justify why they are laying down their weapons. It allows them to keep their sense of honor."

"That works because our government wants agrarian reform, too. We recognize it is a major issue in the country and it needs to be addressed," explained Sergio. "In fact, we are about to present a big bill in Congress on that very subject. So it will be easy for us to discuss as we have many tangible proposals."

"Why don't we delay presenting that bill so the FARC can take credit?" asked Frank.

"Okay," I said. "After agrarian reform, what could the second item be?"

"To address their interest in political power, we can talk about political participation, so that they can see that they will be free to run for public office," proposed Lucía Jaramillo, a close advisor to President Santos.

"This time, we will have to work closely with them on guarantees for their personal security. That will be important to them," Enrique added.

The conversation continued. The final item on the proposed agenda was *dejación de armas*—laying down of weapons. Only when the FARC could see progress on the other items would they be asked to talk about arrangements for demobilization and disarmament.

The draft negotiating agenda was the fruit of the group's creative efforts, which began with imagining the other side's victory speech. Delving deep into each side's interests and needs, the group developed a creative formula for mutual gain. It was intended to serve as the kernel of a final agreement—and that was what it became.

The draft agenda traveled with the government negotiators on their secret trip to Havana a few weeks later. Inspired by the flip chart, Sergio arranged to have a whiteboard in Havana, where the proposed agenda items were presented to the FARC negotiators. Both sides discussed each item at length and made modifications, but the essence remained. The agenda turned into a five-page framework agreement, signed by both sides after six months of negotiations.

On the evening of September 4, 2012, President Santos delivered a televised speech to the nation announcing the results of the secret talks and the beginning of formal peace negotiations:

I am convinced that we face a real opportunity to end the internal armed conflict definitively. . . . If we are successful, we will have ended that dark night of half a century of violence. . . . We cannot allow new generations to continue being born—like mine—without knowing what a single day in peace is.

The framework agreement became the organizing outline for another four years of hard negotiation over the details. The result was a historic peace agreement that brought an end to one of the longest-running wars in the world.

Throughout the many years of challenging negotiation, Sergio Jaramillo, the peace commissioner, liked to remind me of the flip chart standing by the swimming pool in the sweltering jungle:

"It all began there on that flip chart. That was the essence of the deal."

It was a remarkable experience, illustrating the power of harnessing collective intelligence and creativity for the transformation of a seemingly impossible conflict.

## "WHO CAN DO WHAT TOMORROW MORNING?"

In my mind's eye, I can flash back thirty-five years from that flip chart by the pool in the Colombian countryside in February 2012 to another flip chart at the Harvard Faculty Club in February 1977. I can draw an imaginary line from one flip chart to the other. It was at the Devising Seminars, convened by Roger Fisher, where I learned about the power of eliciting human creativity in the face of a challenging conflict.

I was then a graduate student in social anthropology. As I re-counted previously, Roger asked me to coordinate a regular fort-nightly meeting on international conflicts for faculty members and visiting diplomats and policy-makers. During the meeting, my job was to facilitate the flow of ideas and record them with a colored marker on a flip chart that stood in the front of the room.

One session would focus on the Arab-Israeli dispute, another on the violent troubles in Northern Ireland, another on ending apart-heid in South Africa, and yet another on the Cold War between the United States and the Soviet Union.

The first thing I noticed about the seminars was that the ques-tion being asked was radically different. Normally in such academic discussions, the participants would be addressing the questions of *what* was happening and *why*. Sometimes there would be specula-tion: What is going to happen *next*?

In contrast, the main question Roger posed was: *Who can do what tomorrow morning?* In other words, which leader could make which decision that could de-escalate a conflict or interrupt a war?

Instead of *analysis* alone, our focus was *advice*. The aim was to come up with highly practical advice, informed by analysis. Instead of *prediction* alone, our focus was *prescription* and *prevention*. In-stead of just warning that a situation was going to escalate, the aim was to figure out *how* to de-escalate it.

In the academic discussions I knew, it was assumed that we had no agency—no power to affect the situation. The conflict was intrac-table, and we were essentially powerless to do anything except talk about it and analyze it. It was not our job to do more.

Behind the question *Who can do what tomorrow morning?*, the assumption was that the conflict was not impossible to manage, and we might be able to influence it positively. And *it was our job*.

I found Roger's question revolutionary. A conflict may seem impossible, yes. But if you start from that place you are likely to end up in the same place. The assumption of impossibility is a self-confirming prophecy. If you start from possibility instead, there is no guarantee, but you might just end up with a practical possibility that could help. The starting place, the initial assumptions we make, matter hugely.

That simple but powerful question, "*Who* can do *what* tomorrow morning?," has stayed with me all these years. It is the iconic question of the *possibilist*.

The aim of the Devising Seminar was to generate operational proposals in concrete form, such as a draft cease-fire agreement, an outline of a presidential speech, or a UN Security Council resolution.

I would write up the results of the seminar, and then I'd help Roger turn them into a memo intended, ambitiously enough, for a key decision maker who could have a positive impact on the conflict. Roger wanted to offer the decision maker what he called a *yesable proposition*, a concrete and actionable proposal that, if accepted, would lead directly to change. Open to creativity, he also stressed rigor in thinking through the practicalities.

To encourage creative ideas in the Devising Seminar, Roger set a low bar of feasibility. For him that meant at least a 5 percent chance that the decision maker would say yes. He figured that the stakes were so high in terms of human lives and resources that if we could come up with a proposal with even a 5 percent chance of success, it would be well worth all our ideation and effort.

## INVENT FIRST, EVALUATE LATER

The radical redefinition of the question led to a reshaping of the basic rules of conversation.

In academic seminars, I had noticed that the dominant mode was criticism of ideas. Criticism helped test and hone ideas, but it also dampened creativity. Wild, innovative ideas often met with withering objections and ridicule. My fellow students and I had learned to keep our more creative thoughts to ourselves.

In the Devising Seminar, however, we adopted a ground rule from the field of innovation that actively encouraged creativity.

"We want your best ideas," Roger said. "Wild ideas are positively welcome. Many of the best ideas started off as wild ideas. To encourage creativity, we will adopt the golden rule of brainstorming. So for the first half of dinner, no criticism is allowed. Save your criticism for later."

My job was to keep reminding the participants about the elementary ground rule of *no criticism*—and I had to do so often at first. Interestingly, it was easier for the professors and diplomats to take feedback from me, a graduate student, than from Roger, who was their peer; no face was lost.

The ideas, written in different colors of felt-tipped markers, would proliferate and soon fill up the flip chart. I would tear off the sheet of paper and hang it in a place visible to the participants. We could not touch the walls, which were covered in elaborate silklike wallpaper and paintings of deceased faculty in ornate gold frames. So I improvised and found ways to use masking tape to attach the sheets onto windows and doors. And I learned to bring additional flip charts. People walking into the formal room would be slightly taken aback by the chaos of large, brightly colored sheets of paper scattered around the room. I noticed some suppressed smiles.

The results were startling. Instead of shutting one another down, each person vied to be creative. They spurred one another on. The ideas got better, more and more creative.

Think about what stops the flow of creativity in our daily lives—at work or at home. The biggest obstacle is a critical voice that we hear in meetings—and often in our own heads—whenever a creative idea shows up:

"That will never work."

"Be serious."

"We tried that before."

"We've never tried that before."

"Ridiculous."

I think of these as "killer phrases"—phrases that kill off potentially creative ideas.

The simple secret, as I learned from my experience in the Devising Seminar, is to *separate* the process of generating ideas from the process of evaluating them. Evaluation is vital but best done *after* people have had a chance to come up with creative ideas.

Once the participants had generated an initial list of ideas, we asked them to make their criticism constructive. Instead of attacking a creative suggestion, we suggested that they begin by finding one thing they liked about it:

"One thing I like about this idea is . . . One concern I have is . . . One way to improve on the idea is . . ."

The wild ideas started to take shape. Certain ones naturally drew our interest, and we developed them further as a group.

No one's name was attached to an idea. This seemed revolutionary in an academic setting, where customarily names were carefully attached to every idea and often recorded through elaborate citations. The flip chart captured the intelligence of the group. It was an exercise in collective problem solving, not just the individual ideation to which I was accustomed.

Upon entering the Faculty Club, participants would check their overcoats by the door before going upstairs to the private dining room. In a metaphorical sense, I noticed, we were tacitly asking them to check their egos at the door, too.

People built on one another's ideas, so the proposals got better and better as we harnessed the collective intelligence of the group. In other academic seminars, I would often watch participants destroy one another's ideas. Here ideas were built upon. The group intelligence exceeded that of any one individual.

In the end, everyone saw tangibly on the flip chart how the ideas they had contributed were part of the process. No one could say that it was all their idea. It was a bit unsettling to some, I noticed, but in the end more satisfying to all. We were all working together for the common cause of peace.

It helped that we were meeting over dinner. The atmosphere was very different from that of a conference room. The act of breaking bread together cultivated connection among strangers who were often on opposing sides of a conflict: Palestinians and Israelis, Pakistanis and Indians, Catholics and Protestants from Northern Ireland. Back in their home countries, meeting with each other face to face could be a risk, but here, in a non-political university context, far away from home, they were able to come together and talk.

Where possible, we invited participants from opposing sides to sit next to each other rather than face each other across the table.

That way, the seating itself encouraged a *side-by-side* perspective. The problem we were asking them to address was on the flip chart, so we were all quite literally facing a common challenge.

It may be more common these days to have meetings like this, but back then it seemed revolutionary, particularly in the hallowed halls of an institution such as Harvard. I was electrified by the stream of creative ideas flowing forth.

## SEND IN THE WIZARDS

In 1983, US arms control negotiator General Edward Rowny, one of our guests at the Devising Seminar, invited Roger and me to visit the Strategic Arms Reduction Talks (START) between the United States and the Soviet Union in Geneva. I was excited to be there as the conflict between nuclear superpowers was the existential issue that had worried me ever since I was a boy in school—a school not far from where the talks were taking place.

After a morning workshop on negotiation for the US negotiators, Roger and I had lunch with them. I had a chance to ask:

"I'm curious. In the last years, there haven't been any arms control agreements. But before then, there was a whole slew of them. Why then and not now? Can you help me understand?"

As soon as I asked the question, I realized it was a bit indelicate. The negotiators looked at one another to see who would answer. One older man, who had been quiet until then, spoke up.

"Oh, there are several reasons why we were able to reach agreements back then, but one of them was that we had an interesting process we called 'the wizards.'"

"Oh," I said, my curiosity piqued, "what were the wizards?"

"The wizards were two Americans and two Russians who had four characteristics: They were *bilingual* in English and Russian, so they could communicate easily. They were *technically knowledge-able* about the subject. They were *lower level* than the ambassadors. And hence they were *disposable*."

As he said the word "disposable," he cracked a little smile.

"Whenever the talks hit an impasse, these four would get to-gether quietly, sometimes at a restaurant over dinner and sometimes on the ferryboat out in the middle of Lake Geneva. And they would just talk freely and informally.

"They would ask a lot of hypothetical *what-if* questions: What if we were to count the warheads this way? What if we were to count them that way?

"And the funny thing is that we got more good ideas for break-ing impasses from the wizards than from any other source. The wizards never got any credit, which was the whole point."

A few of his colleagues nodded knowingly. I found myself won-dering if the speaker had perhaps been a wizard himself.

"That's amazing," I said. "I am curious: What do you mean by 'they were disposable'?"

"Oh," he answered, "if the conversations went too far, you could always ship them back to Washington or Moscow and say these conversations never took place. They were deniable."

It was a lesson for me. I have noticed often in negotiations that creative ideas and potential breakthroughs rarely emerge in the for-mal talks, where the parties are guarded and wary. They happen most often between individuals who know and trust each other per-sonally. They happen in corridors, during coffee breaks, over a meal, or in retreat settings like the ferryboat on the lake.

Creative ideas emerge more easily when people have gone to the balcony, when they have had a chance to *pause, zoom in* on what they really want, and *zoom out* to see the bigger picture. They happen when people have been able to *listen* deeply to one another. The prior steps create the conditions for creativity. *Sequence matters.*

The wizards served as a "back channel," an unofficial means of communication between two sides. They were behind the scenes and out of the limelight—discreet and deniable. Those are favorable conditions for exploring creative ideas to break through impasses in contentious conflicts.

As at the arms control talks, creative ideas often bubble up more easily at working levels of the organization among people who do not have formal decision-making authority. The top leaders are usually too constrained to be creative. Once the wizards formulate and test out the ideas, they can float suggestions up to their respective leaders who can then discern, decide, and, of course, take credit.

During the difficult and charged negotiations to end apartheid in South Africa, I noticed how the two leaders, Nelson Mandela and F. W. de Klerk, used a similar process. Finding it challenging to negotiate directly with each other, they made creative use of two young deputies: Cyril Ramaphosa, then a trade union leader in the African National Congress (who later became president of South Africa), and Roelf Meyer, a deputy minister in the National Party government.

Ramaphosa and Meyer had first met when they had been invited to go fishing with their families at the country home of a common acquaintance. Meyer, a novice, had promptly gotten a fishhook painfully caught in his finger. Ramaphosa's wife, a nurse, had tried to extract it but without success. After an hour, with Meyer growing faint with pain, Ramaphosa intervened with a pair of pliers.

"If you've never trusted an ANC person before, you'd better get ready to do so now," he told Meyer.

Ramaphosa pushed hard on the hook to make space for the barb and wrenched it out.

Meyer muttered, "Well, Cyril, don't say I didn't trust you."

That interaction began a personal relationship of mutual trust and respect. Not long after, Ramaphosa and Meyer were authorized by their respective leaders to meet quietly to explore creative ways to overcome impasses in the political negotiations. As violence flared up in the streets, the formal talks were often broken off. The quiet "wizard" conversations helped get the talks back on track, averting a total breakdown that might have led to full-on civil war.

As Roelf Meyer told me years later:

"We developed a confidence that, no matter how intractable the issue, we could find a creative way to work it out."

That is the power of using wizards.

So whenever I find myself in the midst of a tough conflict, I like to ask:

*Where are the wizards?*

In other words, where are the people who are trusted and knowledgeable, who can work together informally behind the scenes to overcome impasses and explore creative breakthroughs?

And here's a radical thought as you contemplate the conflicts around you: Could you possibly be a wizard yourself?

## USE THE ONE UNLIMITED RESOURCE

As my fellow anthropologist Angeles Arrien liked to say:

"Conflict is a call to the creative."

Conflict at its best can spur a creative search that can produce better ideas and, ultimately, better relationships. Conflict can be our friend if we unleash the power of creativity.

The essential transformation is to change an *either-or* mindset into a *both-and* mindset. It is to go from a mindset of scarcity to one of sufficiency—and even abundance. It is to turn opposed positions into creative options for mutual gain.

In today's world, many things seem limited, but the one unlimited resource we all possess is our innate creativity. Creativity offers us our greatest opportunity to open up possibilities where none seem obvious. Creativity is the key to making the impossible possible.

## CHAPTER 8

# ATTRACT

## From Harder to Easier

*It always seems impossible until it's done.*
—Nelson Mandela

W hat's he doing in here? Let's *string* him *up*!"

I was in the miners' locker room, preparing to enter the coal mine for the first time. I was getting into my work overalls and strapping on my oxygen mask when I overheard a miner nearby talking about me.

I swallowed, feeling uneasy.

"It's rough down there, I'm telling you," the mine manager, Mike

Johnson, had warned me the day before when I had asked for his permission to enter the coal mine.

"I can't be responsible for your safety—either from machines or accidents. Or men," he had added ominously.

But I had insisted.

"I got it. I'm willing to take the risk. If they won't talk to me up here, maybe they'll talk to me down there."

Inside, I didn't feel as confident as I sounded, but I was determined to give it a try.

As I recounted earlier, this mine in eastern Kentucky was enmeshed in intense conflict marked by a spate of wildcat strikes. My colleague Steve Goldberg, a noted arbitrator, and I had shuttled back and forth for many weeks with the union leadership and management to reach an agreement. We had been elated by our success, but then, seemingly out of the blue, the miners had overwhelmingly voted the agreement down. Our elation had turned to gloom. It turned out that they didn't have an objection to the *content* of the agreement; it included things they wanted. They just didn't trust *anything* management would sign onto.

Rather than give up and go home, I proposed to Steve that we adopt a different approach. This time we would listen to the miners first to learn what was troubling them. And we would encourage both sides to talk out their issues rather than fight. We would try to build trust in the *process*. Steve sounded a bit skeptical but wished me luck as he went off to France for his summer vacation.

I moved down to Kentucky for the summer. Each day, I went to the mine to hang around and talk to anyone who would speak with me. But I found it hard to get even a moment with the miners. They spent all their time inside the mine, and when they emerged at the end of their work shift, they were in a rush to get home. It was not easy to strike up conversations. They seemed distrustful. I was this young guy from faraway Boston who sounded to them much more like a manager than a miner. As far as they were concerned, I was a man from Mars. I wasn't fully shunned, but it felt that way.

Days turned into weeks. I began to wonder if I was wasting my time. Frustrated by the lack of progress, I decided that if the miners wouldn't come to me, I would go to them. I could go down into the mine and talk with them during their shift. Since the mine operated around the clock, I would need to visit the mine during all three shifts, including the midnight one, nicknamed the "hoot owl." I was determined to listen to as many miners as I could.

That was when I approached Mike Johnson for his permission to enter the mine.

"Okay, it's your call." Mike eventually agreed, albeit reluctantly. "You'll have to sign a release form. I'll ask Phil to set you up."

That didn't sound good to me since Phil, the mine foreman, was widely feared and disliked by the miners. He assigned me a locker in the management locker room. I thanked him but demurred. After all, I was trying to win the trust of the miners, so I asked to be assigned a metal basket suspended high up in the miners' locker room, a cavernous space where they all got ready for work.

Phil gave me a hard hat. I noticed that it was white like the managers' hats. All the miners wore black hard hats. So I decided to spray-paint mine another color: green. Phil also handed me a leather belt with a metal plaque with my name and Social Security number engraved on it to identify my body in case of an accident. Lastly, he gave me an oxygen mask and explained how to use it in an emergency.

It was all sounding a bit more dangerous than I had first thought, but I was determined to go ahead with my plan.

The big day arrived. I entered the miners' locker room, pulled on a chain that lowered my metal basket down from the ceiling, placed my street clothes in it, and put on my work overalls. As I was strapping on my leather belt together with the oxygen mask, I overheard that miner talking about me in a threatening fashion.

"Let's string him up!"

I glanced around to see if anyone else was paying attention but noticed nothing.

I proceeded—nervously. The mine, a mile down, accessed by an open elevator, was cold, dank, and pitch black. The only way I could see was with a headlamp attached to my helmet. The ceilings were low, and I had to walk bent over. The noise from the coal-boring machines was infernally loud. And the coal dust was thick—so thick that when I blew my nose, the mucus was black.

But down there, the miners did have time to talk. As they rested, chewed tobacco, and spat out the juice, they talked more freely to me about whatever was bothering them. I was on their turf, and they felt more comfortable talking without managers around watching. They were curious about me, too, and started asking questions about my life and where I came from.

By my third trip down into the mine, I started to relax a bit. My plan seemed to be off to a promising start.

On my fourth trip into the mine, I was listening to a coal miner telling me about a complaint he had about management and how they were treating him. Then suddenly, out of nowhere, I was jumped from behind by four big strong men. They knocked me down and pinned me to the cold, rocky coal surface. As I struggled without avail to free myself, they violently yanked down my work pants. One man wielded a big knife whose ugly rusty blade glinted in the light of my headlamp.

The man with the knife then proceeded to cut from me . . . a patch of pubic hair. I was in shock, naturally, but I can remember the feeling of intense relief that the operation stopped right there. The four men released me from their grip, and I got up on my feet again. To my utter surprise, each man slapped me roughly on the back, congratulating me and declaring loudly for all around to hear:

"Now you've been *haired*! You're a regular coal miner just like us!"

The word spread through the mine like wildfire.

It wasn't how I imagined I would build trust (and I hope those who read this will never have to undergo a similar initiation), but I have to say, it brought about a marked shift in how I was seen. Increasingly, the miners approached me with their grievances. I was able to persuade management to start to listen to their problems and address them through the multistep negotiation process that Steve and I had proposed in the agreement—the one that had initially been rejected.

Gradually, as we were able to settle one grievance after another through negotiation, the miners began to trust the process. The relationship between miners and managers improved. And to everyone's surprise, the wildcat strikes ceased almost altogether. Step by step, little breakthrough by little breakthrough, the conflict was *transformed*. It didn't end, but the form changed from *walking out* to *talking out* their problems.

It was a big lesson for me. I learned that it is not enough just to come up with creative ideas for agreement. It is not enough to focus on the *substance*—the issues in dispute. We need to create an *attractive process*, a path that *attracts* the parties to agreement and a better relationship.

## MAKE IT EASIER TO SAY YES

In my classes, I like to recall Aesop's ancient Greek fable about persuasion. Up in the heavens, a quarrel breaks out between the North Wind and the Sun about who is more powerful. After much argument, the two parties agree to resolve the question with a test. They look down on the earth and spy a wandering shepherd boy. They decide that whoever is successful in plucking the cloak off the shepherd's back will win the argument.

The North Wind goes first and blows and blows—but to no avail. The more the wind blows, the more tightly the shepherd boy wraps his cloak around his shoulders.

Finally, it's the Sun's turn. The Sun patiently bathes the boy in warm sunlight. After a while, the boy remarks to himself, "What a beautiful day! I think I will lie down in the meadow for a moment and soak in the rays." As he lies down, he flicks off his cloak.

So the Sun wins the argument.

I love the wisdom of this fable. The North Wind and the Sun represent two very different forms of persuasion. The North Wind uses *force* and treats the boy as if he were an inanimate object, trying to rip off the cloak against the boy's will. The Sun takes the opposite approach. It exercises its natural power to *attract*. It respects the boy as having a will of his own and creates a conducive environment in which the boy, of his own volition, eventually chooses to remove his cloak. The process may take longer, but it works.

In class, to illustrate the point, I invite a participant to come forward and hold their hands up. I place my hands against theirs. Then I start slowly pushing against their hands.

What do they do? They instinctively push back.

"Did I ask you to push back?" I ask them.

"No."

They just do it naturally.

This is what I see happen in conflict all the time. We believe that our position is right, so we naturally push for it. It is only human. The more we push, the more the other pushes back. On it goes. Unless we are much stronger than the other side, we find ourselves stuck in a standoff. No wonder so many conflicts today are stalemated.

What is the alternative?

Successful negotiators, I find, often do the exact opposite of *push*. Instead, they *attract*.

In a contentious conflict, we may feel like making it *harder* for the other side. That's what the North Wind does, trying to make it harder for the shepherd boy to hold on to his cloak. The Sun, by contrast, makes it *easier*—more attractive—for the shepherd boy to take off his cloak. Taking a lesson from the Sun, our job in difficult situations is to *make it easier—more attractive—for the other side to make the decision we'd like them to make.*

## ATTRACT THROUGH TRUST

There is perhaps nothing more attractive than trust.

I first appreciated this lesson in conflict negotiation as a graduate student in a lively conversation with Lord Hugh Caradon, a retired British diplomat who had spent a half century in the British Foreign Service. He was visiting Harvard, and I was responsible for welcoming him. I had just picked him up from the airport, and we were driving into Cambridge. And he was reminiscing.

Caradon had served as the British ambassador to the United Nations at the time of the 1967 Middle East War. As it turned out, it was Great Britain's turn to chair the UN Security Council, so it was Caradon's job to help the council agree on a resolution to end the war.

Caradon's biggest stumbling block was the Soviets, who had serious reservations. And their vote was critical because they could exercise their veto. After three weeks of arduous negotiation, trying to satisfy all parties, Caradon was under pressure from his government to wrap up, so he called a vote on the proposed resolution.

Ten minutes before the vote, as Caradon was standing outside the Security Council chamber, the Soviet ambassador, Vasily Kuznetsov, approached him:

"Ambassador Caradon, I have a favor to ask. I'm asking you to postpone the vote by two weeks."

"Ambassador Kuznetsov," Caradon replied, "I am sorry, but we've been talking for three weeks now. I think everyone's had a chance to weigh in. It's time to vote."

Kuznetsov looked at him intently.

"Ambassador Caradon, I'm afraid you have misunderstood me. I'm asking you as a *personal* favor if you would postpone this vote by two weeks."

Here Caradon paused his story for a moment.

"So what did you do?" I asked him, my curiosity piqued.

"Well," Caradon told me, "when Kuznetsov added the word 'personal,' I knew I had to grant his request even though I knew I would get a lot of pushback from London and Washington."

"Why did you?" I asked.

"One simple reason," Caradon replied. "Even though Kuznetsov represented a power that did not have a reputation for honesty and fair dealing, he *personally* had that reputation among us diplomats. He had spent years building that reputation.

"Kuznetsov was giving me his personal word. If he was putting his reputation on the line, I knew I could trust him not to use those two weeks to undermine the fragile coalition I had built to support the draft resolution.

"Well, sure enough, the vote took place two weeks later in the UN Security Council chamber. The last country to vote was the Union of Soviet Socialist Republics. To everyone's surprise but mine, Kuznetsov raised his hand and voted yes. True to his word, he used those two weeks to return to Moscow to persuade his superiors to drop their opposition to the proposed resolution."

Caradon's story left a lasting impression on me. Without his personal reputation for trustworthiness, built up over many years, Kuznetsov would never have been able to buy those two weeks. Without his ability to inspire trust in his political adversaries, we might not have UN Resolution 242, arguably the most important resolution ever on the Israeli-Palestinian conflict.

Even in a situation of distrust, Kuznetsov had what you could call *working trust*. His word could be counted on. His counterparts would entrust him with sensitive information, knowing he would not use it to their disadvantage. Thanks to his reputation, Kuznetsov had a better chance of success in the myriad of diplomatic negotiations he engaged in.

*Trust attracts.*

## BUILD A TRUST MENU

But here's the hard question: If neither side trusts the other, how can trust be built?

My work in Venezuela with President Chávez showed me one possible way. As I recounted earlier, Chávez had accepted my proposal to develop a list of practical signals that each side could send the other. The signals would aim to reduce distrust and de-escalate the crisis that was threatening to break out into massive violence. He had delegated his minister of the interior, Diosdado Cabello, to follow up.

Chávez had given me a first signal he would see as a positive sign from his political opponents, some of whom owned the private television channels:

"They could stop calling me a *mono* [monkey] on their TV stations."

Accompanied by Francisco Diez, my colleague from the Carter Center, I went straight from my meeting with Chávez to a meeting with his political opponents, about fifteen of them altogether. Francisco and I briefed them about our conversation with the president. We thought they would be pleased to hear that we had cracked the door open to a possible dialogue. But we were wrong.

"We don't want to engage with him. He's sly. You can't trust him," said Ricardo. The other leaders nodded vigorously.

"I understand you don't trust him one bit," I replied. "That's the whole point of this exercise—to test whether he is trustworthy or not before you would even consider sitting down with him or his people. It's up to you. Do you want to try this out? It costs you nothing but a little time. Otherwise, no problem, I will just send him a message that this won't work."

There was a pregnant pause as everyone stopped to reflect. They looked at one another, then Ricardo spoke again.

"Okay," he sighed. "Let's give it a chance. When do you want to do this?"

"No better time to start than now," I said. I went up to the whiteboard, colored marker in hand, ready to write. I turned to the group.

"Is there anything President Chávez could do now that would send you a credible signal that maybe it would be worth opening a dialogue? Let's brainstorm a list of five or ten possible actions he could take."

"He could resign!" María Eugenia called out. Everyone laughed.

"Of course, that's what you would like," I said, "but I am asking something else. What small but significant steps could he *realistically* take that would be a positive signal?"

"Oh, you mean *besitos*?" Ricardo suddenly asked, with a slight smile.

Everyone laughed. *Besitos* is Spanish for "little kisses." It was a reference to how children—and couples—make up when they have quarreled.

"That's exactly what I mean. *Besitos*."

I turned to the whiteboard and asked them:

"Let's see if we can come up with a list of *besitos*."

"He could stop publicly insulting us, calling us the 'Four

Horsemen of the Apocalypse' and branding us as 'enemies of the people.'"

"That would be something," Juan piped up. "Every morning I used to walk to the cathedral to pray. I can't do it anymore because people on the street harass me and call me an 'enemy of the people,' all because of *him*."

"It would be good to change that, Juan. What else could Chávez do?"

"He could release a political prisoner."

"Okay, good suggestion. Any others?"

They came up with a list of about ten possible ideas. I then asked:

"What about taking these ideas a step further and developing them into a *trust menu*?"

"What's a trust menu?"

"A trust menu is a pre-agreed language of goodwill. It is a list of positive signals that each side can send that have been checked out previously with the other to make sure they will be heard and appreciated. It is not a list of demands. It is a menu of choices.

"One side begins by choosing one signal to send. Then the other side reciprocates by picking a signal to send in return. Then it is the first side's turn and so on. It is like climbing a ladder—one foot then the other. Step by step, you slowly build confidence and climb out of the pit of distrust."

"So what's the next step?"

"Why don't you delegate a couple of people to meet with Francisco and me tomorrow night? We will shuttle back and forth between you and Minister Cabello, without you having to meet, to develop a menu you can both agree upon. Okay?"

"But we can't be seen even going into the same hotel as he does. We don't want to start any rumors that will get us in trouble with our own side."

"Why don't we meet at the *posada* where I am staying?" I suggested. "I happen to be their only guest. It is an old house with a garden surrounded by walls. We can meet at night."

Everyone agreed. At ten o'clock the next evening, Ricardo, María Eugenia, and two other opposition leaders showed up. We sat together conversing on a patio in the middle of the lush garden by the side of a little fountain. An hour later, a black government car showed up at the gate with Diosdado Cabello, the minister of the interior, together with his bodyguards. I invited him to sit on the balcony outside my second-floor bedroom overlooking the garden.

The balcony and the garden seemed fitting places for political enemies to conduct an exercise in building trust. There they could *pause, zoom in* on what they really wanted, and *zoom out* to see the bigger picture.

Francisco and I shuttled back and forth from the balcony to the garden from eleven that night until five the next morning. We asked each side to make a list of what signals the other could send and what signals they could possibly send in response. There were no demands and no commitments, just options. Each item required considerable clarification so that each side understood precisely what the agreed-upon signals would be. By first light, we had our menu.

Significantly, two of the items had to do with showing respect. Chávez agreed to refrain from calling the opposition leaders "coupsters, traitors, drug traffickers, and terrorists," while the opposition leaders, who included the owners of the private media, agreed to refrain from calling Chávez an "assassin, tyrant, animal, crazy, and demented."

In his next public broadcast a few days later, Chávez sent the first signal, asking his supporters not to interfere with the work—or the equipment—of the journalists covering the crisis. The opposition leaders reciprocated with a signal from their list broadcasting a statement condemning violence by any side. And so it began. It was all about *besitos*, baby kisses, intended to cool off the high tensions.

The trust menu exercise was just one little experiment along the path of reducing the threat of civil war, but it served as an important lesson for me. It illustrated how, through little steps, distrustful opponents could engage in a conversation with each other. Although the parties may not agree on the issues, they will usually agree that trust is a big obstacle. Even when distrust is at a high and relations are at a low, progress can be made. A trust menu can be the first step to transforming a strained or broken relationship.

## CHOREOGRAPH THE PLAY

Imagine that the trust menu exercise has been successful. What's the next stage in the process?

If contentious conflict is like a drama, I picture myself on the balcony, looking down at the stage. I see the characters in the play locked in battle with one another. I zoom in to the interests and needs of each. I begin to see how the parties have gotten stuck in a trap.

Then I conduct a little thought experiment and ask myself: If I were the playwright choreographing the play, what steps could each character take that could free them from the conflict trap? What could possibly attract them to a better place? How can this play end well?

At no time was the power of attractive choreography more evident for me than during the Korean Missile Crisis of 2017.

As I recounted earlier, US president Donald Trump and North Korean leader Kim Jong Un put themselves on a collision course from the very outset of Trump's presidency. The crisis continued to escalate dangerously as North Korea tested one nuclear missile after another and then proceeded to detonate a hydrogen bomb. At the end of November 2017, Kim Jong Un tested a third intercontinental ballistic missile, confirming his ability to hit the continental United States.

A few weeks later, in a conversation in the Oval Office, Trump asked his future national security advisor John Bolton:

"What do you think the chances of war are with North Korea? Fifty-fifty?"

"It all depends on China, but probably fifty-fifty," replied Bolton.

Trump turned to his chief of staff, General John Kelly, and said: "He agrees with you."

I learned about that sobering conversation only after Bolton reported it years later in his memoir *The Room Where It Happened*, but it confirmed what my colleagues and I had feared at the time. We had been perilously close to the brink of an unthinkable catastrophe.

On the last day of 2017, looking for some balcony perspective, I took a solitary winter hike, traipsing through the snow and ice up to a mountain lake in Rocky Mountain National Park. On the way down, I paused on a giant rock outcropping with a beautiful view of the valley below.

On an impulse, I decided to call my friend Robert Carlin.

There were few Americans who knew the secretive hermit kingdom of North Korea better than Bob. He had been studying it for
more than forty years, first as an analyst in intelligence and then
in the State Department. He had visited North Korea over thirty
times and had accompanied Secretary of State Madeleine Albright
during her historic meeting with North Korean leader Kim Jong Il,
the father of Kim Jong Un. Retired from government, he had kept
up his daily observation of the ever-changing political dynamics on
the Korean Peninsula.

The next day, New Year's Day, was a key moment for Korea
watchers as Kim Jong Un was expected to give his customary speech
setting out the entire year's political and economic agenda. So I had
a hunch that Bob would be around.

I wanted to ask Bob to help imagine a way to interrupt the dangerous nuclear escalation of threat and counterthreat. What could
be the choreography of steps—the delicate diplomatic dance—that
could steer the leaders away from the brink of catastrophic war?

One of my favorite ways to stimulate practical creativity is to ask
the *magic-wand* question.

"Bob," I said, "I know things are looking pretty grim, but if you
had a magic wand, what could Kim say in his speech tomorrow that
would send a positive signal to President Trump and [South Korean]
President Moon [Jae-in]?"

The magic-wand question gives people permission to suspend
their disbelief and let their imaginations wander. It breaks through
the habit of mind that assumes that tomorrow will be just like yesterday. It opens up new possibilities.

Bob paused and reflected.

"Well, Kim might announce that the DPRK [Democratic

People's Republic of Korea] has completed its historic mission of developing nuclear weaponry. He would declare victory. Then he would announce a moratorium on further testing. Everyone could breathe a little easier."

"That's really good. It would defuse the dangerous tensions and start to build a little trust," I said. "What else?"

"He could also accept Moon's invitation to send athletes to the Winter Olympics next month."

"Great idea. There could be a kind of Olympic truce. That's what happened during the original Olympics. Wars would stop.

"Play this out a bit for me, Bob," I continued. "Could Kim send a high-level political delegation so that there could be discussions on the side on how to de-escalate the situation? If so, who would he send?"

"Yes. I don't think he would go himself, but maybe he would send his sister Kim Yo Jong. She's the closest to him, perhaps the only person he trusts. And maybe Trump could send a personal representative, too. Who knows? They could talk."

"Maybe Trump could send Ivanka," I suggested. "She's the closest to him, the person he seems to trust most. Maybe the two of them could meet."

"Why not?" said Bob. "In Korea, family is very important. The two family dynasties could meet."

"Male egos have gotten inflamed. Maybe the women closest to them could help build trust and cool things down.

"Do you remember Trump once said during his campaign that he would invite Kim to have a hamburger with him and they could make a deal?" I continued. "What if Kim took him up on that and sent a message through his sister at the Olympics?"

"It's not impossible," said Bob.

It seemed almost inconceivable at the time, given all the insults and threats they had hurled at each other. But Bob and I were spinning out a positive scenario.

"If they got together and met, what would they say to one another?"

Bob's mind went to work, and he proposed some phrasing.

My questions continued to flow.

"Where would they meet?"

"Could they meet at Panmunjom on the dividing line between the two Koreas?"

"Would it just be Trump and Kim? Or could there be a three-way with Moon?"

"What do you think they could agree upon? Is it possible they could issue a formal declaration ending the war?" I had in mind that the Korean War had stopped with a temporary armistice in 1953, but had never been officially ended by the signing of a peace treaty.

Bob and I were, in effect, choreographing a play, using grounded imagination based on all that Bob knew about past communications between US and North Korean leaders.

Little did we know at the time that many of those choreographed steps would in fact be taken in the subsequent weeks and months.

## CONSTRUCT A COMPELLING STORY

In his 2018 New Year's speech, Kim Jong Un threatened, "A nuclear button is always on my desk."

Donald Trump was quick to reply by tweet:

"Will someone from his depleted and food starved regime please inform him that I too have a Nuclear Button, but it is a much bigger & more powerful one than his, and my Button works!"

If 2018 started off with the two leaders as mortal enemies threatening death and destruction to each other's country, it ended with Trump telling his supporters at a rally:

"And then [Kim Jong Un and I] fell in love, okay? No, really—he wrote me beautiful letters, and they're great letters."

How did this astonishing turnaround occur?

It happened largely, in my view, through the attractive power of *a compelling story.* As an anthropologist, I have come to appreciate what a central role stories play in human existence. We spend our lives listening to stories and telling stories. They shape how we see ourselves and others. We are creatures of story.

Both leaders began to believe in the story of two strong men meeting and defying the world's expectations to become surprise heroes of world peace. Dennis Rodman was right in his intuitive assessment of their psychology that, if brought together, they could form an unlikely friendship. Egos did not need to produce an escalation to war. They could be placed in the service of peace. Both leaders could appear as heroes to the people they cared about.

In March 2018, I was invited by Ivanka Trump, the president's daughter and close advisor, to give a talk for the senior staff at the White House on the topic of "getting to yes." In my meeting with her, I highlighted the opportunity for her father to make history and confound his critics by becoming a hero of peace. In my subsequent talk, I used North Korea as the lead example, described the victory speech exercise, and underscored the personal victory I believed existed for President Trump.

I underestimated, however, just how powerful and attractive a compelling story could be. I had imagined both leaders delivering victory speeches only *after* reaching a substantive agreement. But I was wrong.

When Trump and Kim met for their historic summit in Singapore in June 2018, they surprised the entire world. Instead of the coldness one might have expected from their previous harsh words, they seemed to take a genuine liking to each other. Trump praised Kim as "a very talented man" with a "great personality."

At the end of their two-day meeting, they agreed to four general principles as a framework for ongoing discussions. At the concluding press conference for the world's eager journalists, Trump, a master showman, did not waste time waiting for a substantive agreement. He proclaimed victory then and there:

> The World has taken a big step back from potential Nuclear catastrophe! No more rocket launches, nuclear testing or research! The hostages are back home with their families. Thank you to Chairman Kim, our day together was historic!

Landing back in the United States the next day, Trump promptly tweeted:

> Just landed—a long trip, but everybody can now feel much safer than the day I took office. There is no longer a Nuclear Threat from North Korea.

North Korean media splashed beaming images of Kim and Trump all over the front pages and on television, hailing the huge, "epoch-making" victory for Kim. The "meeting of the century," would help create "a radical switchover in the most hostile [North Korea]-US relations."

In reality, nothing tangible had changed. No nuclear bomb or bomb-making facilities had been disabled. No peace treaty had been signed. But from the perspective of the story, there had been a dramatic change. The taboo on a US president meeting the North Korean leader had been broken. Two leaders who had been threatening unthinkable destruction had instead constructed a friendly relationship.

From the intangible power of story came a tangible impact: the immediate risk of nuclear war, which had ranged as high as 50 percent, fell back to less than 1 percent, according to experts. And that made all the difference.

The power of a compelling story had prevailed, a vivid reminder of how powerful *framing*—the way a story is presented—can be.

It was a powerful lesson for me. The conflict could be understood as a play—albeit a deadly serious one—in which the players had begun as mortal enemies and ended as friends. The secret was to construct an attractive narrative in which both could appear as heroes to the people they cared about.

## DESIGN AN ICONIC PHOTO

A picture, the old adage goes, is worth a thousand words. One way I've found to bring a compelling story to life is to use Photoshop to create an "iconic" photo of the imagined meeting, agreement, or victory speech that would represent success.

Think of notable moments when seemingly impossible conflicts began to be transformed. They are often preserved for us in iconic photos—leaders smiling, shaking hands, or standing side by side in some historic setting. The images are inspiring.

When I met with Ivanka Trump, I handed her two iconic photos, one of Ronald Reagan at his historic Reykjavík meeting with Mikhail Gorbachev and another of Menachem Begin and Anwar Sadat signing the Camp David Accords together with Jimmy Carter. She asked if she could keep them. When I met with her again a month later, I noticed that they were still on her desk. It showed me just how attractive iconic photos can be.

An iconic photo is the visual tool of a *possibilist*. It helps free our minds and inspire us to imagine possibilities where there seem to be none. At the very least, it can bring a smile to people's faces.

Inspired by the magic-wand conversation with Bob Carlin, I asked my colleague Liza Hester to create a series of photoshopped images of imagined summit meetings with Trump and Kim, and also one of them together with President Moon of South Korea at Panmunjom.

Not long afterward, I traveled to South Korea and met the top South Korean nuclear negotiator. I handed him a photoshopped image of Trump, Kim, and Moon standing side by side in front of the blue guard building at Panmunjom, the iconic setting of the Korean War.

"That's a very interesting photo," he said, smiling. "Why couldn't they all meet there?"

At the end of our meeting, he asked:

"May I keep this photo?"

Six months later, I had a meeting in the State Department with the top US envoy for North Korea.

"I just came back from Seoul and saw my counterpart there," he told me with a smile. "He has your photoshop of the three leaders' meeting framed on his wall."

In early June 2019, I met with Jared Kushner, President Trump's son-in-law and senior advisor, in the White House and brought up the idea of a quick, informal summit meeting with Kim at Panmunjom in connection with an upcoming presidential trip to Japan. I gave him a one-page memo on the idea, half of which was an attractive iconic photo of the meeting.

"I'll pass it upstairs," he said, pointing his thumb up.

Two weeks later, to universal surprise, Donald Trump had a quick informal summit with Kim Jong Un at Panmunjom. South Korean president Moon joined them after their bilateral meeting. The iconic photo from eighteen months earlier became a reality.

When the unexpected summit took place, I received an email from the South Korean nuclear negotiator who had just returned from the historic meeting:

"Congrats! Your idea has come true. I have in front of me the photo of the three leaders that you gave me."

## PUT THE "GOLDEN" IN GOLDEN BRIDGE

Attracting puts the "golden" in the golden bridge.

To appreciate the power of attracting, a power available to each of us, you may find it helpful to apply it to a conflict of your own. I invite you to ask yourself:

If trust is an issue, what steps might you take to create trust—and what steps might the other side take? What would a *trust menu* look like that could begin to transform a strained relationship?

If you were to choreograph your own play, what would be the sequence? If you had a magic wand, what would you make happen?

Can you imagine a shared victory? What would an iconic photo look like?

Imagining yourself as the playwright might open up new possibilities that you had not imagined before.

This brings us to the last of the three victories to achieve on the path to possible. If we are to succeed in transforming the polarizing conflicts of today, we need to go beyond the balcony and the bridge. We need to engage the *third side*.

# THIRD VICTORY

# ENGAGE THE THIRD SIDE

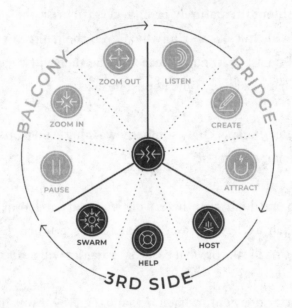

The US-Soviet War of October 1962 was the most catastrophic war in human history that didn't happen.

In October 1962, I was just nine, but I remember the frightening headlines and the feeling of deep unease and dread. President John F. Kennedy made a riveting speech to the nation on the evening of October 22:

This secret, swift, and extraordinary buildup of Communist missiles . . . in violation of Soviet assurances . . . cannot be accepted by this country.

He announced a naval blockade of the island of Cuba to stop the Soviet ships from landing their nuclear cargo and urged Soviet premier Nikita Khrushchev "to move the world back from the abyss of destruction." He declared ominously:

We will not prematurely or unnecessarily risk the costs of worldwide nuclear war in which even the fruits of victory would be ashes in our mouth—but neither will we shrink from that risk at any time it must be faced.

He ended his speech by somberly warning Americans to brace themselves for the worst:

Let no one doubt that this is a difficult and dangerous effort on which we have set out. No one can see precisely what course it will take or what costs or casualties will be incurred.

A quarter of a century later, in January 1989, I was in Moscow in the icy depths of winter to find out what had really happened and how close to Armageddon we had come. A group of Soviet and American former policy makers and experts came together to try to piece together the full story of those tense thirteen days in which the world's survival hung in the balance. What had been going on behind closed doors in Washington and Moscow as the leaders pondered life-and-death decisions for their nations and others?

Seated at the conference table around me were the surviving participants of the crisis. It was hard to believe. There they were: the main advisors to President Kennedy and Premier Khrushchev. Robert McNamara, who had been Kennedy's secretary of defense, was sitting next to McGeorge Bundy, who had been national security advisor. Khrushchev's foreign minister, Andrei Gromyko, was sitting across the table next to the former Soviet ambassador in Washington, Anatoly Dobrynin. Khrushchev's son and close advisor Sergei was there. So, too, was Sergio del Valle, the former commander of the Cuban armed forces.

If that crisis had escalated into war, there would have been no table and no people, either. All of us in the room, including my Harvard colleagues and me, would likely have been incinerated in an atomic blast or poisoned in its aftermath, joining hundreds of millions of other deaths in the United States, the Soviet Union, Europe, and around the world.

What my Harvard colleagues and I knew about the crisis was this: In October 1962, as President Kennedy was making his speech, US armed forces were preparing to launch an all-out invasion of Cuba to stop Russia from deploying its nuclear missiles. Southern Florida looked like a massive parking lot of military equipment. A tentative decision had been taken in Washington to invade if there was any interference with the US U-2 spy plane making its daily flyover to inspect progress on the installation of nuclear missiles.

Then it happened. On Saturday, October 27, at the very height of the crisis, the spy plane was shot down over Cuba by a Soviet ground-to-air missile. An invasion seemed imminent.

What my American colleagues and I learned at that meeting shocked us. The Soviets had already secretly succeeded in bringing nuclear weapons to Cuba, 162 of them. Missiles had been activated and were ready for use.

"Had a U.S. invasion been carried out," Robert McNamara burst out, with emotion in his voice, ". . . there was a 99 percent probability that nuclear war would have been initiated."

As secretary of defense, McNamara knew what he was talking about. He also knew that the only thing that had stopped the imminent invasion and a nuclear Armageddon was a last-minute deal negotiated between the president's brother Robert Kennedy and Anatoly Dobrynin. Premier Khrushchev agreed to withdraw the Soviet missiles from Cuba; in return, President Kennedy pledged not to invade Cuba and made a secret commitment to withdraw US nuclear missiles from Turkey. Dobrynin read out to us the telegram he had sent to Moscow at the time detailing the secret deal.

As we learned at the conference from Sergei Khrushchev, his father was taken by utter surprise when the plane was shot down. He had not given the order, as Washington had naturally assumed. Instead, two Soviet generals on the ground in Cuba had made the decision to fire independently *without* any instructions from Moscow. As we received more details during that meeting, we understood that this had been just one of many miscommunications and miscalculations that had almost precipitated an unthinkable worldwide catastrophe.

I emerged from those freezing cold days in Moscow haunted by how close we had come to mutual annihilation and deeply appreciative of how lucky we had been to survive the Cold War. I found it hard to fully digest the reality of what had almost happened.

Thankfully, as the frank exchange of information during the

meeting showed, the Cold War was coming to an end. We had dodged the proverbial bullet. But as an anthropologist concerned with the longer-term future of humanity, I was left wondering how we and future generations could continue to live on this planet, given our genius at devising weapons of mass destruction and our propensity to go to war. I felt a heightened sense of urgency to answer the question I had long asked myself: How can we deal with our deepest differences without destroying all that we hold dear?

In intense conflicts, it is not easy to go to the balcony or stay there. Nor is it easy to build a golden bridge. And what if leaders in crisis cannot reach agreement? Is war the only alternative—or is there another?

Where can we turn for help?

## OUR BIRTHRIGHT

I did not need to wait long for a clue. Weeks after my trip to frozen Moscow, I departed for an anthropological research visit deep inside the Kalahari Desert of southern Africa. Ever since college, I had wanted to visit the indigenous peoples of that region, one of the most ancient surviving cultures in the world.

Until recently these peoples had lived as semi-nomadic hunters and gatherers, the way humanity had lived for more than 99 percent of its history. I had studied the anthropological literature about their culture, and I was eager to learn firsthand about their ancestral ways of managing conflicts. I had the privilege of visiting two groups—one in Botswana who called themselves the Kua and another in Namibia who called themselves the Ju/'hoansi.

"It is natural for human beings to have disputes," the Kua elder Korakoradue told me as we sat around his campfire in the middle of the desert.

"When disputes happen, all of the friends and relatives of the parties are approached and asked to put in a calming word."

The Kua, like us, are perfectly capable of violence. Indeed, each man has in his possession hunting arrows coated with a deadly poison. All it takes is one man getting angry at another for the first to pick up a poison arrow and shoot him. But the poison takes three days to kill the man, so he has plenty of time to take revenge. Things can easily escalate from there.

In a small-scale society of roughly twenty-five, with five active hunters, two or three deaths can wreak havoc on the group's ability to survive. In terms of its potential impact, a poison arrow is the rough equivalent of a nuclear bomb. How, I wondered, do such groups deal with their disputes given the ever-ready access to weapons of enormous destructiveness?

I learned that whenever tempers rise and violence seems imminent, people near the disputing parties gather up the poison arrows and hide them far away in the bush. Meanwhile, others try to separate the antagonists.

That's when the talking begins. All the men and women—even the children—gather around the campfire and talk and talk . . . and talk. No one is excluded, and each person has a chance to have their say. This open-ended process, which the Kua call a *kgotla*, can take days until the dispute is literally talked out. At night, the community gathers around the campfire to chant and dance so as to appeal to the gods for help and insight into how to resolve the dispute.

They all work hard to discover what social rules have been

broken to produce such discord and what needs to be done to restore social harmony. They don't rest until they find a solution that is good for everyone—not just for the parties but for the whole group. They frame the conflict as the community's problem because any conflict threatens the community.

It is not enough to reach an agreement. They are keenly aware that if the underlying relationship is not healed, a dispute can easily erupt again. There must be a reconciliation of the parties through repair, apologies, and forgiveness.

If tempers run too high, the elders counsel the parties to go off and spend time with relatives at other waterholes. I recognized the technique; in labor-management conflicts I had worked on, we called it a "cooling-off period."

It was with the Kua that I began to appreciate the full power and influence of the third side. *Their secret to managing conflicts is the vigilant, active, and constructive involvement of the surrounding members of the community.*

The community acts for the benefit of the whole. The whole is the good of the community, the children, the future. *The third side is the side of the whole.*

The third side is not just an idealistic vision; it has genuine power. As powerful as any one person might be, that person is not more powerful than the surrounding community if the community unites. In negotiation terms, the third side serves as the BATNA, the best alternative to a negotiated agreement. The alternative to violence and war is the constructive intervention of the community.

The third side, I came to appreciate from my research into the anthropology of war and peace, is our most ancient heritage for transforming conflict. It is our *birthright*.

Many of our ancestors were, I suspect, practicing *possibilists*. It is how we survived and thrived.

My visits with the Kua and the Ju/'hoansi left me wondering how the third side could work in highly populated urban societies. My next clue began to emerge days later as I traveled next to South Africa.

## HOPE FOR US ALL

For decades, South Africa had been the leading symbol of racial injustice in the world, governed by apartheid, a harsh and cruel system of discrimination and segregation based on the color of one's skin. After decades of patient nonviolent resistance, the African National Congress (ANC) had turned to guerrilla warfare, bombings, and riots that the National Party government had met with massively violent suppression in which thousands of people had died.

"Awful things were happening in our land," explained Archbishop Desmond Tutu, describing the moment. "People were dying as if they were but flies. Very many were predicting that the most awful racial confrontation was waiting to overwhelm our land—that we would be devastated by a racial bloodbath. We did seem to be on the brink, on the verge of the most awful catastrophe."

"How long can this go on?" I asked a foreign ambassador whom I met in Capetown. He was one of the most informed and perceptive observers of the conflict.

"My best guess is we will see an end to apartheid in thirty years," he ventured.

I had arranged to meet with a fellow anthropologist and university professor, David Webster, a determined opponent of apartheid, but just a few days before our scheduled meeting, he was assassinated on his doorstep in front of his partner by a government-sponsored death squad.

The conflict appeared almost irreconcilable. Yet to universal surprise, over a period of five short years, the conflict was dramatically transformed and the formal system of apartheid came to an end.

When I made a return visit to South Africa in January 1995, I felt as if I had entered an entirely different country. I had to pinch myself to believe that it was real. Nelson Mandela, who had been in a decades-long imprisonment on my first visit, was now president of the country. F. W. de Klerk, who had been president, was now serving as second deputy president to Mandela. At a dinner in Johannesburg, I listened to both leaders speak movingly about their experiences.

Bullets had given way to bridges. The immense changes seemed almost miraculous to South Africans and to the world community, but, as I came to understand, they resulted from the exact same phenomenon I had observed among the Kua: the engagement of the community, the third side.

"You must believe," declared Archbishop Tutu, present at the dinner, "that this spectacular victory [over apartheid] would have been totally, totally impossible had it not been that we were supported so remarkably by the international community."

Tutu was right. During the prior years, the world community came together to create a critical mass of persuasive influence. The United Nations provided political and economic support to the African National Congress. Eminent statesmen from many countries came to offer counsel and mediate. Governments agreed on financial sanctions, restricting trade and investment in South Africa.

Churches mobilized the public conscience. University students around the world carried out protests, demanding that corporations and universities divest from their investments in South Africa. Sports federations voted to ostracize South African teams operating under a system of racism.

Just as influential as the work of *external* thirdsiders was the work of *internal* thirdsiders—those inside South Africa. Business leaders, feeling the financial pressure of sanctions, sought to persuade the government to negotiate. So did leaders of faith and civic movements of women and students, who mobilized to reach across ethnic lines.

Under all these conditions, de Klerk was persuaded to release Mandela from prison after twenty-seven years and initiate negotiations with the African National Congress.

Negotiations did not prove easy, however, and political violence continued. Business, labor, faith, and civic leaders then worked together with the government and the ANC to create the National Peace Accord. The Accord formed an unprecedented network of committees across the country, made up of citizens of all races and classes. The committees worked together with the police to interrupt and reduce the violence in the streets so that a genuine and inclusive democracy could emerge. The third side was fully engaged.

While fighting staunchly for his cause as the leader of the ANC, Mandela became a third-side leader. The core of apartheid was exclusion. Ironically, the wound of exclusion was also felt by the white Afrikaner people, who carried the traumas of war and domination by the British. Mandela's leadership genius was to reach out to include the Afrikaners and other white people. It was a bold third-side move.

To heal the deep wounds left by apartheid, he appealed to the traditional African spirit of *ubuntu*. *Ubuntu* means simply "I am because you are. You are because we are."

*Ubuntu* is the essence of the third side, the recognition that we all belong to a wider community. *Everyone is included; no one is excluded.*

In his inaugural address, Mandela declared:

We have triumphed in the effort to implant hope in the breasts of the millions of our people. We enter into a covenant that we shall build the society in which all South Africans, both black and white, will be able to walk tall, without any fear in their hearts, assured of their inalienable right to human dignity—a rainbow nation at peace with itself and the world.

Here in South Africa, I found a clue to the question I had found myself asking after that deeply sobering meeting in Moscow. Violence and war have traditionally served as the last—and sometimes the first—resort when two parties cannot agree. Could there be a viable alternative? The South African people and their leaders had taken our oldest human heritage for dealing with conflict—the third side—and re-created it in a large-scale society to deal with a deep-seated, intractable conflict.

A whole country had seen, created, and acted on new possibilities. Its citizens had shown how, within the container of the larger community, even the most difficult conflict can be contained and slowly transformed. They had demonstrated in the clearest way how we today might choose to interrupt the pattern of destructive fighting that exists today at home, at work, and in the world.

When we get caught up in a heated conflict, we tend to think small, reducing it to two sides: us against them. Everyone else is expected to take one side or the other. "Which side are you on?" becomes the salient question. With two-sided thinking, it is so easy to get trapped in an escalating, destructive power struggle.

But as I observed in the Kalahari and in South Africa, there is never, in any conflict, large or small, just two sides. There is never just "us versus them." Every conflict takes place within a larger social context. Whether we perceive it or not, there is always "all of us together." It is an anthropological truth that we are all connected in a seamless web of sociality, however torn that web might seem.

In seemingly impossible conflicts like those we face today, it is only natural to wonder where we can turn for help. What I learned from my experiences in Africa—and elsewhere—is that help can come, as it has for eons, from the engaged community—the third side. Here was a constructive alternative to the path of endless destruction, violence, and war.

It was a ray of hope for humanity.

## THE THIRD SIDE IS US

The third side is *people power*—people using the power of peers, adopting the perspective of the whole, and supporting a process of conflict transformation.

In the conflicts around us, each of us is a potential thirdsider—as a family member, a friend, a colleague, a neighbor, or a fellow citizen. When conflicts affect everyone, it is our responsibility to help. Transforming conflict is not just the job of specialists. It is everyone's job.

*The third side is us—each of us and all of us working together.*

Before my experiences in Africa, my image of a third party was of a mediator, a neutral outsider who could assist the parties in negotiating a mutually beneficial agreement. Mediation was what I had learned to practice. Mediators have an important role to play. But now I came to understand that there is a much broader and ultimately much more potent way to transform conflicts: *a community that can mediate its own disputes.*

An analogy for the third side is our body's immune system. There are trillions of viruses in our bodies, more apparently than there are stars in the universe. The vast majority of them are benign, but what keeps the threatening viruses in check is our immune system. It is our natural resilience. The third side can be understood as a *social immune system* that helps keep the virus of violence and destruction in check.

We don't have to be *neutral* to be a thirdsider. Often we are not. Among the Kua and the Semai, thirdsiders are close relatives who urge their family members to calm down and talk it out. Even the parties themselves can sometimes act as thirdsiders if they take the perspective of the whole. Mandela became a third-side leader even as he remained a strong defender of his own side. He advocated for the whole even as he led one particular party.

The third side is motivated by more than altruism. Whether we are family, friends, or neighbors, we are impacted by conflicts around us. We are acting out of collective self-interest because this is our community.

When Roger Fisher, Bruce Patton, and I worked on *Getting to Yes*, we focused on mutual gain—a classic "win-win"—an outcome good for both sides. What I learned from my experiences in Africa and elsewhere is that if we are to fully mobilize the third side, we need to take a big step beyond our previous thinking about win-win. From win-win, we need to move to *win-win-win*. We need to think in terms of a *third win*—a win for the larger community, for the future, for our children. This third win catalyzes and sustains the efforts of the third side over the long term.

To be an effective thirdsider is not easy. If we are reactive and intrusive, we risk making things worse. As thirdsiders, we can help others go to the balcony only if we have gone to the balcony ourselves. We can help the parties build a golden bridge only if we ourselves have built bridges of trust with the parties. That's why in the logical sequence of the path to possible, the third side is the final victory, building on the work of both the balcony and the bridge.

The third side is an invisible resource that we have barely begun to tap, perhaps the greatest power we have for transforming conflict. If we activate it fully, it has the potential to be the much-needed antidote to today's troubling polarization, extremism, and demonization of the other.

## UNLOCK THE POTENTIAL AROUND

If going to the balcony unlocks the potential *within* us and building a golden bridge unlocks the potential *between* us, engaging the third side unlocks the potential *around* us.

To activate the third side, we deploy three natural powers. Each is an innate human capacity, something we may already know how to do but simply need to develop and hone.

The first is the power to *host*—to welcome and connect the parties. When the Kua circle around the campfire in their *kgotla*, they are effectively hosting the conflict and the parties. No one is left out of the circle.

The second is the power to *help*—to help the parties go to the balcony and build a golden bridge when it is not at all easy to do. Among the Kua, the friends, relatives, and elders help the parties by facilitating resolution and reconciliation.

The third is the power to *swarm*—to apply a critical mass of ideas and influence. As a flock of birds swarms an intruder attacking a nest, the third side can swarm a difficult conflict. In South Africa, external thirdsiders combined with internal thirdsiders to create a strong force of influence and persuasion.

The three powers have a logical sequence. We begin by *hosting*, which creates a propitious psychological atmosphere. We intensify our engagement with *helping*, which focuses on addressing the actual issues. The process culminates in *swarming*, which brings the full influence and leverage of the community to bear. Together, all three powers unlock the full potential *around* us.

The third side is a sleeping giant. It is a latent "superpower" that exists within each and all of us. Our challenge today is to find ways to wake it up.

## CHAPTER 9

# HOST

## From Exclusion to Inclusion

*He drew a circle that shut me out—*
*Heretic, rebel, a thing to flout.*
*But Love and I had the wit to win:*
*We drew a circle that took him in!*
—Edwin Markham

Are you William Ury? My name is María Elena Martínez. I've been on a bus all night for twelve hours, and I have been waiting here since six o'clock this morning just to meet you," said the stranger who came up to me as I entered the doors of the Teatro Ateneo de Caracas in the capital of Venezuela in February 2003.

Five heavily armed national guardsmen and a US Embassy official were escorting me into the theater. Immediately, the embassy official tried to shoo away the woman, explaining that we were busy, but I insisted on hearing her out.

"I've just come from a gathering of indigenous leaders deep in the rainforest," María Elena told me. "Yesterday, they held an all-day ceremony for the peace of the country. The leaders recited many prayers to bless this necklace and sent me here to present it to you so that it may bless this conference. May I put it on you?"

She held out her hands, offering me the necklace. It was strikingly beautiful, made of red and white seeds from the jungle with a large brown hard nut in the center.

I paused for a moment and looked into her eyes.

*"Por favor,"* I said. *"Gracias."*

I bowed my head as she placed the necklace around my neck.

As soon as we entered a private room in the theater, the embassy official said to me:

"I suggest you take off that necklace. It looks ridiculous on you."

I chuckled. "I bet it does look a little strange with my suit and tie," I replied. "But all the same, the indigenous leaders and that woman went to a lot of trouble to bring it to me for this meeting. I don't want to let them down."

I neglected to say that I was an anthropologist and it didn't seem so strange to me. The embassy official gave me a hard look and turned away.

I was in Venezuela at the invitation of the Carter Center and the United Nations to provide ideas on how to deal with a conflict that was tearing the country apart. In between meetings with government officials and opposition leaders, I was invited by my friend and colleague from the Carter Center, Francisco Diez, to co-facilitate a conference for citizens. The theme was *El Tercer Lado*, the third side, the title of a new book of mine just translated into Spanish.

"How many people are you expecting?" I asked him.

"I don't know since it's open to the public. But this is an all-day meeting on a weekday. Maybe a hundred and fifty people will show up, maybe two hundred if we're lucky. Frankly, things here are so polarized that I'm not sure how much interest there is in a public dialogue. But just in case, we rented a theater that holds five hundred seats. Don't worry, though. If the numbers are small, we can all sit up front."

But when Francisco and I got to the theater, to our surprise, we found the street teeming with more than a thousand people clamoring to get into the theater and dozens of armed soldiers holding them back. Since *chavistas*—supporters of President Hugo Chávez—and anti-*chavistas* had never met in such numbers except to protest and fight, the National Guard had been called out for fear of violence. It didn't seem to bode well for the peaceful public workshop Francisco had intended.

"What do we do now?" I asked Francisco in the car as we eyed the wild scene around the theater. "Is there a larger venue that can fit all these people? Or should we postpone it until we can find one?"

"At this point, unfortunately, we have no other options. I think we should just proceed," he replied. "We can do another one later. Everything has been planned. Secretary General Gaviria is about to arrive."

"Okay," I agreed. I felt a little unsure, never having facilitated a large meeting of angry, polarized citizens like this before. "Let's do our best."

As I stepped out of the car into the chaos, I recalled the gathering of the Kua around the campfire in the Kalahari, what they called a *kgotla*. That was the third side in action, *hosting* a live conflict: taking care of the parties, listening to them, and making sure everyone felt included. I was wondering if somehow, in a very different context, we could create a modern-day version of hosting a conflict. What would it look like?

Going into the theater foyer was when I met María Elena Martínez. I felt strangely fortified by her unexpected gift of the necklace with the prayers of the first peoples of the country. The necklace reminded me of the people all over Venezuela whose lives were deeply impacted by the dangerous political conflict. It made me aware of why I was there.

## LET THE THIRD SIDE BE HEARD

When I entered, every seat in the theater was filled, with people standing in the aisles or sitting on the stairs in the upstairs sections. Everyone seemed to be speaking at once. Many voices sounded agitated and fearful.

The conference began, as planned, with brief introductory remarks by César Gaviria, the secretary general of the Organization of American States. As he spoke, I tried to collect my wits, remembering to breathe. Then Francisco introduced me. I went onto the stage and stood behind the podium, looking out at all the people in the theater. Many faces seemed drawn and anxious.

"Thank you for having the courage to come here today for a conversation," I began. "This is the hardest work we human beings can do—to face our fears and listen to others with whom we may disagree.

"I know a lot of people wanted to participate in this conference, many more than the organizers expected. I am truly sorry that many people who wanted to come today were not able to because the theater is too small. We will try to find a way to include them very soon.

"You may be here today as individual citizens, but you carry the fears and hopes of many others around the country. One of you took an all-night bus for twelve hours just to be here. She came directly from a meeting of indigenous leaders in the forest. They performed a ceremony yesterday for the peace of Venezuela and asked her to bring a necklace that holds their prayers to bless the conversation we will hold today. She was instructed to place it around my neck so that it can be here with all of us. María Elena, will you please stand so we can thank you and the indigenous leaders?"

As María Elena stood up, people clapped.

I continued, "I have to tell you up front that I am still learning about Venezuela and your conflict here. There is much I do not know. But I have worked in many other conflicts around the world, many civil wars. And I believe that you have an enormous opportunity here in Venezuela—to prevent a civil war *before* it begins. I can tell you from my own experience that it is so much better and easier to *prevent* a war. Once blood starts to flow, it is extremely difficult to stop it.

"In almost every one of the conflicts I have worked in, there are common early-warning signs before civil war. People start buying weapons. Rumors spread of impending violence. People stigmatize the other side not just as political opponents but as evil. They begin to perceive the danger as existential, threatening everything they hold dear. That's when the violence begins.

"So let me ask you a few questions: How many of you in recent months have bought weapons or know people who have?"

Almost every hand in the theater went up.

"How many of you have heard rumors that your neighborhood will be attacked?"

Again, the hands went up.

"How many of you have heard words calling the other side evil, devils?"

Once again, most hands were raised.

"In your conflict, like in others, it seems like everyone has to choose one side or the other. People who don't take a side are criticized and attacked. I have heard there is even a name for those people here in Venezuela. It is *ni-ni* [Spanish for "neither-nor"], and people who are *ni-ni* are shamed by people around them. Is that right?"

People nodded their heads.

"How many of you have been called that?"

Some hands went up.

"What can stop a civil war? I can tell you from my experience elsewhere that the key is the whole community coming together to stop violence. Beyond the two sides, there is a *third side*. It is the side of all Venezuela—the side of your children and their future. And your future. The third side is the engaged community that opposes violence and stands for dialogue and finding ways to live together peacefully, even with deep political differences.

"Any of you can be a thirdsider. You can be a thirdsider if you are a *chavista* or if you are an anti-*chavista*. Or if you are neither. To take the third side simply means to take the side of the whole community.

"Think for a moment about how this conflict has hurt you and those you love. Maybe someone you know has been beaten up or even killed. Maybe your family members or friends no longer speak to each other. Maybe you or someone around you has lost their job. Maybe you or your child have had a nightmare about violence.

"In the places I have known where the community comes together to unite against violence, it is the third side saying *no*. If you were to say no to violence here in Venezuela, what word would you pick?"

*"Basta!"* someone yelled from one of the distant rows. "Enough!"

"I would love to hear for one moment the voice of the Venezuelan people saying no to violence. Until now, this voice from the third side has been silenced. As you think about how this conflict has hurt you and those around you, I ask you to call out *'Basta!'* together, with all the emotion you feel. Will you do this for me?"

They nodded their heads.

"Ready? On the count of three. *Uno . . . dos . . . tres.*"

*"BASTA!"* they shouted.

It was powerful, but I could tell that people were still holding back.

"Do me a favor, and just repeat it one more time. *Uno . . . dos . . . tres.*"

*"BASTA!!"* This time it was louder.

"One last time. See if you can give it all your strength."

*"BASTA!!!"* The sound was deafening as the theater shook to its rafters.

That was the voice of the third side I had been wanting to hear.

At that moment, the emotional atmosphere in the room seemed to change. The negatively charged emotions of fear and anger began to give way to a positively charged intention to put an end to the destructiveness of the conflict. It seemed that everyone in that theater suddenly remembered what it meant to be Venezuelan, part of a larger family. In that moment, the latent power of the third side was activated to interrupt the escalation toward violence.

In the theater after lunch, the participants broke up into small groups, *chavistas* together with anti-*chavistas*, and then gathered in larger groups to discuss how they could work together to prevent violence and preserve the peace of the country. The theater positively hummed with excitement and creativity.

## MEET EXCLUSION WITH INCLUSION

My experience in the theater brought to mind the short poem by Edwin Markham that I quoted at the beginning of this chapter. I first heard this poem from my friend Landrum Bolling, a noted peacemaker then in his nineties. Landrum told me he had heard it when he was a boy from the lips of the poet himself at a high school in Tennessee in the 1920s.

Landrum described how Markham had stood up on the stage, with his big shock of white hair, and begun reciting "He drew a circle that shut me out—/Heretic, rebel, a thing to flout" while dramatically drawing a circle in the air with his finger. Then, equally dramatically, the poet, stretching out his arm fully, drew a much larger circle: "But Love and I had the wit to win:/ We drew a circle that took him in!"

In that one stanza, the poet summed up a key obstacle to transforming conflict and offered up an ingenious strategy—a surprising action that met exclusion with inclusion. It was emotional jujitsu. That little poem and its wisdom have stuck with me ever since.

*At the core of almost every deep-seated conflict I have ever worked on is the wound of exclusion.* Palestinians and Israelis, Protestants and Catholics from Northern Ireland, Serbs and Croats, and coal miners in Kentucky—I have listened at length to their stories of feeling discriminated against and humiliated, stories that often go back many generations or even centuries. These feelings and traumas fuel conflict and often trigger acts of violence and war.

In business, I have seen relationships break down and conflicts break out because of perceived slights such as the exclusion of a colleague from an important meeting. And family feuds, I find, are frequently fed by one family member's feelings of being treated as less than another.

*The only remedy I know for the wound of exclusion is inclusion.* It is to meet the universal need to belong. That is what the Kua do when disputes arise. They begin by forming a circle around the campfire, a circle in which everyone belongs and everyone can be heard. To include those who feel excluded is an ancient and time-tested way of dealing with differences.

The shift from exclusion to inclusion is what I felt happen in the theater that day in Caracas, reminding me how, at any moment, we human beings have the capacity to change our way of approaching conflict from excluding the other to including them.

The inclusive conversation did not stop there in the theater. The participants agreed to meet the next day. They went on to organize public dialogues across the country. They put on street theater and school programs. They went on radio shows. The dialogue in the theater that day was turned into a nationwide television broadcast. It was titled *El Tercer Lado—The Third Side.*

The participants founded a national civil movement whose purpose was to remind Venezuelans that what united them was greater than what divided them. The organizers called the movement *Aquí Cabemos Todos,* meaning "Here there is room for everyone." Here everyone belongs. That is the quintessential message of the third side.

Before that moment, there had been just two salient sides in the Venezuelan political conflict. There had been no room for nuance or complexity—or for conversation. Now there was a place for the third side to stand, a community that included people of all opinions. In that moment of intense exclusion between the two polarized sides in Venezuela, a home for the third side was born.

*Aquí Cabemos Todos* was just one community-building initiative in a larger society torn apart by destructive conflict. While the political strife, sadly, continues to this day, Venezuelans were able to avert a widely feared civil war. To transform an entire society's pattern of toxic conflict, the third side needs to become even stronger. If the third side is like a social immune system, then, just as we strengthen our individual immune systems to preserve our health, so we need to strengthen our social immune system to preserve our social health.

As I recount the story of the dialogue in the Venezuelan theater that day twenty years ago, I can't help but think about my own country today. Buying weapons? Fears of impending violence? Stigmatization of vast numbers of fellow citizens? If Americans are able to prevent the civil war that many fear may happen in the years to come, it will be because we are able to strengthen our social immune system and rally to the third side, no matter what political side we are on. It will be because we will recognize that here, in the end, everyone belongs.

## TO HOST IS HUMAN

We probably all know how to host. When we host, we welcome our guests and ask them if they are hungry or thirsty. We attend to their needs. We listen to them and make them feel at home. We introduce them to others. We can all recall a moment when we hosted someone as a guest—or a moment when we were hosted by someone as their guest. To host is perhaps the most basic act of our humanity. Taking care of another in need, perhaps more than any other activity, is what makes us human.

To host means to *take responsibility*. Responsibility means response-ability—the ability to respond constructively to a conflict. Hosting means to give a conflict our *attention* with the *intention* to transform it. To host is to *take care* of the parties. Hosting is exactly what is needed when arguments arise around us.

Hosting is contagious. The day before the conference in Caracas, the conflict was hosted by indigenous leaders in the rainforest holding a peace ceremony. The conference was hosted by outside thirdsiders: the Organization of American States, the Carter Center, and the United Nations Development Programme. By the afternoon, the citizens themselves assumed responsibility as internal thirdsiders, creating a movement, *Aquí Cabemos Todos*, to host the conflict nationwide.

Hosting draws a larger circle of community around the parties.

By creating that circle, real or metaphorical, the act of hosting makes the third side manifest. Before, there may have seemed to be just two sides, but now, thanks to the power of hosting, it becomes clear that there are three.

Hosting includes. It welcomes everyone and treats all as worthy, with a voice that deserves to be heard. It recognizes their inherent dignity. It creates a safe container within which everyone belongs, no matter who they are or what political opinion they hold.

*To host means to welcome the parties, witness their stories, and weave a web of community around them.*

## WELCOME

Hosting begins by *welcoming* the parties—and their conflict. Rather than avoid them or join them, we turn toward them with a spirit of curiosity. We bring them into our circle of concern. We offer them basic human respect. We let them know they belong.

Have you ever had the experience of being a stranger in a strange land? Have you been welcomed by someone you hardly knew and offered food and drink? Have you experienced an act of hospitality and kindness from a stranger?

I have worked for many years on an out-of-the-box project to give birth to a long-distance walking path across the Middle East that retraces the legendary journey of Abraham and his family four thousand years ago and celebrates his spirit of hospitality toward strangers.

It started with a group of friends having dinner on a summer night under the stars. Two of them had just returned from the Middle East, and we found ourselves discussing the wall of fear and separation dividing the world. It was August 2003, less than two years after the tragic attacks of 9/11, which had led in turn to the devastating wars in Afghanistan and Iraq. The global "war on terror" launched by the United States was being widely perceived in the Islamic world as a war on Islam.

My friends and I were being hosted that evening, and in turn, in a small sense, with our attention and concern, we were beginning to "host" those divisive conflicts.

"We could be facing a new world conflict, a bit like the Cold War, with the world divided into two giant camps with religion in the mix," remarked my friend Rabia Roberts.

"With so much fear and separation, what could possibly bring people together?" asked my friend Elias Amidon.

Rabia and Elias had just returned from leading a pilgrimage of Westerners to Syria—as a small step to bridge the chasm between people in the West and people in the Middle East.

It got me thinking. Over the years I had worked on the conflicts in the Middle East, focusing on political negotiations, but I found myself wondering if there was some other more down-to-earth way we could approach those conflicts. As a passionate traveler and walker, I said:

"It's a wild idea, but what about doing what you just did on a larger scale?"

"What do you mean?" my friends asked.

"I don't know. Has anyone ever retraced the footsteps of Abraham? He's the legendary ancestor of all the peoples of the Middle East—and much of the world besides."

Everyone looked at me quizzically for a moment.

"When the Iraq War broke out, I remembered that's the land

where Abraham is believed to have been born. I know it sounds far-fetched, but as an anthropologist, I know there can be something powerful in retelling an ancient mythic story. It stirs something in us all. Maybe a walking trail in his legendary footsteps might help remind us all that no matter what divides us, there is something greater that we share: a common story, a common humanity, a common future. And there is something about walking. Who fights while they walk?"

I didn't know it at the time, but that little wild idea over dinner was the start of two decades of hard work—and a lot of walks—to bring the dream to fruition in the midst of intense political conflict and wars.

Skeptics said it couldn't be done. But my colleagues and I persevered. We studied other long-distance paths around the world, notably the world-famous Camino de Santiago, which ends in Spain.

In October 2006, we set out on an inaugural journey, traveling with twenty-three people from around the world, including an imam, a priest, a rabbi, and a minister, to retrace the remembered footsteps of Abraham, or Ibrahim, as he is known in much of the region. Our aim was to show that it could be done and to consult communities along the way for their views on a long-distance cultural route. For almost two weeks, we journeyed by bus, and occasionally on foot, starting from Harran in southern Turkey, where Abraham is believed to have set forth, and ending in Hebron, or Al-Khalil, just south of Jerusalem, where he is believed to be buried.

Responding to the interest of local communities, my colleagues and I launched the Abraham Path Initiative in 2007. Working in partnership with local organizations, the initiative has supported the mapping out of many hundreds of miles of path in a half-dozen countries across the Middle East. The initiative received support from the United Nations as well as from the World Bank, which was interested to learn how paths could create jobs and livelihoods for people living in fragile political environments. Within a few short years, the Abraham Path was listed in first place by *National Geographic* among the ten best new walking trails in the world.

Thousands of people, young and old, local and foreign, from many different cultures and nationalities, have walked the different national trails that have sprung up along the ancient cultural route. Many stay in people's homes along the way. Walking paths could well outlast any of the current conflicts in the region that grab the headlines today. And they might even contribute to their transformation.

The aim of the path is to host differences in an unusual way by inviting people to walk in the ancient footsteps of Abraham in order to get to know other peoples, cultures, and faiths. Overtly, there is no conflict resolution, but indirectly, old stereotypes are challenged and mutual understanding grows. As my friend and fellow walker David Baum likes to say, the secret is to *have the conversation without having the conversation.*

Abraham is famous for many things but perhaps most of all for his hospitality. The ancient stories recount how he left the home of his ancestors and became a stranger in a strange land. He received hospitality, and he gave hospitality. It is said that he kept his tent open on all sides to be able to receive strangers and attend to them with food and care. He is regarded as the quintessential *host.*

That quality of hosting is what I—and many others—have

experienced over the years when walking along the different paths in the region. All we had heard and read conditioned us to expect *hostility*. Instead, we have received the most astonishing *hospitality*.

A shepherd boy runs after my fellow walkers and me to offer us fruit from his tree. He has nothing but wants to give. A Bedouin woman and her daughter call out insistently for a group of ten of us straggling hikers to come join her in her goat-hair tent for a cup of coffee. In a village, various families reach out to offer us hospitality. Along the path, we often hear the traditional greeting in Arabic to visitors, *"Ahlan wah sahlan"*: "Be at ease. You are among family."

Walking the Abraham Path, I learned a big lesson: The impulse to connect, to give, and to welcome others is deeply human. It is the hidden power of community that we can tap when it comes to dealing with differences. The simple act of hosting and being hosted opens up new possibilities for transforming human relationships.

Hosting doesn't have to be a big project. Any of us can host any-time and anywhere, as I learned on the Abraham Path. It could be as simple as inviting a coworker who is having a conflict to have a cup of coffee—and to listen to their story.

## WITNESS

Once we have welcomed the parties and helped them relax, the next step is to *witness*. It is to listen deeply to our guests and bear witness to the loss and pain that accompany any difficult conflict.

I am reminded of an old legend about King Arthur. A young knight from the Round Table sets out on a quest to find the Holy Grail, the legendary symbol of that which is most precious. After years of searching in vain, the knight finally comes across a mysterious castle that suddenly appears in the mist. The knight musters up his courage and enters the castle, where he finds a great dining hall with an old, wizened king sitting at a long table with all his courtiers. The king looks deeply troubled. There on the table in front of the king is the Holy Grail, a beautiful silver cup. The knight can hardly believe his eyes. But there is a magical question that the knight must ask to persuade the king to give him the Grail. What is that question?

That all-powerful question, the ancient legend suggests, is a simple one. The young knight asks the old king, "What ails thee?" As the knight listens to the king's woes and uncovers his deepest needs, a human connection of friendship grows between the two. And in an act of unexpected generosity, the king gives the Grail to the young knight.

The conflicts that I have worked on all my life and that trouble us most today are often deeply rooted in trauma, both individual and collective—enormous suffering that is so overwhelming that people's nervous systems can only freeze in order to numb the painful feelings. The trauma becomes a deep well of pain that unceasingly feeds fear and anger and drives much of the conflict, often without the person even being aware of it. Perhaps the only way to release that pain is through compassionate attention—of the kind that the young knight gave to the old king.

True witnessing is an exercise in compassion. Compassion goes one step farther than empathy. In addition to understanding what the other may be feeling, compassion means deep well-wishing and a desire to help.

When the parties get a chance to be truly heard, they can begin to let go of the past and are better able to focus on the present and the future. I had a vivid glimpse of the potential of this kind of witnessing during the Colombian peace talks.

Negotiations between the government and the guerrillas had been dragging on in Havana when President Santos made a radical proposal. Rather than wait for an agreement to be reached, he proposed to invite the victims of the conflict to give public testimony *during* the negotiations. The victims would travel to Havana, where the negotiators would listen to their stories.

I remember the skepticism and resistance that arose to the president's proposal.

"It will only further delay the talks," the critics argued.

"It will only stir up the past and all the hatred and resentment."

"The victims will call for retribution and that will only make it harder to reach agreement."

But in fact, the opposite happened.

Five delegations of victims were carefully chosen by the United Nations and universities to represent those who had suffered at the hands of all the parties to the conflict. They came to Havana and, with extensive media coverage, offered their vivid and painful testimony to the negotiators.

After their personal stories were collectively witnessed by the negotiators, and by the Colombian people, the victims surprised the critics. Most of them urged the negotiators to work harder, show more flexibility, and come to terms on an unprecedented peace pact.

I heard from several of the negotiators who told me how deeply moved they had been by the victims' stories. Instead of slowing down the talks, they felt, the hearings had re-energized them to work vigorously through their differences.

President Santos himself was moved. Hearing personal stories helped him continue the negotiation despite often feeling intense pressure to call off the effort. He told me one story that had touched him and gave him the strength to continue. It was the story of a woman, Pastora Mira, who had lost her father, her mother, and two brothers. Her son had been tortured and killed.

About ten days after she buried her son, a wounded man came to her house and asked her for help. She put him into her son's bed and nurtured him back to health. When he was leaving, he saw a photograph of the woman and her son. Suddenly he fell to his knees and started crying.

"Please don't tell me that this is your son."

"Yes, it is. Why do you ask?"

"Because I was the one who tortured and killed your son," he cried as he wept and kept repeating, "I'm sorry. I'm so sorry."

The mother looked at her son's killer and lifted him to his feet. To his utter surprise, she embraced him, saying:

"Gracias!"

"Why on earth are you thanking me?" the man exclaimed.

"Because by recognizing what you did and asking for my forgiveness, you have liberated me from hatred for the rest of my life."

Santos was so moved by Pastora's story that he invited her to go with him to Oslo when he was awarded the Nobel Peace Prize.

"This Nobel Prize is not for me," he told me, "but for the victims of this conflict, like this remarkable woman, who gave me the courage and the energy to continue in the peace process."

Never to my knowledge had the victims of any conflict been formally included in the negotiation process as they were in Havana. It was a historic first, an innovation that I hope will inspire other peace negotiations in the future as we humans learn how to deal more effectively with our toughest conflicts.

What I took from my experience in Colombia was this lesson:

It's not just the way we *talk* to each other that is important. It's the way we listen and *witness* each other. If we can witness the other's pain with empathy and compassion, we can change the quality of the talking. Feelings of exclusion can give way to feelings of inclusion. Separation can give way to connection. New possibilities can emerge to deal with even the toughest conflicts.

That is the power each of us possesses to witness the pain of others around us.

## WEAVE

Ultimately, hosting a conflict means to *weave* a web of community that connects the parties. To weave is to bring the conflicting parties together, helping them appreciate that they are indeed part of a larger community, however torn that community might be. Weaving means reminding the parties that there are not just two sides in any conflict but a larger third side, a shared social context with common interests in the future. Weaving changes the frame from "us against them" to "all of us together." Weaving is how we strengthen our social immune system.

Few conflicts are more resistant to this kind of weaving than partisan politics. Twenty years ago, in the wake of the impeachment of President Clinton, I was invited to facilitate a conversation among a small group of members of the US Congress, Democrats and Republicans, who found themselves bitterly polarized and not speaking to each other.

For two years, there had been a plethora of personal attacks and insults on the floor of the US Congress. The leaders of the House of Representatives organized a weekend retreat in Hershey, Pennsylvania. Some two hundred members and their families participated.

After dinner the first night, the members broke up into small groups of eight, four Republicans and four Democrats, joined by their partners. In my group, everyone seemed a little tired after a day of work and travel. I felt tension and discomfort in the air.

As the "host," I arranged all the chairs in a circle. Rather than sit at a long table with two sides facing each other like opposing armies on a battlefield, I like using a circle because subtly it implies community, evoking the eons in which our ancestors gathered around the campfire. There is a head of a table, but there is no head of a circle; all are equal.

"I would like to ask you to share a little of your personal experience of these last two years. What has been the price of this conflict for you?"

"It was a witch hunt!" grumbled one Democrat.

"Your leader lied under oath!" snapped a Republican.

"My children hardly ever saw their father for dinner," said one spouse. "He always came home late because the proceedings kept him away—often on weekends, too!"

Feelings were still raw.

Then, out of the blue, one of the members showed up late.

"I'm sorry," she said. "My babysitter didn't show up. Do you mind?"

And she laid her six-month-old baby on a blanket on the floor in the middle of the circle.

The baby lay there, wriggling her arms and legs and making gurgling sounds.

All attention went to the baby for a moment.

The tone of the conversation suddenly softened.

"This was not the same Congress I joined," said one Republican member. "We used to speak with each other. Now we hardly ever do. I had more time talking with a Democrat on the train ride up here than I did in the last two years."

Heads nodded.

"We've got to do better," said another member. "We can't do this to our families."

"Our country deserves better."

Everyone looked at the baby, who had fallen asleep.

I suddenly realized that the baby, lying there in the middle of our circle, was the third side, the symbol of the whole, the newest citizen standing for the future of the country.

The baby was a silent witness who, without a word, had reframed the conversation, reminding people of the bigger picture. For a moment, it was no longer "us against them." It was "all of us together."

I was reminded of an anthropological study I had read as a student of two adult male chimps who were fighting with each other and chasing each other around. One of the males approached a mother chimp with an infant and gently borrowed the infant to hold it momentarily in his arms. As they gazed at the infant, both male chimps immediately calmed down, and the fight came to an end.

I am not suggesting that we need to find a baby whenever a fight is going on. The broader question to ask yourself is: What resources do you have as a thirdsider to help the parties reframe the conversation—like that baby did?

In this case, for instance, I seized the opportunity to ask a follow-up question that I sensed could stimulate more connection among the rival leaders.

"Tell me a story of when you were young," I asked. "What inspired you to get involved in public service in the first place?"

The participants began to share their personal stories. One person's vulnerability stimulated another.

"I cheated on a high school exam," said one member. "The principal called me into his office and told me I could choose to make this the worst thing that ever happened to me or the best thing by learning a life lesson."

"I got pregnant as a teenager," another told the group. "That motivated me to get my life together, and it gave me empathy for people less fortunate than me."

Hearts opened. Distrust began to subside. The participants became more aware of all they shared, not just what divided them.

We were beginning to weave a web of community around the conflict. It was just a beginning, of course, but it revealed the possibilities for creating a broader and deeper context in which toxic polarization can be diminished. It is a lesson we need to remember now more than ever.

## HOST A CONFLICT NEAR YOU

As I was about to write this chapter, I was cohosting a large family reunion with my cousin Claire. Family reunions can be fraught with tensions and unspoken conflicts, and this one was no exception.

One afternoon, a dozen cousins, ranging in age from their forties to their seventies, were sitting around in a circle outside the old family summer home on the shore of Lake Michigan. The home had been in the family for nearly a hundred years. My mother and her six siblings had spent their summers there. I had many warm childhood memories of this beautiful place all throughout my life. So did my cousins.

Everyone was in good spirits, relaxed, well nourished, and enjoying the natural beauty. Some of the younger-generation cousins were curious, asking the older cousins about family history, events that had taken place almost seventy years before.

"What happened to the family business after the war?"

"Why was the eldest son asked to leave the business?"

Each of us had heard different stories from our parents.

A lot of it had to do with a dispute about the family business founded by my grandfather. My uncle had come back from World War II and taken over the business from his father, who had withdrawn from active participation. Ten years in, the previously thriving business was suddenly badly in debt and in grave danger of bankruptcy. There had been serious conflict in the family and even the threat of a lawsuit.

My uncle had been asked to leave the business. He had left Chicago with his family. It had created a rift that was not discussed for more than forty years and was never fully healed.

"What was the real story?" the younger cousins asked.

"Was it because of running up gambling debts—and borrowing money from the business to pay?"

We tried to go deeper and understand each person in the story.

My cousin Lynne, my uncle's daughter, spoke up.

"Did you know that, at the age of twenty, my father landed at Normandy and then fought on throughout Europe all the while watching his buddies being slaughtered around him? Did you know he was part of the army unit that liberated the concentration camp at Dachau? Imagine what he saw. He could never talk about it."

"Maybe he suffered from PTSD—post-traumatic stress syndrome," one cousin suggested.

Our understanding deepened as we collectively witnessed the painful story and began to understand the depths of trauma.

"So many years have gone by and most of the older generation is no longer with us, but let me at least offer an intergenerational apology," said my cousin Claire.

"I will gratefully accept that and offer one back," said my cousin Lynne.

Old unspoken family feelings of exclusion began to give way to feelings of inclusion and deeper community.

None of that healing had been intended. It had just naturally arisen out of an informal, seemingly casual conversation as we were hosted at the family reunion.

What worked here to help address these deeply emotionally charged issues was the power of hosting. It created a propitious psychological atmosphere. The community of cousins served as a safe container within which it felt safe to discuss delicate, emotionally fraught issues.

It was the third side—the surrounding community—naturally at work. It made me think back to the Kua, sitting in a circle around their campfire, discussing a conflict that had arisen between people in their group.

Hosting is a first step any of us can take. We all know how to host. At its most basic, it simply means to pay attention to the parties and their situation, extending our circle of concern. It means to turn feelings of exclusion into feelings of inclusion. And it means to change our attitude from "this is not my concern" to "this is my community."

It makes me wonder:

What would a world look like where we reinvented the inclusive circles around the campfire that our ancestors used to host the issues that naturally arise in any human society? What would be the modern-day equivalent of those campfires?

What if "host a conflict near you" became the norm?

That is the kind of world I dream of for our children and grandchildren.

I believe it is within our reach.

## CHAPTER 10

# HELP

## From "I Can't" to "I Can"

*There is always a large horizon. . . . There is*
*much to be done. . . . It is up to you to contribute*
*some small part to a program of human*
*betterment for all time.*
—Frances Perkins

The president asked me to call you. The talks are at a standstill,
and our time is running out."

My friend Sergio Jaramillo, the Colombian peace commissioner, sounded worried on the phone.

"Can you come to Bogotá to help us sort this out?"

I wasn't sure if I could help since I wasn't knowledgeable about the issue in contention—and yet I still felt the urge to respond.

"How can I *help*?" I asked.

It was April 2015. The peace talks to end the civil war in Colombia had been going on in Havana, Cuba, for three years. While progress had been made, there were still a couple of big issues, of which the most delicate was the question of transitional justice and accountability. There were more than 8 million victims of the war. Who was going to be held accountable for the multitude of war crimes so that the country could heal and move forward?

"We have a real problem *inside* our delegation," explained Sergio over the phone. "We've tried for a month to explain to the general in every way why the language about institutional responsibility for war crimes is absolutely necessary. It's the international legal norm now. But he absolutely refuses to accept it. After a month of arguing, he left Havana and flew back to Bogotá. It's all over the news in Colombia, and it threatens the entire peace process. How is the public going to support a peace agreement that is not supported by the military?

"We need your *help* to reach an internal agreement on language we can propose to the other side."

I packed my bags and left early the next morning.

After I arrived in Bogotá late at night, I went straight to Sergio's home. I found him in a state of agitation—understandably, because all his hard work over many years was now in peril. With emotion in his voice, he burst out:

"If the president ends up siding with the general, it's clear that I will have to resign."

The next morning, I had a breakfast meeting with the general, a highly respected and popular former chief of the Colombian armed forces. In my previous conversations with him, I had found him to be upright and forthright. I approached him with a tone of curiosity:

"*Mi general*, I think I understand your concern, but I would really like to hear it directly from you so I can understand it better."

"It's quite simple," he replied.

"The language my colleagues propose specifies the collective responsibility of 'institutional actors.' We all know that is just a code name for the army. We in the military have talked to our colleagues in El Salvador and Guatemala about what happened to them after their civil wars. The politicians eventually got off without repercussions, and the guerrillas got off free, while the military were used as scapegoats."

He paused.

"We will be tied up in endless lawsuits. Some of us will end up in jail. It's grossly unfair. And it dishonors all those who have fought bravely for their country. I will resign rather than accept this language."

"I understand."

I then met with the chief negotiator, a constitutional lawyer and former vice president. I had known him for some years and had always found him open and reasonable, sensible and intelligent.

"I would love to hear directly from you how you see the situation and why this language about collective responsibility is so important," I said.

He responded without hesitation:

"Sadly, there were war crimes committed by all sides—the guerrillas, the military, and the paramilitary forces. The individual combatants who committed them did not act alone but on behalf of their institutions. We cannot stand in front of the whole world and say that our institutions are not in any way collectively responsible for all the tragic events that have happened in this country. Otherwise, no one will trust our judicial system in Colombia to deal with the question of justice. We absolutely must include the language around collective responsibility."

The different interests were now much clearer to me.

My next meeting was with the whole delegation together. I requested a whiteboard so that the entire team could visualize the problem.

"It is a pleasure to see you all again," I told them. "I know this issue has been deeply frustrating for all of you. I would like to ask you for a moment to be patient with me as I try to understand exactly where the difficulty is."

I asked Sergio to tell me the sentence that was causing so much trouble. I wrote it on the board and read it aloud:

"'Institutional actors will be held collectively responsible for any crimes committed.'"

I asked the general to explain his concerns.

"The phrase *institutional actors* is just a code name for the army."

I turned to the general and said:

"I understand that your concern is that the word *institutional* means the army. What if we found a way to make it clear that it is the entire government, including all the political leaders, who are collectively responsible, not just the military?"

I looked at the general, and he looked back at me, quizzically.

"What other word could we possibly use?" I asked.

"What about 'state actors'?" Sergio suggested.

I walked up to the whiteboard, crossed out the word *institutional*, and replaced it with the word *state*.

I looked at the general and asked:

"What about the phrase *state actors* instead?"

He paused for a moment and reflected.

"Well . . . I guess the word *state* doesn't single out the army but includes all the government decision makers."

"So would that address your concern sufficiently?"

He paused again.

"I guess . . . that might work."

I turned to address everyone else in the room.

"Is this new phrasing acceptable to you?"

Starting with the chief negotiator, each one nodded their head.

Everyone looked around in a state of surprise and disbelief. It slowly dawned on them that the problem that had paralyzed the peace talks for well over a month had been solved by them in twenty minutes. We all trooped over to the presidential palace to report to President Santos. With a smile on his face, he promptly approved the language and dispatched the negotiators back to Havana.

It was an important lesson for me. When we find ourselves trapped in conflict, our vision often becomes constricted. Conflict creates blinders. Those who are outside the conflict can often help the parties see possibilities that are hard to perceive from inside. *What you see depends on where you sit.*

We may assume that to *help* the parties in conflict, we need to have *answers*. We need to have substantive suggestions for how to resolve their problem. But, in fact, we don't. To help, we just need to be curious, listen carefully, and ask questions that can open up new possibilities.

## TO HELP IS HUMAN

Helping is an innate human capacity and inclination. When someone we know is in distress, we are naturally moved to ask the simple question "How can I *help*?"

It is not easy for those who are trapped in conflict to go to the balcony or build a golden bridge. We all need help at times—even those who might seem capable of handling conflicts. That has certainly been my experience when I feel stuck in a dispute.

I recall the issue of a family inheritance in which I had been asked by my mother, when she was dying, to serve as executor of her will. She had assumed that I could mediate the sensitive issues involved but, in fact, as I discovered as one of the parties, I could not. It took my brother's suggestion of using our cousin Paul as an informal mediator to resolve the matter to everyone's satisfaction.

Paul was a family member, not a professional mediator. He was a little reluctant to get involved, as we all might be in such a situation, but agreed to help because he cared about us. It was a good and humbling reminder to me of the value of seeking and accepting help.

Help was around me if only I had eyes to see. What was hard for me proved much easier for my cousin. He, who had never mediated before in this fashion, was able to help in a way that I, who had mediated a lot, could not. The principal obstacle in this case was not the objective problem of dividing the estate. It was the emotional problem of distrust. As one of the parties, I was naturally not perceived as neutral. Paul was trusted and seen as neutral, so a process that had been blocked was able to flow.

It was a huge relief to me personally. I had little capacity at the time to deal with all the logistical and financial details but, far more important, I felt the heavy burden of fulfilling my mother's request lifted. And most precious of all was the transformation of my relationship with my siblings. Freed from this lingering issue, we could all begin to heal.

As I was writing this chapter, I saw Paul and thanked him again for his help.

"That was the most satisfying work I think I've ever done," he said.

*Help* is a short way to say *help the parties go to the balcony and build a golden bridge*. It means to help them *pause, zoom in* on what they really want, and *zoom out* to the bigger picture. It means to *help* them *listen* to each other, *create* possible options, and *attract* the other to agreement. In short, it means to help the parties see possibilities where they may not see any.

In the face of heated conflicts, we may feel powerless as potential thirdsiders, believing there is little or nothing we can do. In fact, each of us may be capable of helping one or all the parties in some way. All it takes to start is a shift in mindset from *"I can't"* to *"I can."*

## ASK CLARIFYING QUESTIONS

Most people do not like to be told what to do, particularly in a sensitive situation. They are likely to find their own insights most persuasive. The key, in my experience, is to begin by asking *clarifying questions* that bring out the parties' own insights. Clarifying questions help uncover underlying interests and generate possible options.

The questions may be as simple as:

"Can you please explain why this creates difficulty for you? What is your concern? *Why* is this important to you?"

Or "How can we satisfy the *interests* of both sides?"

Or "If you can't agree now, under what *conditions* could you possibly agree?"

Or "What have been the *costs* for you of fighting? And what would be the *benefits* to you of agreement instead?"

These are questions any of us can ask.

Asking these questions helps people discover within themselves the clues that can help them address their issues.

"I have had many consultants come and give their best advice to me," the president of Afghanistan told my colleagues and me as we sat in a circular gazebo in his garden inside the Arg, the fortified palace that had been built by the former kings of Afghanistan.

Brilliantly colored parrots flew above us among the flowering trees. Far above them, military helicopters whirled in the sky as the tragic war raged on.

"But you, my new friends," the president continued, "are the first ones to listen carefully, ask good questions, and tailor your ideas to the real problems we face here."

To offer counsel is different, in my experience, from simply offering advice. Advice starts from the advisor's perspective. What are the brightest ideas one can offer? Counsel, by contrast, starts from the other person's perspective. If we put ourselves in their shoes, experiencing their problems, what would be the most useful questions to ask?

*Advice is 80 percent talking. Counsel is 80 percent listening.*

This is a lesson I came to appreciate deeply in my experience in Colombia. When I was invited to meet with President Santos in June 2011, I thought it might involve just one trip. I was too busy working on other conflicts to take on one more. I would offer some advice based on my experiences elsewhere and make a referral if further work was requested. But when I was there, I saw that something very different was needed. The civil war had been going on for more than fifty years, and the task of making peace was widely considered impossible. President Santos did not need general advice; he needed counsel adapted to his specific situation.

I ended up making twenty-five trips to Colombia over the ensuing seven years, working closely with other conflict advisors. We delved deeply into the complexities of the conflict, asking a lot of questions. We listened at length to many of the key players, and offered ideas that were highly tailored to President Santos's needs and political realities.

To offer useful counsel, I find it helps to make a distinction I learned as a budding anthropologist between *general knowledge* and *local knowledge*.

*General knowledge* is what we usually refer to as knowledge. It is what we learn in school. It is often acquired through reading books and articles. *Local knowledge*, however, is the close-up knowledge of people and context that is often unspoken and rarely written down. It is acquired through experience. It is the things we sense about people, and their behavior and motivations. It is the way decisions are actually made—not just the formal procedures but the informal ways. We often don't even realize we have been accumulating this kind of knowledge about the people and situations around us.

As I have come to realize in my negotiation work, advice based on general knowledge alone is usually not very useful. People don't know how to apply it to their specific situation. It may not even be applicable. The trick is to blend general knowledge with as much local knowledge as possible.

The best way to do that, I have found, is to listen carefully and ask questions of people who are full of local knowledge. If you are close to one or more of the parties, you are likely to have local knowledge. With this kind of knowledge, you can do more than give general advice; you can offer genuine counsel.

## FACILITATE GENUINE DIALOGUE

What if people are so much at odds that they can't even talk to each other without coming to blows, either metaphorically or literally?

This highlights another valuable role we can play as thirdsiders: We can *facilitate* clear communication and genuine dialogue. We can create a *safe environment* and an *inclusive process* in which people can have an open interchange to deepen their mutual understanding and address the issues in contention.

In the spring of 1996, I was invited by a well-known conflict resolution organization, Search for Common Ground, to facilitate a confidential conversation in France between Turks and Kurds. A terrible civil war had raged for decades in Turkey, resulting in more than twenty-five thousand deaths and the destruction of three thousand villages.

The organizer, David Phillips, had worked for months to bring together five prominent leaders from each side, drawn from politics, business, and retired military. Hostility and suspicion were so high that even talking with the other side was condemned as treason. The leaders were risking their reputations and perhaps even their lives by engaging in conversation with the other. David found a confidential setting, far away from the scene of the conflict, in an old château, complete with a moat. It served as a balcony.

From the start of the meeting, two of the leaders caught my eye, as they seemed to represent the strongest views on either side. Ali (as I will call him) was well known as a passionate defender of Kurdish national rights. He was the leader of a Kurdish political party, elected to the national parliament. He had been jailed many times for his outspoken beliefs and had been released from prison only recently. Mehmet (as I will call him) was a Turkish nationalist. As a university student, he had been a leader in a violent extremist group called the Grey Wolves. Over breakfast, one of his colleagues told me:

"Mehmet would just as soon shoot a Kurd as talk to one."

On the first morning, the tension in the room was high. Early on, I introduced the distinction between positions and underlying interests, and asked the participants the basic question:

"What do you *really* want for your people?"

Ali spoke first. He talked eloquently about how much ordinary people had suffered during the civil war. He declared that his aim for his people was "self-determination."

Hearing that phrase, Mehmet jumped to his feet in protest.

"It is high treason to use that phrase! I cannot stay in this room and listen to this traitorous talk! I am packing my bags!"

He stormed angrily out of the room. I asked the group to take a break and went after him.

"Mehmet," I told him, "you have traveled a very long way to

come here. All of us need to hear your views. Please give us another chance and come back to rejoin our discussion."

One of his colleagues spoke with him quietly in Turkish.

"Okay, I will come back and give it one more chance," he said testily to me. "But please understand that my colleagues and I are breaking the law to be present in a meeting where that offensive phrase is used."

As we began our dialogue again, I explained to the group:

"Listen, this work of dialogue is the hardest work we humans can do. It requires us to listen to other points of view that we absolutely don't want to hear, and that can make us angry.

"When I listen to Mehmet, I understand it is painful to hear a phrase like the one Ali used. For Mehmet, it implies the division of Turkey and brings up the traumatic events that followed the breakup of the Ottoman Empire."

I looked directly at Mehmet, who nodded his head.

"When I listen to Ali, I am hearing him talk about the deep wounds of the past and the intense sufferings of his people. I hear the need for respect and for people to have a say in decisions that affect their lives and destinies."

Ali and his Kurdish colleagues were nodding their heads.

Ali rose to speak as people shifted nervously in their chairs.

"I want to finish explaining what I was saying. Yes, I believe that Kurds, like all peoples, have the God-given right to self-determination. But I also believe that we should exercise our right to self-determination by choosing to remain as equals in Turkey."

He paused and looked around.

"In fact, personally I would defend Turkey against any external threat with my blood and my life."

I looked at Mehmet. He seemed extremely surprised—and relieved. I felt the whole room breathe more easily.

With tensions, fears, and mistrust, it takes work to bring parties together—and to keep them together. *It requires building a neutral container as strong as the emotions of the parties.* As a thirdsider, my job was to hold the container so that participants such as Mehmet could have their natural reactions but without destroying the dialogue.

Ali took it from there. In his eloquent speech after the tense break, he succeeded in taking all three sides of the conflict. He was able to advocate for his side, claiming the right to self-determination. He was able to build a bridge to the other, choosing to remain as equals in Turkey. And he was able to take the third side by proclaiming his solemn commitment to defend the whole community with his life.

It was an important reminder for me: It is not just outsiders who can play the role of thirdsiders. As Ali brilliantly demonstrated, even if you are a party to the conflict, you can take the third side while at the same time advocating strongly for your own side.

Each of us, even the parties, is a potential thirdsider. Each of us, if we choose, can take the side of the larger community.

That night at dinner, I saw Mehmet, Ali, and others sitting together for a long time in animated conversation. I wondered what they were discussing so heatedly.

The next morning, I found out. As we began, Mehmet raised his hand and asked to speak.

"Yes, Mehmet?"

I felt a little nervous about what he might say. I think the whole group felt the same way.

Mehmet rose to his feet.

"Last night, I could not sleep. I could not stop thinking about what Ali and others told us about the suffering of the Kurdish people in this war. I had no idea what ordinary people were going through just for speaking their language or practicing their customs at home. Or what Ali experienced in prison. I kept asking myself, if I had been born a Kurd, wouldn't I have fought for my rights like he has?"

He paused.

"If someone had told me a few months ago that I would be sitting here with a group of Kurds who were using the word 'Kurdistan' for the land in which they live, I would have thought I was living in my worst nightmare.

"Now, however, I think I'm living in a dream."

He paused and looked at Ali.

"I want to thank Ali for helping me understand. And while I am and will forever be a strong defender of Turkish national interests, I want to acknowledge here that everyone, Turkish or Kurdish, has the right to express their identity as they see fit."

Mehmet sat down. Everyone looked at him, eyes wide with astonishment.

If there was to be a way forward in this seemingly impossible conflict, it would come from the parties themselves. My job as facilitator was simply to help them bring it out. I got the conversation started, but Ali, Mehmet, and their colleagues continued it over dinner themselves. They helped facilitate their own conflict.

In my experience, the hardest work is done by the parties. It is much easier to remain at a distance, casting stones at the other. It takes real courage to face the pain of human differences. It takes courage to talk with vulnerability about what really matters.

As I have often witnessed in conflicts both large and small, dialogue has the power to change hearts and minds. The parties are frequently surprised to discover that their enemies are human beings like themselves. They sometimes end up concluding, like Mehmet, that, placed in the same position, they might feel and act the same way.

I find it deeply moving to witness these courageous break-throughs. As people work through their conflicts, they come alive and grow as human beings, as Ali and Mehmet did. And the break-throughs bear fruit. This group of Turkish and Kurdish leaders ended up bonding and working together for years afterward to promote mutual understanding and political dialogue between their peoples.

This experience vividly demonstrates that the real magic comes from the parties themselves. I came to appreciate how the task of those around them is to help facilitate dialogue until they themselves can facilitate their own conversations. Our work as thirdsiders is to help them learn to take the third side as they stand up for their own side. Our job ultimately is to work ourselves out of the job.

## MEDIATE A SATISFYING AGREEMENT

What if people have real trouble reaching agreement?

This is where we can help by mediating—even informally, as my cousin Paul did when he helped my family settle the family inheritance issue. He brokered a mutually beneficial agreement that allocated the fair value of my mother's estate among her children and distributed her art and furniture in a way that left everyone satisfied. To mediate means to actively assist the parties in reaching an agreement they can all live with. Mediation is simply assisted negotiation.

Mediation is often confused with arbitration, but the two are very different. In mediation, the agreement belongs to the parties. They are central, and the third party simply helps. In arbitration, by contrast, the third party decides. I came to appreciate this vital distinction early on when, after my mediation work at the Kentucky coal mine, I was invited by the national union and employers association to serve as an arbitrator in West Virginia for grievances that arose under the terms of the national labor contract.

My first case as an arbitrator was held in a hotel conference room in Charleston, West Virginia. There was a long table. Five union representatives sat on one side together with the miner whose job was on the line. Five management representatives sat on the other side. The mood was somber. I was expected to sit at the head of the table and conduct the proceedings very much as a judge in court might. I was only twenty-seven at the time, but all the representatives treated me as if I had gray hair.

Over the course of a long day, each side argued its case. Management wanted to fire the miner for repeated absenteeism. The union contested the decision. I asked questions, but the only issue for both sides was whether management had fully complied with the contract. Management's objective was to protect its management rights. The union's objective was to challenge those rights under the contract.

No one really seemed interested in the miner, who was on the verge of losing his job. I had a hunch that there might be another possibility that could satisfy both sides and save the miner's job. One of the managers admitted that the miner had been good at his work.

There seemed to be a reason for the absences, but I was not allowed to surface it in the proceeding as it was not relevant to the contract. There was an overlooked possibility to repair the relationship.

As the arbitrator, I was limited simply to deciding who was right and who was wrong according to the contract. It felt deeply frustrating. In the end, when I had to write up a brief decision, I had no choice but to rule based on the contract. Management had a decidedly more persuasive case in this situation. It was entitled to fire the miner. But even if management won the point, it seemed to me that everyone ended up losing. The mine lost a good worker, the union lost a case, everyone lost a lot of time and energy, and the miner lost his job and livelihood.

It was a big lesson for me and felt completely different from my previous experiences as a mediator. As a mediator, I had a chance to probe deeply into what the real problem was: What were the underlying interests and needs of all sides? As a mediator, I could explore with the parties the full range of possibilities and not be forced into a narrow binary yes-no decision about the contract. Mediation can help unlock the full potential within, between, and around us.

There is a valuable place for arbitration to settle disputes that cannot be resolved by negotiation and mediation and that would otherwise go on to costly lawsuits. What drew me to mediation, however, was the way that it allows parties to explore options for mutual gain. To mediate literally means to *sit in the middle*.

We may not be aware of it, but in an informal sense, everyone has the chance to mediate in everyday situations. Parents mediate among their quarreling children. Managers mediate among their employees and among their bosses. Marriage counselors mediate between contending spouses.

We may not be neutral, but we are interested and motivated to help the people around us transform their conflicts in a way that benefits our families, workplaces, and communities. Each of us has the opportunity to sit in the middle and help the people around us reach satisfying agreements and repair their relationships.

## GO HELP

When my mother was ill with cancer in December 1997, I received an urgent request to facilitate a meeting intended to stave off a resurgence of war between Chechnya and Russia. The cease-fire that my colleagues and I had helped negotiate was in grave danger of breaking down. The meeting was to be hosted by the president of Tatarstan in his presidential palace in the Ural Mountains.

In my daily phone call with my mother, I told her about the request.

"Aren't you going to go?" she asked.

"No, I don't think so. I don't feel right leaving the country right now with you being ill. I want to stay close."

"You have to go. They need your help."

"I know, but you're not well. I need to be here."

"I want you to go. Please go for my sake," my mother insisted.

"Mom . . . I'm not sure."

*"Go help!"*

She had the last word.

Perhaps the biggest obstacle to helping is within us. It is the mistaken belief that we can't really be of much assistance.

*Help* may be *easier* to provide than we think. We think we need to have an answer to help. We don't. Instead, we can listen and ask

basic problem-solving questions. We can offer counsel. We can facilitate genuine dialogue. And we can help mediate. The best answers
emerge from a process in which the parties are fully involved and
they themselves create and own the agreement.

*Help* can also be more *useful* to the parties than we may think.
Asking good questions helps them zoom into what they really want
and zoom out to see the bigger picture. Bringing people together
to talk in a safe atmosphere can help people connect with and understand one another better. Mediating can help them reach a satisfying agreement they can all live with. The right kind of help can
often make the difference between a destructive stalemate and a
satisfying yes.

Last, if we are one of the parties in conflict, *help* from the third
side is more *available* and accessible than we may think. The third
side is all around us. As I learned in dealing with my family's inheritance, we may be able to find help more easily than we can
imagine.

Each of us is a potential thirdsider, and each of us has a supportive role to play in the conflicts around us.

*Go help.*

# CHAPTER 11

# SWARM

## From Latent to Mobilized

*When spider webs unite, they can halt even a lion.*
—Ethiopian proverb

W ho can do what tomorrow morning to interrupt the escalation to nuclear war with North Korea?"

That was the question I posed to twelve volunteers assembled for a two-week social experiment in a rental house in Boulder, Colorado, in October 2017.

It had all begun with a conversation five weeks earlier with Patrice Martin, a leading practitioner of design thinking. I was asking her advice about how design thinking—a human-centered approach to innovation—could help tackle seemingly impossible conflicts.

"What is your dream?" she asked me.

"What's so often missing in these conflicts, Patrice, is a critical mass of creative collaboration. In Silicon Valley, they *swarm* tough, seemingly impossible software problems. My dream is high-performing teams of people swarming the world's toughest conflict situations."

"What does *swarm* mean to you?" Patrice asked.

"Come at the problem creatively from all sides. Deploy a team with diverse perspectives. Use radical collaboration. Continue intensively until you crack the problem open with new possibilities."

"Why don't you just simulate what you want to see happen?" asked Patrice. "Just do it for two weeks. That would give you an idea of what to do next. In design thinking, we call this rapid prototyping. You try out something rudimentary as an experiment and keep on improving it until you have something that works."

"Sounds great. How would we start?"

"First, pick a problem."

I had just returned from a second meeting with Dennis Rodman, and North Korea was very much on my mind.

"Is it better to pick a smaller problem that seems more solvable, or is it okay to pick a big, seemingly impossible problem?" I asked. "I'm thinking about how we can prevent a nuclear war with North Korea."

"Pick the one where you have energy. There is magic in setting a date and just starting. Don't wait," Patrice urged.

My colleague Liza Hester and I picked a date five weeks out.

We put out a call to our network of colleagues to see who would, with little notice, free themselves up for two weeks to participate in this unusual experiment. We interviewed and selected twelve people with a diverse set of perspectives and backgrounds. They included an international lawyer, a couple of trained mediators, a strategic storyteller, and a military veteran. None had expertise on North Korea, but the point was simply to simulate a swarm.

I asked my friend Rob Evans, a masterful facilitator of collective intelligence and creativity, if he would help, and he readily agreed. He brought a gifted graphic artist with him. We rented a house nearby and filled it with huge display boards, flip charts, colored markers, plenty of sticky notes, and collaborative workspaces.

The social experiment began. We nicknamed ourselves a SWAT team for peace. Our job was to swarm the US–North Korea conflict from all perspectives to see if we could discern possible ways to avert a catastrophic war.

## SWARM TO TRANSFORM

In the tech world, "swarming" refers to the self-organizing collaboration of a network to solve a problem in a flexible and innovative fashion. Instead of each person working on a separate project, team members focus their attention collectively on one project until it is solved. The goal is to deliver high-quality results in the time required with every team member playing to their strengths.

Swarming is precisely what we need to transform the challenging conflicts we face in today's world.

*To swarm a conflict means to surround it with a critical mass of ideas and influence.*

Swarming uses the power of the many, *mobilizing* the *latent* potential of the community.

Just as birds gather in a swarm to defend their nest from a marauding hawk and interrupt an act of destruction, people from the community can work together in a concentrated way to interrupt a destructive conflict and set it on a more constructive path.

When the Kua people of the Kalahari hide the poison arrows and gather around the campfire, they are swarming the conflict. When business, labor, faith, and civic leaders came together to create the National Peace Accord in South Africa, they were swarming the conflict to put an end to apartheid.

Whereas *hosting* takes care of the *people* and *helping* addresses the *problem*, *swarming* adds to the mix the critical missing element of *power*. When conflict escalates and one party tries to impose its will on the other with force, it can take the *power* of a united community to halt the fighting and start the talking.

With power comes responsibility. The more power is exercised, the more respect needs to be shown if that power is not to backfire. The intention of a swarm is to transform the conflict for the long-term benefit of the parties and the community.

I appreciate that the word *swarm* is an intense one, bringing up connotations of menace for some, as when bees or insects swarm. It may help to remember that it is not a *person* who is swarmed; it is the *conflict* that is swarmed. *Attack the problem, not the person.*

## SWARM WITH IDEAS

*Swarming* is the culminating move on the path to possible. It integrates the balcony, the bridge, and the third side.

"We are on the *balcony*," I told the volunteers on the SWAT team for peace, "a place where we can see the bigger picture and focus on what really matters. We are trying to build a *golden bridge* for the parties. And we all belong to the *third side*, the larger community worried about a conflict that threatens our world right now.

"You have one job, and that is to figure out *who* can do *what* tomorrow morning to interrupt the escalation toward nuclear war. That is the question I want you to live and breathe for the next two weeks. Read as much as you find useful, call up and interview experts, be open to new ideas, and see what you can come up with.

"I'd like us to write a script in which these two leaders, each with their finger on the button, end up finding a better way to deal with their differences. What are their victory speeches?

"Our motto is *humble audacity*. Let's be audacious enough to believe we might make a contribution. At the same time, let's be humble enough to know how little we know so we can listen with a beginner's mind to all the knowledge and experience out there."

We broke up into small groups and set up a Team Trump and a Team Kim. The teams were assigned the task of learning as much as possible about the leaders both as human beings and as decision makers. What motivates them? What was their childhood like? How do they see the world? How do they make decisions—who influences them, and what can change their minds?

"Even if you disagree with the person, try to put yourself in their shoes. What does it feel like to be in their place? Practice *strategic empathy*—empathy with a purpose. Only by understanding them do we have a chance to influence them to make the right decision."

Team Trump researched every statement and tweet Donald Trump had made on the subject of North Korea going back twenty-five years. They wrote each one on a sticky note and placed them in a row on a display board to see if any patterns could be discerned.

The team also researched specific instances in which Trump had changed his mind on a political decision. How had that happened? Who had he listened to, and what factors had influenced him most? We came to appreciate Trump's unusual flexibility—how he could change his mind on a dime and still frame it as a win.

One team member, Gia Medeiros, who worked in marketing and strategic communication, called up a reality TV producer who had worked with Donald Trump on *The Apprentice*.

"If this were a reality TV show, how could it end well?" she asked him.

"Well the first rule of reality TV is 'Whatever you do, don't be boring.' The same person can't always be the villain. You always need a surprise or plot twist."

That was an *aha!* for us as we thought about how to find a way out for Trump.

We reached out to speak on Zoom with experts: professors who had studied the conflict, ex-diplomats who had dealt with North Korea, ex–intelligence analysts, anyone who could give us insight. We also sought out unlikely perspectives such as that of a former gang member who talked to us about effective methods for interrupting violence between gang leaders. The team listened carefully for any insights and wrote them down on sticky notes. We posted them on the flip charts and analyzed them for clues and further questions to pursue.

The entire house was filled with display boards with large sheets of paper capturing all we were learning, almost as if we were trying to solve a crime and track down all the missing data. We listed all the key players in the drama—from Washington to Pyongyang to Seoul to Beijing, Moscow, Tokyo, and beyond. The team wrote up background profiles of the key individual decision makers. That was the virtue of having twelve minds single-mindedly focused like a laser for two weeks on a single question: *Who* can do *what* tomorrow morning to reduce the risk of nuclear war?

At the end of every day, we assembled in the living room and listed on a wall chart:

"What have we learned today?"

"What worked?"

"What needs to be changed for tomorrow?"

And every morning, we assembled again to ask ourselves about any insights or new questions and plan the day accordingly. Our relentless focus was on learning and improving what we were doing. We were practicing "rapid prototyping."

Our aim was to swarm the problem with multiple perspectives and ideas and to find multiple points of contact that could open the way for productive negotiations. Many creative possibilities emerged and were posted on the walls.

"Keep the ideas flowing," I told the team. "But take them lightly, remembering how little we know. The key for us is to listen even more carefully to those who have thirty years of experience. Creativity that is ungrounded is useless. Experience without creativity won't bring us a new approach. It is the blend of creativity with experience that is needed. *Grounded imagination* is the key."

Understanding that it takes great teamwork to overcome tough challenges, we engaged in *radical collaboration*, sharing our ideas and perspectives freely, cheering on the creativity of others, and helping one another every step of the way. Each person felt encouraged to contribute their full potential. Together, our collective intelligence was far greater than the intelligence of any one of us.

The work pace was intense. At the same time, it felt satisfying to be tackling such a dangerous problem instead of just worrying about it. And—perhaps odd to say because of the gravity of the topic—it was fun. We ate together, went for walks together, took exercise breaks outside in the garden together. Our facilitator, Rob, played music during the breaks and encouraged us to move our bodies, dance, and shake out the worry.

We tried any modality that could open our minds, sharpen our creativity, increase our ability to collaborate, and augment our dogged persistence as we pursued one angle after another.

As we know from sports and music, the spirit of play can bring out our best performance and highest potential. In this experiment, I got a glimpse of the same *power of play* applied to the serious task of transforming a dangerous conflict.

It was a simulation of what I had dreamed of: a dedicated team swarming a difficult conflict. But it was not *just* a simulation; there was a real-time emergency in the world. As we spoke with those in the know, from former diplomats to academic experts, we heard from three separate people:

"This situation is getting really dangerous. We're glad *someone* is doing something about it."

That concerned us. Our two-week simulation had been intended, after all, as a social experiment. None of us was an expert on North Korea. Given the enormous gravity and urgency of the situation, one might be forgiven for thinking that there would be real teams of knowledgeable specialists working single-mindedly, day and night, on how to practically avert a potentially imminent catastrophic war. To our dismay, however, none of the many Korea experts with whom we spoke could name even one.

A great deal of intellectual effort was focused on *analyzing* the danger but comparatively little on *averting* the danger. There was *a lot of prediction* but *very little prevention*.

So even though we had initially planned for only a two-week simulation, the team and I made a decision: We would find a way to keep it going. We would try to turn our simulated swarm into a real swarm.

## BUILD YOUR *ACT*

Good ideas are vital but useless unless there is a way to get them in front of key decision makers for their consideration. For that, we need *ACT*: *A for access, C for credibility, T for trust.*

*Access* means a connection to the people in conflict. *Credibility* is believability based on competence and track record. It is rational and comes from the head. *Trust* is believability based on intent and integrity. It is emotional and comes from the heart.

Among the Kua, the family and friends of those in conflict work together to persuade the parties to sit down, listen to each other, and eventually reconcile. The community, in effect, pools its access, credibility, and trust to sway the minds of the parties in conflict.

*ACT is the basic currency of the third side*, enabling the community to influence the parties to stop fighting and start talking.

If we don't have *access*, *credibility*, and *trust*, we need to either build them or work with others who have them. When I became concerned about the risk of war with North Korea, I reached out to one of the few people I knew who had actually been to North Korea, my old negotiation colleague Jonathan Powell. I remembered a dinner in Colombia with him during which he had explained to me that once a year, he traveled to North Korea as part of a regular European political exchange with that country. I called Jonathan for advice.

"I am getting worried about what's going on with North Korea. With Trump and Kim in a showdown, where is the off-ramp?

"When are you going back to North Korea?"

"Soon. So far our talks haven't really produced anything useful. We just get the party line, but this time might be different. As luck would have it, our new interlocutor for the exchange is Ri Su Yong. He was the North Korean ambassador to Switzerland in the 1990s, when Kim studied there at a boarding school under a cover name."

"Sounds like an opportunity."

"Let's see," said Jonathan. "Meanwhile, why don't you speak with Glyn Ford, who goes with me? He's an ex–Labour MP and former European parliamentarian who has been traveling to North Korea for twenty-five years. He has been there almost forty times."

I called Glyn, who told me:

"Meeting Ri Su Yong offers a real opportunity. He's the highest-ranking foreign policy official in North Korea. Word has it that he took care of Kim and his sister while they were in Switzerland and was a kind of surrogate father. My guess is that Kim listens closely to him, given their longtime relationship."

I arranged for Jonathan and Glyn separately to speak by Zoom to the SWAT team in Colorado to offer their impressions and ideas for a negotiated off-ramp. I tasked the team with this assignment:

"Jonathan and Glyn have built some *ACT*—access, credibility, and trust—with the North Koreans that could be useful. But how best should they use it? In a few weeks, they will be in Pyongyang. Imagine they have only an hour of substantive conversation with Ri Su Yong, who is close to Kim. Without naming names, I want you to get our experts' advice on what questions Jonathan and Glyn should ask and what main points they should convey. What can they say to Ri that could possibly help de-escalate the situation?"

From that beginning, a swarm effort began as Jonathan, Glyn, and I worked closely together, supported by a team of researchers and analysts. In the year that followed, we made twenty-one trips to Washington, DC, Seoul, and Pyongyang. As a US citizen, I could not go to North Korea, but as British citizens, they could and did. Thanks to pooling and building our *access*, we ended up having more than eighty-five meetings with key policy officials in the three capitals.

It wasn't easy to get those meetings—especially the first ones. The initial *access* required quite a bit of networking and referrals. But once we started, one meeting opened the door to the next. Each official we met was curious about what we were learning from the others. As they found our conversations helpful, our *credibility* increased. And as we followed up on those relationships, maintaining repeated positive contact and preserving confidences, we built *trust*.

On the basis of what we heard at those meetings, listening keenly to their concerns and questions, we sent follow-up advisory memos. These short memos, two or three pages in length, were masterfully drafted by Jonathan, drawing on his long experience as chief of staff for British prime minister Tony Blair. The memos, of which there were forty-eight in that one year, were supported in turn by more than two hundred background profiles and issue papers that we called "get smarts," prepared by the team that grew out of the swarm experiment.

What was the impact of these collective efforts? We will never know. I did get a call, however, from a veteran political reporter from the *Washington Post*, known for his inside access to the White House, who told me:

"I honestly believe your efforts influenced the negotiation process and contributed to bringing the American president and the North Korean leader to the table for the first time ever."

The North Korea swarm allowed me to glimpse my dream of teams using collective intelligence and *ACT* to swarm the toughest conflicts that face us today.

## TO SWARM IS HUMAN

Mobilizing the surrounding community to act as a swarm to interrupt destructive conflict is not new. As I learned from my anthropological research into war and peace, swarming may be our most ancient human heritage for dealing with contentious conflicts.

"What happens if someone hunts on someone else's territory without asking permission?" I once asked the Kua elder Korakoradue.

"The injured party will call three people as witnesses. He will show them the offender's footprints. Then they all go talk to the offender and admonish him not to do it again."

"Supposing the offender ignores them and hunts again without asking permission?"

"This time the injured party will call *four* witnesses. They will speak very loudly this time to the offender and tell him not to do it again."

I couldn't resist following up.

"And what if the offender repeats his offense a third time?"

Korakoradue looked at me closely and pronounced slowly:

"No community member would ever *dare* to violate the norms like this and offend again!"

The community mobilizes a critical mass of collective influence. The offending party may be more powerful than the injured party but is never more powerful than the community acting together. Swarming is the application of collective power, needed to deal with injustice.

"Do you see these sticks in my hand?" Tsamko, a member of the Ju/'hoansi community in Namibia, once asked. "One stick breaks easily, but if you pick up lots of sticks like this, you can't break them."

When I ventured deep into the Malaysian rainforest to visit the Semai people, I found them using a similar approach of swarming conflict situations.

"It is not proper to take sides," one Semai elder explained to me. "What is proper is for *everyone* to urge their relatives and friends to resolve their disputes."

Everyone is expected to take the side of the whole community—the third side. Taking the third side doesn't mean ignoring the needs of your family or friends. It means refraining from making the dispute worse. It means using your constructive influence to help the parties go to the balcony and focus on what truly matters.

The Semai start learning to take the third side when they are children. When one child strikes another, the adults, instead of punishing the child, will call a children's *bcaraa'*, or council. All the children sit down in a circle, discuss what happened, and talk about how to resolve the issue and repair the injured relationship. Everyone profits from the dispute by learning the lesson of how to handle frustrations and differences peacefully. The Semai mobilize *the power of peers* to transform conflict.

Swarming is an innate human capacity that we can apply in any conflict. We may already do so without even recognizing that that is what we are doing. That was my experience some years ago in a family situation.

My son was nineteen. He was living back in the family home, taking a break after a year of college. He had been hanging out for many years with a group of high school friends who were lost in their lives, adrift and drinking. Like many adolescents, he had become distant and uncommunicative. The sensitive boy I knew with a deep heart who loved improvising music on the piano had seemingly disappeared. In his stead was a young man who got into trouble, wrecked more than one family car, and felt that the world was somehow arrayed against him.

Naturally, these behaviors led to family tension, angst, and worry. It all came to a head one day when Lizanne and I traveled to visit family and asked our son not to have his friends in the house. He gave us his promise. When we returned from our trip, the person we had hired to look after the house in our absence came to us in tears.

"I am afraid to tell you this, but, from what I could tell, your son had friends over last week, and they partied in the house. The place smelled of smoke and alcohol. When I asked him about this, he threatened to tell you about how *I* wasn't doing *my* job. But I need to tell you anyway."

She was trembling.

"It breaks my heart as a mother," my wife, Lizanne, cried out to me later that day, "but I cannot live with him anymore in the house. I can't stand the way he is right now."

Up to that point, I had been a little more accepting, understanding that our son was going through a difficult phase of life. But now I felt a wave of anger rising in my gut. This could not continue.

I went for my favorite solitary walk in the canyon near my home. It was my balcony. Walking amid natural beauty, I could listen better to my anger. I paused and started to zoom in. Why was I angry? What was my anger trying to tell me? It was partly the breaking of a promise and trust, but this time, it was more that had set me off. It was the abuse of power by a member of my own family over a trusted employee who was simply doing her job for us. He had threatened her livelihood, leaving her in fear and tears. That was a bright red line for me.

I asked myself: How can we begin to turn around a destructive pattern of behavior that has generated repeated family arguments for years? I realized that we were stuck and that my wife and I alone did not have enough influence to stop our son's destructive behavior. We needed help. We needed a community. In short, we needed a swarm.

Later that day, Lizanne and I called our son into a meeting in our home office. He sat on the couch, and we sat facing him. She began:

"I've always loved having you living in our home. I've always wanted you to come back anytime you want. But the truth is that I don't like living with you. It hurts me to say this, but it's true."

She had tears in her eyes.

I then spoke up.

"Your mother and I love you very much, I hope you know that. And this is serious. It is one thing when you violate a promise you made to us. That is wrong. But to threaten and create fear in someone who depends on us for her livelihood and is just doing her job makes me *really* angry."

I looked at him. He was very quiet, looking startled, with his eyes wide open.

"Here's what your mother and I propose. We want you to make a full apology to her. We want you to leave home and go away for two months to work out your issues. We have a program in mind where you will be with a counselor and other people your age. We hope they can help you remember the person we know you really are."

Our son's journey began with an intensive workshop led by a counselor we knew. The workshop focused on understanding oneself, seeing one's strengths and limitations, and learning to assume responsibility for one's own life. The twenty people in the workshop became close and gave one another peer support. My son ended up spending the entire two months in that community, focused on learning more about himself and making new friends. He rediscovered the joy of music and learned to meditate. He had regular sessions with the counselor. He also spent considerable time with his two uncles, who supported him in the work of personal transformation. It was a complete immersion in a supportive community.

When he returned two months later, the changes in his behavior were striking. He took full responsibility for his actions and apologized sincerely to his mother and me. He came back with a renewed passion for his music and went on to form a band. He returned to his university studies. The destructive arguments about his behavior subsided entirely and were replaced with more constructive conversations about other issues such as space where his new band could practice.

I do not mean to suggest that this kind of process is in any way easy or guaranteed to work. Every case is different. Nevertheless, it was a big lesson for me. It was a conflict in which I personally felt stuck and lost. It took the intervention of an entire community to help our son transform a destructive pattern.

As I write these words fifteen years later, I have just returned from visiting my son with his wife and new baby. I feel touched to witness him as a father—tender, loving, and playful with his infant son. I watch him in his role as husband, the way he gladly shares the work of child rearing and household chores. At the same time, I am impressed by the leadership he shows at work, responding this past week with wisdom, support, and empathy as he helped his team adapt to layoffs at one of the world's most demanding high-tech companies. To me, he is a shining example of someone who is working to fulfill his potential as a human being.

As I look back on the experience of dealing with a thorny family situation that threatened to become a destructive conflict, I realize that it is an example of swarming with the third side. My wife and I, our son's counselor, his peers in the workshop, his new friends, and his uncles constituted a dynamic community that surrounded him and supported his personal work and transformation with encouragement, feedback, and support. Working together, individually and collectively, we were able to help him unlock the potential within. None of us alone could have helped him break through. It took all of us together.

As the saying goes, it takes a village.

## ASSEMBLE A SWARM TEAM

To *swarm* is a team sport.

For many years, I have been impressed with the innovative example of hostage negotiation teams. I have had the chance to teach police hostage negotiators and always found their stories inspiring.

A generation or two ago, hostage negotiations in the United States were often handled by violent methods. The police would pull out a bullhorn and shout:

"You have five minutes to come out with your hands up!"

If the hostage taker did not surrender, in would go the tear gas and out would come the guns blazing. Not only would the hostage taker die, but often the hostages and police would die as well. A tragic example was the debacle in Waco, Texas, in April 1993, when a tear gas attack by the FBI ended in a fire in which scores of people died, including many children.

Over time, police departments learned that there was a better way: quiet, persistent negotiation carried out by a trained team of police negotiators. The police surround the site to prevent any escape and then start talking.

"When I'm dealing with an armed criminal, for example, my first rule of thumb is simply to be polite," explained Dominick Misino, who, in his career with the New York Police Department, negotiated with his colleagues more than two hundred hostage incidents, including a plane hijacking, without losing a single life.

"This sounds trite, I know, but it is very important. A lot of times, the people I'm dealing with are extremely nasty. And the reason for this is that their anxiety level is so high: a guy armed and barricaded in a bank is in a flight-or-fight mode. To defuse the situation, I've got to try to understand what's going on in his head. The first step to getting there is to show him respect, which shows my sincerity and reliability."

Success lies in building credibility and trust in a very short period of time.

Police hostage negotiators work in teams. It is not uncommon to have a dozen or more people trying to understand what is going on in the hostage taker's head and to figure out how to persuade him to surrender peacefully.

One person is speaking to the hostage taker, and eleven are on the balcony. One may be passing the negotiator notes. One may be tracking down relatives or friends of the hostage taker who can talk with them and calm them down. One may be coordinating with the SWAT team that is standing by in case it is needed.

It is a genuine swarm team effort—and has proven to be astonishingly successful. As my negotiation colleague George Kohlrieser explained:

"Hostage situations can be dramatic and intense, but you don't hear about most of them in the news. That's because more than 95% are resolved peacefully, without casualties, and with the hostage-takers accepting the consequences."

I found myself inspired by similar swarm team efforts to reduce gang violence in big cities. I have learned a lot from my friend Dr. Gary Slutkin. Gary spent twenty years as a public health doctor specializing in stopping epidemics around the world, only to return to his home city of Chicago to find an epidemic of gang shootings. He founded an organization to interrupt violence called CeaseFire (now a worldwide initiative called Cure Violence Global).

Gary wanted to apply the same public health tools that were effective in interrupting disease to interrupt the virus of violence. Just as public health campaigns recruit local citizens to reach out to their peers to change the behaviors that spread disease, Gary experimented with using community interrupters.

"Our violence interruption workers come from the same community as the gang members and are in fact often former gang members themselves," Gary explained to those of us involved in the initial swarm on North Korea.

"Every Wednesday, we gather together to review what is going on in the neighborhood, compare notes, and see what needs to be done. We call it an *interruption table*."

I encouraged the North Korea swarm team to watch an extraordinary documentary about Gary's work by Alex Kotlowitz entitled *The Interrupters*. In the film, Alex shows an interruption table at work. A dozen or more people are gathered around a conference table, all talking excitedly, when the meeting is called to order.

"All right, let's close up. Everybody that's in the meeting, this is serious now, okay? We're in a crisis mode, and we need people to step up at this table and go over and beyond. Guys are getting killed for just anything. Have there been any conflicts mediated on the front end? From last week to this week?"

The other interrupters are quiet for a moment. Then one pipes up:

"Two guys were arguing. One guy threatened to blow the other guy's wig back. I got him to calm down, tell him, 'He didn't shoot you, he was just talking.' We stopped that one on the front end."

One lead interrupter explains:

"I have the 'dirty dozen' at the table. We've always had outreach workers, but the violence was not necessarily going down at that point. So in the year 2004, we began a new concept called the 'violence interrupters.' Most of the violence interrupters come from the hierarchy in some of these gangs. Because ain't just nobody can come in and tell a guy to put his gun down. The violence interrupters have one goal in mind: to stop killings. They're not trying to dismantle gangs. What they're trying to do is save a life."

One of the most effective interrupters, whom I once had the pleasure of meeting, is an inspiring young woman named Ameena, a former gang member. As one of her colleagues explains:

"Ameena Matthews, as a violence interrupter, she's the golden girl. She gets in where a lot of guys can't get in. She knows how to talk to these high-risk young men. And a lot of guys that I know that have a lot of murder in their background, they respect her."

As Ameena says, she can relate because she has been there herself:

"The life that I lived, being in shootouts, looking at the devil face to face. . . . And I look at my sisters and my brothers today, you know, that was once me."

She is a genuine thirdsider, emerging from within the community itself.

In a very different context, I witnessed another kind of swarm team cooperation in my work with Colombian president Juan Manuel Santos on ending the civil war. As I mentioned earlier, Santos assembled a team of five key negotiation advisors. We brought with us a wide range of perspectives and experiences from different parts of the world.

What we shared was a common zeal for peace and a desire to help the president. A willingness to be team players. A respect for the other's strengths and skills. And a willingness to stay in for the long haul. Even though we were advisors to one of the sides, we were also thirdsiders, working for the benefit of the whole. Our role was to stay on the balcony, keep an eye on the bigger picture, and help Santos build a golden bridge that could end the war.

We would show up, usually on a day's notice, from different parts of the world. We would be whisked through airport security so our presence would not be detected. We would spend three intense days working closely with one another, the president, and the government negotiation team. We would meet with the officials and receive special intelligence briefings. We would then have dinner alone with the president. Our job was to listen carefully to the president, understand his dilemmas, and give him our best counsel.

We repeated that routine twenty-five times over seven years.

We worked remarkably well together, building on one another's strengths. We had different lanes. Jonathan Powell was a masterful synthesizer and memo writer. From his prior experience as chief of staff to the British prime minister, he knew intimately how politics and government worked. Joaquín Villalobos, as a former guerrilla commander, had a deep understanding of the minds of guerrilla leaders.

Shlomo Ben-Ami, drawing on his long experience with the Arab-Israeli conflict, proved to be a highly able strategist. Dudley Ankerson knew Latin American politics from the inside out. I focused more on negotiation strategy and psychology. I also helped facilitate strategy meetings and occasionally mediate among the government negotiators.

Our collaboration felt seamless. We developed what is called *swarm intelligence*, collective intelligence that is much greater than the intelligence of any one of us.

"You and the others serve as my balcony," President Santos once remarked to me at a crisis moment during the peace negotiations. Later, when it was all over, he told an audience at Harvard:

"Our conflict was so difficult I realized we needed help, the best we could find, drawing on lessons from mistakes and successes made in other conflicts elsewhere. If I have one piece of advice to another head of state embarking on a challenging peace process, it would be to convene a team of world-class negotiation advisors like I had."

## BUILD A WINNING COALITION

Swarming a conflict succeeds through the principle of critical mass. Critical mass provides the persuasive power that is needed to overcome resistance and power imbalances. Individually, people may not be sufficiently influential, but collectively they are potentially more powerful than any conflicting party.

As part of my research into the evolution of human conflict, I went to visit the distinguished primatologist Frans de Waal at his research center. De Waal was conducting extensive studies of our closest primate cousins, the bonobo chimpanzees. I was curious about how the bonobos handle conflict.

As we were walking around, de Waal explained to me:

"When a male bonobo gets aggressive with a female, I have often observed the other females responding by building a coalition. The females will line up shoulder to shoulder like linebackers on a football team and slowly back the offending male away. It's as if they are saying 'Back off, big guy. You've gone too far. Now, behave!'"

That is the power of the third side in the form of a *winning co-alition*, a gathering of community power so strong that it can bring about a peaceable outcome. As powerful as any one party may be, it is never more powerful than the community acting together.

So how can you build a winning coalition of thirdsiders? That was the immense challenge confronting President Santos as he faced the seemingly insurmountable task of ending a war that had gone on for almost fifty years.

The guerrilla group, the FARC, was in the jungles, and its members had known nothing but fighting for decades, fortified by funds from the drug trade and kidnapping. They had sanctuaries in the neighboring country of Venezuela. Many of the young fighters were reluctant to set down their weapons. Many of the leaders were reaping substantial material gains from the drug trade. In a prior negotiation three decades earlier, guerrilla leaders had emerged to participate in an election and then had been assassinated, along with hundreds of their supporters. Why risk everything for a highly un-certain peace with a government that could not be trusted?

There had been many previous attempts at negotiation, but all had failed, and the last, a decade earlier, had failed disastrously in the public's eyes. Santos's predecessor, President Álvaro Uribe, had achieved a lot of success, with Santos serving as his defense minis-ter, in attacking the FARC in its strongholds and putting its fight-ers on the defensive. Feelings of animosity toward the FARC ran high. People favored peace, but most were deeply skeptical about any realistic prospect for it. Why risk everything to negotiate with a group that could not be trusted?

To make matters even more difficult, Uribe opposed a peace agreement, arguing that the FARC could be defeated militarily. He traveled the country mobilizing opposition, particularly among the military and business sectors of society. With daily tweets, he accused Santos of being soft on terrorists and communists.

In effect, the challenge Santos faced was to overcome a formidable *blocking coalition*, forces arrayed against a possible agreement. This is a serious problem in many of the intractable conflicts I have worked on: those parties who work hard to block a possible agreement, perhaps because they feel left out, perhaps because they derive benefits from the conflict, or perhaps simply because they believe an agreement would go against their interests.

The first surprising move Santos made in his first weeks in office was to reach out to Colombia's neighbor and prickly adversary, President Hugo Chávez of Venezuela. Although he denied it publicly, Chávez was a friend, mentor, and main supporter of the FARC, quietly offering its fighters sanctuary in Venezuela. A month earlier, President Uribe had publicly accused Chávez of harboring terrorists. Furious, Chávez had broken off diplomatic relations with Colombia, accusing it of having plans to attack Venezuela.

At a conference of Latin American leaders, Santos met with Chávez, tried to put the relationship between the two neighboring countries back on track, and took the opportunity to ask him boldly for his help in bringing the FARC leaders to the negotiating table. Expecting hostility, Chávez was naturally surprised. He was attracted by the idea of hosting a historic peace as his legacy. He went on to persuade the FARC leadership that winning elections as he had, not guerrilla warfare, would be their best avenue to advance their cause.

Not long thereafter, Santos boldly reached out to the FARC's most important mentor and revolutionary model, Cuban president Fidel Castro. Santos surprised Castro by asking him to host the secret talks. Pleased to be invited to be a host, he agreed. He also played a key role in convincing the FARC leaders to come out of the jungle to negotiate.

To the astonishment of outside observers, Santos succeeded in moving both Chávez and Castro from the blocking coalition to the winning coalition. Both revolutionary leaders became active third-siders. When the public talks started in Havana, Santos added Norway and Chile to balance them out so that each side would have two friendly governments to help facilitate an agreement.

Just as important as the thirdsiders outside Colombia were the thirdsiders inside Colombian society. A peace process would require the support of many domestic constituencies, particularly the military and the business sector. To help assuage their concerns, Santos appointed as negotiators a popular former head of the armed forces and a former head of the business trade association.

All of those thirdsiders, both external and internal, constituted a winning coalition and made a crucial difference in ending the fifty-year civil war. Thanks to the mobilization of the third side, the winning coalition proved stronger than the blocking coalition. The lesson was clear: To transform a difficult conflict, it is vital to identify and win over potential blockers and to recruit new allies. Critical mass matters.

## SWARM TO SAVE THE DAY

The historic signing of the peace agreement by President Santos and Timochenko took place outside by the sea in Cartagena.

Everyone was dressed in white. I sat near mothers who had lost their children and loved ones. They were visibly weeping. I listened as the FARC commander apologized to the victims. Those who had met in battle were now meeting in peace.

I conversed with a high government official I knew, Luis Carlos Villegas, who introduced me to his daughter, Juliana. She had gone through the harrowing experience of being kidnapped by the guerrillas many years earlier, at the tender age of seventeen. She was marched through the mountains and jungles and held hostage for more than three months. For her parents and her, it had been absolute hell.

I remembered Luis telling me that when President Santos had asked him to join the negotiating delegation, he had demurred because of his wife's and his strong personal feelings, but Juliana had insisted that he play his part, saying "Father, we must do everything possible to end this war." Here they were together to celebrate the surprise peace that, just a few years earlier, had been widely believed to be impossible. I felt the emotions of father and daughter—they were palpable and contagious.

In peace, however, as in war, nothing goes according to plan. A week later, there was a huge upset.

As part of his efforts to win support for the peace process, President Santos had promised the people of Colombia a referendum. They would have the last say on any agreement that was negotiated.

The referendum, unfortunately, was plagued by low turnout. A hurricane suppressed the vote precisely in those coastal regions where the war had taken its highest toll and where support for peace was strongest. A powerful and sophisticated disinformation campaign was waged on social media against the peace agreement. In the end, the referendum was lost by the tiny margin of a fifth of 1 percent.

Everyone was shocked. What could be done? Was the peace process at an end?

My friend Sergio, the peace commissioner, called me:

*"William, now what?"*

It was time to mobilize the third side with another swarm effort. The team of peace advisors showed up the next day to help President Santos figure out what to do to save the agreement. All the outside friends and supporters of the peace applied their influence: Venezuela, Cuba, Norway, Chile, and also the United States, Europe, and the United Nations. Fortuitously, the very same week, the Nobel Peace Prize was awarded to President Santos, boosting international recognition of the peace deal.

Just as important, inside the country, a powerful social movement arose, supporting the peace agreement. Colombian citizens filled the main public squares, vowing to remain there until a new agreement was reached. I will never forget leaving the presidential palace late one night and walking around a huge encampment with hundreds of tents set up outside the presidential palace by citizens who had come from all over the country to ensure that the historic opportunity would not be lost. The encampment was buzzing with life and energy.

It constituted a genuine third-side swarm of the conflict—from both inside and outside the country. Following an intensive set of listening sessions with those who had opposed the agreement and another round of challenging re-negotiations with the FARC leaders, the government and the FARC signed a revised agreement in the Teatro Colón in Bogotá on November 12, 2016. The agreement was then taken to the Colombian congress for ratification. That time, to widespread relief, the effort was successful.

Over the ensuing months, the guerrilla army proceeded to do what no one had believed possible: under the supervision of the United Nations, they gathered together in camps and laid down their weapons. Some of the leaders began to enter politics. While the political conflict continued, the war ended. The peace process was messy, slow, and uneven, as such processes often are. That is the nature of transformation.

## SWARM IS THE NEXT FRONTIER

"Six years ago," President Santos began his Nobel Prize acceptance speech in Oslo a few weeks after the signing of the final peace agreement, "it was hard for we Colombians to imagine an end to a war that had lasted half a century. To the great majority of us, peace seemed an impossible dream—and for good reason. Very few of us—hardly anybody—could recall a memory of a country at peace.

"Today, after six years of serious and often intense, difficult negotiations, I stand before you and the world and announce with deep humility and gratitude that the Colombian people, with assistance from our friends around the world, are turning the impossible into the possible."

An extraordinary swarm by the community, inside and outside, had succeeded in ending one of the longest-running wars in the world. In these troubled times, we are so focused on what *doesn't* work that we often neglect to pay attention to what *does*. We can now permit ourselves to ask an audacious question: If we humans can begin to end war in *one* of the world's hemispheres, why not one day in *both* hemispheres?

As my old colleague Kenneth Boulding liked to say, *"What exists is possible."*

If we are to succeed in transforming today's conflicts, there is no more important power for us to activate than to swarm. Swarming is the culmination of the path to possible. It combines all our natural powers, harnessing our full human potential. If the path begins in the quiet of a pause, it ends in the noisy, creative collaboration of a swarm.

Swarming is the patient, persistent application of critical mass. It is radical collaboration in action. Swarming pools access, credibility, and trust—*ACT*—to build a winning coalition. It represents the full activation of our social immune system.

Swarming is the next frontier—the work I personally find most exciting. Our challenge today is to re-create, in today's very different conditions, the strong third side that I believe enabled our distant ancestors to survive and thrive so that we can be here today. We must learn to tap into the creative power of the community around us.

There is an old Irish saying, "Is this a private fight, or can anyone get in?" Truthfully, there are few private fights these days, if only because destructive conflicts directly and indirectly affect the people who surround the parties. Because we are affected, each of us rightfully "can get in"—in a curious, compassionate, and constructive way. We can assume "response-ability"—the ability to respond.

Whenever I hear that a particular conflict is impossible, I wonder: Have we really tried? In other words, have we swarmed it? Have we applied our collective intelligence and influence on a scale that is commensurate with the difficulty of the conflict?

"When spider webs unite, they can halt even a lion," goes the Ethiopian proverb that begins this chapter. When we are able to unite as thirdsiders, even the most difficult conflicts at work, at home, or in the world can eventually yield to the power of all of us working together.

# A WORLD OF POSSIBILITIES

*Hope is not a lottery ticket you can sit on the sofa
and clutch, feeling lucky. It is an axe you break
down doors with in an emergency. . . . To hope is to
give yourself to the future—and that commitment to
the future is what makes the present inhabitable.*
—Rebecca Solnit

"Has anyone here ever done a plank before?"

My daughter, Gabi, aged sixteen, was standing on a big stage asking this question to an audience of several thousand people at a TEDx event in Copley Symphony Hall in San Diego. The plank, as you may know, is an abdominal exercise where you prop yourself up horizontally on your forearms and toes and then hold your body straight like a plank of wood. My family and I sat in the audience as Gabi proceeded to tell everyone her story:

"Up until the day I was born, my parents were expecting a perfectly normal baby girl; then I popped out. You see, no one, not even the doctors, realized that I was one of the one out of forty thousand babies born with VATER syndrome every year. For me individually, it affects my spine, spinal cord, legs, feet, and a number of my organs. That's a lot of problems for a tiny baby. The doctors weren't sure if I'd ever walk or even live, and, well, . . . here I am!

"In order to fix all those problems, I had to undergo about fifteen major surgeries, casts on both my legs and my back for eleven years, physical therapy every single day for years, and literally hundreds and hundreds of doctor's appointments.

"My philosophy ever since I was little was basically: Complaining about my situation wasn't going to help, so what was the point? I didn't care that I was smaller or couldn't run as fast as any of my friends, and neither did anyone else. The way I saw it, the only thing wrong was when people thought I couldn't do something.

"[When I was fifteen], I was trying out for my school's volleyball team. When everyone else had to go out for a run, I explained to my coach that I couldn't since I was born without calf muscles and, let's be honest, running isn't really my thing. So she told me to get on the ground and do the plank for as long as I could.

"When everyone else came back, it had been twelve minutes. When I saw everyone else's surprise that I had held it that long, I instantly thought:

*Oooh, Guinness World Record.*

Everyone laughed.

"That day I went home and applied for the record."

I remembered the evening when Gabi came home and told us about her plan with a tone of excitement and determination in her voice. My wife and I were surprised but also not surprised, as we knew that Gabi had long entertained a dream to set a world record. We wanted to support her in achieving whatever dream she had. Privately, however, we worried about the disappointment she might feel if she did not achieve what seemed like an impossible goal.

Gabi waited two months until after another major surgery to begin her training. Weeks went by as she practiced on her bedroom floor after school, distracting herself with YouTube videos and with her puppy, Mia, by her side. The world record at the time stood at forty minutes, one second. In her first session, Gabi held the plank for a full twenty minutes. She then gradually moved upward incrementally. She decided that she would try to break the record on her sixteenth birthday and asked my wife and me to make the necessary preparations.

Finally, the big day arrived. My wife and I awoke and felt more nervous than I think we had ever felt before. But Gabi seemed calm and excited about the event. At her birthday party, her friends and family gathered around to watch her make the attempt.

Gabi got into position and, as we all looked on, held the plank position for an astonishing thirty minutes. But then she hit a wall of discomfort. She was clearly hurting, and her arms started to tremble a little. Her tears began to fall on the mat. My heart was in my stomach.

Thankfully, Gabi's friend Leah and her sisters stepped in and began to sing and entertain her in order to distract her from the pain. As the minutes slowly went by, everyone started to clap, and my friend Robert played the piano with energetic verve. The power of community was palpable.

Just after forty minutes, Gabi broke the world record. We all broke into applause. I felt an overwhelming sense of relief and wonder.

And then, unbelievably, she continued. Finally, at an hour and twenty minutes, double the world record, she asked me to ease her out of her rigid position onto the mat. She proceeded to eat her birthday cake with her friends just as any other sixteen-year-old would.

The following Tuesday, she was invited onto the national television show *Good Morning America* in New York City, where a Guinness official presented her with the world record award.

"It felt amazing," Gabi told the audience in San Diego, "especially to know that all those people—including my family, who had given me a funny look when I said I wanted to break the world record for planking—now knew I had done it. Whenever I would get those kind of odd looks, I would just think to myself: everything is impossible until someone has done it."

I smiled, hearing echoes of my grandfather Eddie and his motto "Wanted: a Hard Job." Gabi was a *possibilist*, too.

I felt awed and moved to tears as a father to witness her persistence, courage, and sheer grit. There is no one I've learned more from about the spirit of possibility. Witnessing her accomplish the seemingly impossible renewed my faith in the indomitable human spirit to open up new possibilities where at first none may seem evident.

Where others saw obstacles, Gabi saw opportunities.

In her words:

*"I see it differently, and that makes all the difference."*

## HUMANITY NEEDS *POSSIBILISTS*

We are all born as *possibilists*. I need only observe my new baby grandson, Diego. He spends his day exploring and marveling at all the possibilities around him—whether a plant to touch or a pot to bang. I look at the joy in his eyes. Watching him reminds me that we don't need to learn to be a possibilist. It is innate. We just need to turn the switch back on.

More than ever, humanity needs *possibilists* to transform conflicts of all kinds—personal, professional, and political.

Destructive conflict seems to be increasing all around us, threatening everything we hold dear—from our families to our democracy, from our workplaces to our world.

We live in an age of accelerating change and disruption—in the economy and the environment, in politics and society. New technologies from genetic engineering to artificial intelligence are changing the fundamental patterns of our lives, including what it means to be human. More change naturally brings more conflict.

In this last year, as I have been writing this book, I have watched with mounting concern as the world slides back into the age of cold war among the great powers that I remember all too well from my childhood and early adulthood. The war in Ukraine has brought Russia and the United States—and its NATO allies—dangerously close to nuclear conflict again. Meanwhile, in Asia, the United States and China are plunging deeper into tensions around the future of Taiwan with a heightened risk of hostilities that, if we are not careful, could escalate into a showdown with unthinkable consequences.

We need *possibilists* to transform these destructive conflicts—and to stop wars everywhere.

In relation to the natural world, too, political stalemates often get in the way of protecting the environment we want for ourselves and our children. At a time that new technologies promise abundant clean energy, we are facing the grave impacts of our energy habits on the climate around us. Extreme weather increasingly assails communities everywhere.

We need *possibilists* to help us transform political and economic conflicts so that we can make a speedy transition to clean energy for all.

Meanwhile, political polarization is increasing around the world. Here, too, we need possibilists to transform our toxic politics.

As I was finishing this book, I went for a walk around the lake in front of my home with my old friend Mark Gerzon. He and I have worked closely together over the years on bridging the political divide in the United States.

"I read your book," Mark said. "I loved it, but it leaves me with one question. You are inviting us to make a choice. When we choose the balcony, the bridge, and the third side, what are we leaving behind?"

"That's a really good question," I replied. "Things usually become clearer if you know their opposite. What do you see?"

"Take a look at some of the gutter politics in our country today—the name-calling and demonizing of the other. Going to the *balcony* is the opposite of going to the *gutter*."

"You're right. What else do you see?"

"Right now, we're destroying the relationships that used to connect us. We're *burning* bridges."

"That's it. *Building* bridges is the opposite of *burning* them."

"And it is getting purely adversarial with no common ground," Mark added. "We're forcing everyone to take one side or the other."

"That's true. Reducing everything to *two sides* is like a straitjacket. It leaves us no room to breathe. The opposite is to make room for the *third side*—the side of the whole."

"So," Mark concluded, "to sum up, the choice we face today is: Do we go to the gutter or do we go to the balcony? Do we burn bridges or do we build them? Do we force everyone to take sides or do we make room for the third side?"

"That's it, Mark. The key word is *choice*."

If I were an anthropologist of the future looking back, I would see this era as one of the great transitional ages of humanity, just as significant as—and perhaps more than—the agricultural and industrial revolutions. I would take note not only of the enormous dangers but of the equally enormous opportunities.

Thanks to our collective intelligence and cooperation, we live in a time of extraordinary potential. Although our world today is burdened by unacceptably high levels of inequity, poverty, and war, the truth is that thanks to the knowledge revolution, there is enough to meet everyone's needs. We are fast learning how to end hunger, how to cure previously incurable diseases, and how to use clean energy to fuel our activities without destroying our environment. We are even learning how to prevent wars.

We live in a world of possibilities, some quite hopeful and some quite scary. In the end, our future depends on us. There is virtually no problem we cannot address and no opportunity we cannot realize *if only* we can work together. What stands in the way is destructive conflict. Fortunately, what is created by us can be changed by us. *The choice is ours.*

## THE PATH TO POSSIBLE

It has been almost a half century since I arrived at Harvard and began to study anthropology and negotiation to find answers to the question that had absorbed me ever since I was a boy: How can we humans learn to deal with our deepest differences without destroying all that we hold dear?

Since then, I have had the chance, in a multitude of difficult settings around the world, to test out what works and what doesn't. My experiences have amply confirmed my boyhood hunch that there is a better way—a much better way—to deal with our differences. And that way is available to each of us at any time. That way is the *path to possible*.

Here's the secret: The problem isn't conflict. Conflict is natural. We actually need more conflict, not less—if we are to learn, grow, and evolve. The problem is the destructive way we handle conflict—destroying relationships, lives, and resources. Thankfully we have a choice.

We can't end conflict, but we can *embrace it and transform it*. We can *choose* to handle conflict *constructively*, using our innate curiosity, creativity, and collaboration. While conflict can clearly bring out the *worst* in us, it can also bring out the *best* in us—*if* we unlock our full potential. We are capable of so much more than we may think. The key is to "see it differently."

This book, as you may recall, started with a challenge from my friend Jim Collins as we were hiking up a mountain near our homes. Jim asked me to sum up in a single sentence everything I'd learned about negotiating difficult conflicts that could be of use in these troubled times. After a month or two of rumination, on our next hike, I offered him an answer:

*"The path to possible is to go to the balcony, build a golden bridge, and engage the third side—all together, all at once."*

Throughout this book, we have taken a walk on this path. We

started with the balcony, which unlocks the potential that exists *within* us. The balcony focuses on *I*—the self. We proceeded with the bridge, which unlocks the potential that exists *between* us. The bridge focuses on *You*—the other. We ended with the third side, which unlocks the potential that exists *around* us. The third side focuses on *Us*—the community. In this way, we unleash our full human potential to deal with our deepest differences.

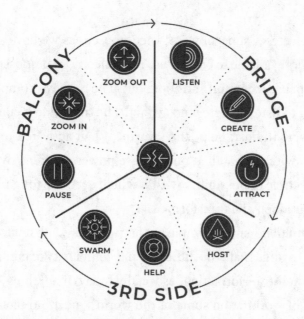

Perhaps my biggest realization since writing *Getting to Yes* forty years ago has been that building a bridge *between* parties in conflict, while necessary, is not sufficient. The bridge is the middle part of the path, but what is a middle without a beginning and an end? If we are having so much trouble dealing with conflicts, it is often because we skip over the necessary work on the *I*—the balcony—and neglect to seek adequate help from the *Us*—the third side. If we want to transform the conflicts of today, we need to address the *I*, the *You*, and the *Us*. The bridge needs to be supported by the balcony and the third side.

As you face the conflicts around you, as either a party or a third-sider, I hope that the balcony, the bridge, and the third side will become your friends and allies, part of your everyday vocabulary. They are our innate human "superpowers"—natural capacities that each of us can activate to achieve the three victories on the path to possible.

Each of these "superpowers" is composed, as we have seen, of three powers available to each of us. The balcony is composed of the powers to pause, zoom in, and zoom out. The bridge is composed of the powers to listen, create, and attract. The third side is composed of the powers to host, help, and swarm. When activated together, like lights switched on all at once, these powers create a dynamic, synergetic circle of possibility within which even the toughest conflicts can gradually be transformed.

The path to possible is simple but far from easy. I do not for a moment wish to understate the difficulty and complexity of human conflicts and their transformation, especially today. If anything, almost fifty years of working on some of the world's most intractable and dangerous conflicts have taught me realism, humility, and patience.

While the task of the *possibilist* may be hard, I have found no work more rewarding. It is fulfilling to help people who are stuck—oneself included. When people bridge the chasms that separate them from their adversaries, when enemies reconcile in an unexpected fashion, I feel deep elation. The greater the initial differences, the greater the sense of wholeness and satisfaction when a conflict is transformed.

This work has often brought me the kind of joy I feel when climbing the high mountains that I love. And along the way, I have found that the companions I have met have inspired and sustained me. Even when the mission has seemed impossible, the company has always been good.

We are coming to the end of the imaginary walk on the path to possible that I invited you to take with me in the very first chapter. My single purpose in writing this book is to pass on what I've learned about the art of finding new possibilities in difficult situations. More than a *method*, the path to possible is a *mindset*. It is a *way of living in these challenging times*—needed now more than ever.

If I have one request, it is that you try out this *possibilist* mindset and see how it works for you. Adapt it to your needs. If you find it helpful, please pass it on in whatever way suits you so that others may benefit, too. That's how, step by step, person by person, we can reclaim our power, fulfill our potential, and begin to create the world we want.

*The path to possible is how we survive—and thrive—in this age of conflict.*

## MY DREAM

Fifty years ago, a Tibetan lama came to Colorado and brought with him from his homeland high in the snowy Himalayas an ancient prophecy that was more than a thousand years old. The prophecy was this: Sometime in the distant future, the entire world would find itself in peril. In that moment, there would arise in the places of danger a new kind of warrior.

These brave warriors would be armed with two special weapons. The first is compassion. The second is insight—understanding the connections that link us all.

Here is my dream for the coming generations:

I dream of a world of brave, compassionate, and insightful *possibilists* who fearlessly lean into challenging conflicts and listen for new possibilities.

I dream of a world where each one of us develops our natural ability to go to the balcony, build a golden bridge, and engage the third side—at home, at work, and in the larger community.

I dream of a world where we unlock our full human potential to deal with our differences constructively.

I dream of a world where each of us exercises the fundamental choice we have, at any moment, to *transform* our conflicts so that we can learn, grow, and evolve.

I dream of an anthropologist a thousand years from now who will look back and see the coming generations as the ones who seized their evolutionary chance and exercised their innate human capacities to create a future that works for everyone.

Where conflicts prove truly difficult, I dream of teams of courageous *possibilists* swarming them, animated by a spirit of humble audacity.

I dream of an emerging community, a worldwide *League of Possibilists*, learning from and inspiring one another.

I have a hunch that you might be one of them.

So I ask you: *If not you, who? If not now, when?*

# ACKNOWLEDGMENTS

In this book, I have sought to distill lessons I have learned over a lifetime of immersion in the world's conflicts—lessons I have learned *from* and *with* others—mentors, colleagues, clients, and parties in conflict. To each and all of them, I feel deeply grateful.

Collaboration and community—central themes in this book—have been vitally important in the process of writing. It has been a collaborative effort that has benefited greatly from the support and suggestions of a community of colleagues. For all that is of value here, credit is shared with them while all failings in formulation and expression are mine alone.

As I recounted in chapters 1 and 2, the idea for this book began with a hike in the mountains near my home with my friend Jim Collins. I am forever grateful to Jim for asking the question that inspired me to write this book and for generously contributing an eloquent foreword.

Since this book sums up a life's work, let me begin by thanking my first teachers in the two fields that led me into this work. Triloki

Pandey surprised me with a comment at the end of my first essay in his undergraduate course at the University of California: "You must become an anthropologist!" Loki's passion about the field was positively contagious.

Roger Fisher generously initiated me into the theory and practice of mediation and negotiation. He was an iconic *possibilist*. Undaunted by any conflict, he would cheerfully pound out a practical proposal on his trusty old Smith-Corona typewriter with a twinkle in his blue eyes. I am profoundly indebted to Roger for setting me on the path I have been on ever since.

The Program on Negotiation at Harvard Law School, which I had the privilege to help found, has been my intellectual community from the very beginning. Frank Sander, Howard Raiffa, Thomas Schelling, Lawrence Susskind, Jeffrey Rubin, Deborah Kolb, Jeswald Salacuse, and Robert Mnookin were some of the giants in the field from whom I had the pleasure to learn as colleagues. David Lax, James Sebenius, and Bruce Patton were peers from whose friendship and ideas I benefited greatly.

The core lessons in this book I learned from experiences in conflicts around the world. I would like to thank my old friend Stephen Goldberg, a master arbitrator, for introducing me to the coal mines of Kentucky, offering me my first real work as a mediator in a complex dispute. I am grateful to former president Jimmy Carter— a true *possibilist* and selfless peacemaker—for entrusting me with assignments in Venezuela and elsewhere. For my experiences in Colombia, I am indebted to former president Juan Manuel Santos, another dedicated and courageous *possibilist* who never lost hope even in the darkest of times.

Stories are the core of this book, essential for communicating core lessons. For the stories in which they played key roles, I would like to thank Francisco Diez, Dennis Rodman, Dwight Manley, Abilio and Geyze Diniz, Ana Maria Diniz, Sergio Jaramillo, Enrique Santos, Jonathan Powell, Luis Carlos Villegas and his daughter Juliana, Glyn Ford, and Robert Carlin. For personal stories, I would like to thank my family: Lizanne Ury, Melvin Gray, Claire Lieberman Goulding, Lynne Gray Garman, Paul Gray, Thomas Modern, and Gabi Ury.

This book benefited greatly from my anthropological visits and interviews. I would like to register my deep gratitude to the Kua and Ju/'hoansi communities of the Kalahari and to the Semai community of Malaysia, whose elders shared their timeless wisdom with me. From them, I came to appreciate the true power of the third side.

Without the support of friends, a book would be hard to write. I owe heartfelt thanks for their warm encouragement and valuable feedback to my close friends David Friedman, Robert Gass, David Baum, David Lax, Jill Bolte Taylor, Mark Gerzon, Anne Silver, Paula Rocha, Josh Weiss, Alex Chade, Nicholas Dunlop, Carolyn Buck-Luce, and Rob Evans.

I would like to express my immense gratitude to my old friends Marcel Arsenault and Cynda Collins Arsenault, with whom I share a common passion for creating a world without war. Their generous support and long-term philanthropic backing for my conflict work through One Earth Future Foundation made this book possible. I would also like to acknowledge my colleague Jon Bellish, OEF's executive director and chief operating officer, who played a key role in the realization of this work and the incubation of side3, a nonprofit intended to support the work of *possibilists*.

I had the good fortune of having an extraordinary team who supported the writing process from start to finish. I feel deeply indebted to Gia Medeiros, who, ever creative and positive, skillfully led the process, shaped the book's framing, and offered valuable edits with every successive draft. Haven Iverson, savvy and insightful, brought her talented editorial eye and ear to every page and helped the stories come alive. Daniel Medina, smart and enthusiastic, was unfailingly supportive with suggestions and daily encouragement. He is responsible for the end notes, aided by the careful eye of Olivia Grotenhuis.

Rick Bolton and Kae Penner-Howell served as advisors, offering invaluable ideas on how to frame the message of the book. Jessica Palladino and Kristin Weber designed the elegant book graphic and creative icons that provide a map of the path to possible.

While the book was in gestation, it benefited greatly from insightful feedback from Liza Hester, my close colleague of seven years, as well as from David Lander and Ian Scott. Other members of our side3 team joined in with helpful comments—including Rob Sokol, Olivia Grotenhuis, Mary Denmon, and Hildy Kane. Hildy also provided essential administrative support. To each of them, I offer my profound appreciation.

This book benefited from other careful readers who were generous with their constructive suggestions. I am much indebted to Aditi Junjea, Alexis Sanford, Ameya Kilara, Amy Leventhal, Christian Modern, Claire Hajaj, Claudia Maffettone, Cody Smith, Diane Tompkins, JB Lyon, Kim Syman, Jonathan Powell, Lior Frankiensztajn, Lizanne Ury, Pete Dignan, Rick Bolton, Sameer Kassan, Tom Bassett, and Victoria Keziah.

My friend Jim Levine has been a consummate agent and valuable advisor throughout every stage of the process. I feel very lucky to have Hollis Heimbouch as my editor at HarperCollins; she embraced the book from its inception and offered wise counsel. James Neidhardt skillfully guided it through the publishing process.

Finally, I owe a deep debt of gratitude to my parents and grandparents and to the loving support of my immediate family—Lizanne and our children, Christian, Thomas, and Gabi. Family means more to me than I can possibly express. During the time of writing this book, I also had the great fortune to become a grandfather. I affectionately call my new grandson Diego "my new boss." I fervently hope this work will serve his generation around the world.

I feel extraordinarily grateful to each member of this goodhearted and talented community, for they are the ones who made *Possible* possible.

*William Ury*
Boulder, Colorado
July 2023

# NOTES

## CHAPTER 1: THE PATH TO POSSIBLE

1  *We are continually*: This quote is attributed to the anthropologist Margaret Mead (quoted material extracted from a quote compendium). See Quote Park, https://quotepark.com/quotes/702384 -margaret-mead-we-are-continually-faced-with-great-opportunities/.

6  Unthinkable as the prospect: "Two in Five Americans Say a Civil War Is at Least Somewhat Likely in the Next Decade," YouGov, August 20, 2022, https://today.yougov.com/topics/politics/articles -reports/2022/08/26/two-in-five-americans-civil-war-somewhat -likely; "Survey Finds Alarming Trend Toward Political Violence," UC Davis Violence Prevention Research Program, July 20, 2022, https://health.ucdavis.edu/news/headlines/survey-finds-alarming -trend-toward-political-violence/2022/07.

7  For the first time: For more on global trends in conflict, see "A New Era of Conflict and Violence," United Nations, https://www.un .org/en/un75/new-era-conflict-and-violence#:~:text=ENTRENCHED %20CONFLICT,criminal%2C%20and%20international%20ter rorist%20groups.

11  Transforming conflict is: For further reading, I recommend John Paul Lederach, *The Little Book of Conflict Transformation:Clear Articulation of the Guiding Principles by a Pioneer in the Field* (New

York: Good Books, 2003); Georg Simmel, *Conflict and the Web of Group Affiliation* (Glencoe, IL: The Free Press, 1955); and Lewis Coser, *The Functions of Social Conflict* (New York: The Free Press, 1956).

13  Hundreds of thousands: "Hay Futuro, Si Hay Verdad. Hallazgos y Recomendaciones para la No Repetición." *Comisión de la Verdad* 127 (August 2022), https://www.comisiondelaverdad.co/hallazgos -y-recomendaciones.

16  Thirty years ago: For more about the Semai, see Clayton A. Robarchek and Carole J. Robarchek, "Cultures of War and Peace: A Comparative Study of Waorani and Semai," in *Aggression and Peacefulness in Humans and Other Primates*, edited by James Silverberg and J. Patrick Gray (New York: Oxford University Press, 1992), 189–213.

17  Some years ago: I highly recommend Jim Collins's books on leadership, which you can browse through here: https://www.jimcollins .com/books.html.

## CHAPTER 2: THE THREE VICTORIES

21  *The Possible's slow fuse*: To read the full poem, see Emily Dickinson, "The Gleam of an Heroic Act," in *The Complete Poems of Emily Dickinson* (Boston: Little, Brown, 1960), 688.

24  "We had 700 days": "Brokering Peace," John F. Kennedy Presidential Library and Museum, https://www.jfklibrary.org/events-and -awards/forums/past-forums/transcripts/brokering-peace.

29  One of my favorite teaching: There are a few different versions of the seventeen-camel story. The first known written version has been attributed to the Iranian philosopher Mulla Muhammad Mahdi Naraqi. See Pierre Ageron, "Le Partage des dix-sept chameaux et autres exploits arithmétiques attribués à l'imam 'Alî: Mouvance et circulation de récits de la tradition musulmane chiite," *Société Mathématique de France* 19, no. 1 (2013): 13–14.

32  "It won't happen!": Donald J. Trump (@realDonaldTrump), Twitter, January 2, 2017, https://twitter.com/realDonaldTrump/status/81605 7920223846400?lang=en.

32  Expert estimates of the risk: Nicholas Kristof, "Slouching Toward War with North Korea," *New York Times*, November 4, 2017, https://www.nytimes.com/2017/11/04/opinion/sunday/nuclear-war-north-korea.html.

32  The expected consequences: The Congressional Research Service published a document in October 2017 noting that "hundreds of thousands of South Koreans would die in the first few hours of combat . . . and if this war would escalate to the nuclear level, then you are looking at tens of millions of casualties." See "The North Korean Nuclear Challenge: Military Options and Issues for Congress," Congressional Research Service, November 2017, https://sgp.fas.org/crs/nuke/R44994.pdf.

34  The leader of the most: Tania Branigan, "North Korea Executes Kim Jong-Un's Uncle as 'Traitor,'" *Guardian*, December 13, 2013, https://www.theguardian.com/world/2013/dec/13/north-korea-executes-kim-jong-un-uncle-jang-song-thaek; Merrit Kennedy, "Kim Jong Un's Half-Brother Reportedly Dies in Kuala Lumpur," NPR, February 14, 2017, https://www.npr.org/sections/thetwo-way/2017/02/14/515170332/kim-jong-uns-half-brother-reportedly-dies-in-kuala-lumpur.

34  The casualties were staggering: "New Evidence on North Korean War Losses," The Wilson Center, August 1, 2001, https://www.wilsoncenter.org/article/new-evidence-north-korean-war-losses.

## FIRST VICTORY: GO TO THE BALCONY

40  More than 215,000: "Sistema de Información de Eventos de Violencia del Conflicto Armado Colombiano," Centro Nacional de Memoria Histórica y Observatorio de Memoria y Conflicto, https://micrositios.centrodememoriahistorica.gov.co/observatorio/sievcac/.

40  I had just arrived: If you want to learn more about my work in Venezuela with Francisco Diez and the Carter Center, which I reference throughout this book, I suggest this report: *The Carter Center and the Peacebuilding Process in Venezuela: June 2002–February 2005*, The Carter Center, February 2005, https://www.cartercenter

.org/resources/pdfs/news/peace_publications/americas/peace building_venzuela_feb05.pdf. For a more in-depth read, I recommend this excellent book: Jennifer McCoy and Francisco Diez, *International Mediation in Venezuela* (Washington, DC: The United States Institute of Peace, 2011).

44 "Señor Presidente": A Christmas truce had been proposed the year before but had been rejected by the opposition. See "Venezuelan Strikers Reject a Truce Call," *New York Times*, December 24, 2002, https://www.nytimes.com/2002/12/24/world/venezuelan-strikers -reject-a-truce-call.html.

## CHAPTER 3: PAUSE

49 *Do you have*: Lao Tzu, *Tao Te Ching*, translated by Stephen Mitchell (New York: Harper Perennial, 1991), 63.

50 "It felt like you": "Recollections of Vadim Orlov (USSR Submarine B-59), 'We Will Sink Them All, but We Will Not Disgrace Our Navy,'" National Security Archive, The George Washington University, January 1, 2002, https://nsarchive.gwu.edu/document/29066 -7-recollections-vadim-orlov-ussr-submarine-b-59-we-will-sink -them-all-we-will-not.

50 "Arm the nuclear torpedo!": The conversation of the B-59 crew is reconstructed from Svetlana V. Savranskaya, "New Sources on the Role of Soviet Submarines in the Cuban Missile Crisis," *Journal of Strategic Studies* 28, no. 2 (2005): 233–59, https://doi .org/10.1080/01402390500088312; Marion Lloyd, "Soviets Close to Using A-bomb in 1962 Crisis, Forum Is Told," *Boston Globe*, October 13, 2002; Robert Krulwich, "You (and Almost Everyone You Know) Owe Your Life to This Man," *National Geographic*, March 25, 2016, https://www.nationalgeographic.com/culture /article/you-and-almost-everyone-you-know-owe-your-life-to -this-man.

51 "If that torpedo had": Gary Marx, "Old Foes Recall '62 Scare," *Chicago Tribune*, October 14, 2002, https://www.chicagotribune .com/news/ct-xpm-2002-10-14-0210140181-story.html.

51 "Arkhipov stood out": Ryurik Ketov in "Secrets of the Dead: The Man Who Saved the World," PBS, video, 45:15, premiered Octo-

ber 22, 2012, https://www.pbs.org/wnet/secrets/the-man-who
-saved-the-world-about-this-episode/871/.

54  When we feel threatened: To read about the science behind
    fear, see Arash Javanbakht and Linda Saab, "What Happens in the
    Brain When We Feel Fear," *Smithsonian Magazine*, October 27, 2017,
    https://www.smithsonianmag.com/science-nature/what-happens
    -brain-feel-fear-180966992//.

55  "Speak when you are": This quote is attributed to Ambrose Bierce
    (quoted material extracted from a quote compendium). See Good-
    reads, https://www.goodreads.com/quotes/9909-speak-when-you
    -are-angry-and-you-will-make-the.

55  In one of my favorite: You can read a version of the myth here: "Her-
    cules and Pallas," Original Sources, https://www.originalsources
    .com/Document.aspx?DocID=QN9XAAIDT2VCV1Z.

56  In May 1997: My participation in the negotiations was under
    the auspices of the Strengthening Democratic Institutions Proj-
    ect (SDI) at Harvard and the Conflict Management Group. You
    can read more about it here: "BCSIA Annual Report, 1996–1997:
    Strengthening Democratic Institutions Project," Harvard Ken-
    nedy School Belfer Center for Science and International Affairs,
    https://www.belfercenter.org/publication/bcsia-annual-report
    -1996-1997.

57  The war had claimed: "Official: Chechen Wars Killed 300,000,"
    Aljazeera, June 26, 2005, https://www.aljazeera.com/news/2005/6
    /26/official-chechen-wars-killed-300000.

58  The room was hot: For a lively description of the negotiations, see
    Doug Stewart, "Expand the Pie Before You Divvy It Up," *Smithsonian
    Magazine*, November 1, 1997, https://www.williamury.com/smith
    sonian/.

59  Many of the intractable: For further reading on collective trauma,
    I recommend my friend Thomas Hübl's books, especially *Healing
    Collective Trauma: A Process for Integrating Our Intergenerational
    and Cultural Wounds*, co-authored with Julie Jordan Avritt (Boulder,
    CO: Sounds True, 2020). I also recommend Bessel van der Kok's
    book *The Body Keeps the Score: Brain, Mind, and Body in the Healing
    of Trauma* (New York: Penguin Books, 2015).

60  Breathing decreases the level: On the effects of breathing on stress,

see Christopher Bergland, "Diaphragmatic Breathing Exercises and Your Vagus Nerve," *Psychology Today*, May 16, 2017, https://www .psychologytoday.com/us/blog/the-athletes-way/201705/diaphrag matic-breathing-exercises-and-your-vagus-nerve.

60 "When a person reacts": For further understanding of the ways in which we can help control our natural reactions, I highly recommend Dr. Jill Bolte Taylor's book *Whole Brain Living: The Anatomy of Choice and the Four Characters That Drive Our Life* (Carlsbad, CA: Hay House, 2021.)

61 This has been confirmed: Jared Curhan et al., "Silence Is Golden: Silence, Deliberative Mindset, and Value Creation in Negotiation," *Journal of Applied Psychology* 107, no. 1 (2022): 78–94, https://doi .org/10.1037/apl0000877.

61 *the ultimate power*: C. W. Headley, "MIT Researchers Say This Is the Ultimate Power Move in a Negotiation," *Ladders*, March 29, 2021, https://www.theladders.com/career-advice/mit-researchers -say-this-is-the-ultimate-power-move-in-a-negotiation.

61 "Observe all men": This quote is on Brainy Quote at https://www .brainyquote.com/quotes/benjamin_franklin_151641.

63 In between the state: Daniel J. Siegel, *The Developing Mind: How Relationships and the Brain Interact to Shape Who We Are* (New York: The Guilford Press, 2012).

71 "The cell is": Nelson Mandela, *Conversations with Myself* (New York: Macmillan, 2010), 7.

72 In that little cell: Nelson Mandela, *Long Walk to Freedom* (New York: Little, Brown, 1994).

## CHAPTER 4: ZOOM IN

73 *Who looks inside*: This quote is attributed to Carl Jung (quoted material extracted from a quote compendium). See Goodreads, https://www.goodreads.com/quotes/492843-who-looks-outside -dreams-who-looks-inside-awakes.

77 This story was inspired: Mary Parker Follett, *Dynamic Administration: The Collected Papers of Mary Parker Follett*, edited by Henry Metcalf and Lyndall Urwick (London: Harper, 1942).

77 "prophet of management": "Wise Words from an (Almost) Un-

known Guru," BBC, December 18, 2013, https://www.bbc.com/news
/business-25428092.

79  In January 2000: For an analysis of the negotiations, see: Konrad
    Huber, *The HDC in Aceh: Promises and Pitfalls of NGO Mediation
    and Implementation*, Policy Studies 9 (Washington, DC: East-West
    Center, 2004).

81  Five years later: James K. Sebenius and Alex Green, "Everything
    or Nothing: Martti Ahtisaari and the Aceh Negotiations," HBS Case
    Collection, Harvard Business School, December 2010, https://www
    .hbs.edu/faculty/Pages/item.aspx?num=39807.

82  Elections were held: "Resounding Victory for Democracy in
    Aceh," Tapol, January 14, 2014, https://www.tapol.org/briefings/re
    sounding-victory-democracy-aceh.

84  "perhaps the biggest": Joe Leahy and Samantha Pearson, "Brazil's
    Billionaire Baker Who Came of Age in Captivity," *Financial Times*,
    July 4, 2011, https://www.financialexpress.com/archive/brazils-bill
    ionaire-baker-who-came-of-age-in-captivity/812359/.

84  The clash centered on: For more on the dispute, see Samantha
    Pearson, "Brazil Tycoon Closes Lid on Supermarket Feud," *Financial
    Times*, September 6, 2013, https://www.ft.com/content/9e9f8280
    -175e-11e3-bced-00144feabdc0.

91  Santa Rita had: For more about Santa Rita, see "The Story of
    Saint Rita of Cascia," The National Shrine of Santa Rita of Cascia,
    https://www.saintritashrine.org/saint-rita-of-cascia.

## CHAPTER 5: ZOOM OUT

93  *The garden of the world*: This quote is attributed to Jalāl al-Dīn
    Rūmī (quoted material extracted from a quote compendium). See
    Goodreads, https://www.goodreads.com/quotes/472665-the-garden
    -of-the-world-has-no-limits-except-in.

94  Mike Johnson: The names in this story, including "Mike Johnson,"
    are pseudonyms to protect the individuals' identities.

97  As we learned: That negotiation was the topic of my doctoral the-
    sis in anthropology; see *Talk Out or Walk Out: The Role and Control
    of Conflict in a Kentucky Coal Mine*, Harvard University Graduate
    School of Arts and Sciences, July 22, 1982.

106 wrote a report: William Langer Ury and Richard Smoke, *Beyond the Hotline: Controlling a Nuclear Crisis: A Report to the United States Arms Control and Disarmament Agency by the Nuclear Negotiation Project* (Cambridge, MA: Nuclear Negotiation Project, Harvard Law School, 1984). See also a short follow-up article I wrote in 1985: William Ury, "Beyond the Hotline," *Washington Post*, February 24, 1985, https://www.washingtonpost.com/archive/lifestyle/magazine/1985/02/24/beyond-the-hotline/9eac0f91-73a4-495c-937da7235f8bc1e0/.

108 The misfire of a: William Ury, *Beyond the Hotline: How Crisis Control Can Prevent Nuclear War* (Boston: Penguin Books, 1986).

108 In March 1983: Ronald Reagan, "'Evil Empire Speech,' March 8, 1983," Voices of Democracy, The U.S. Oratory Project, https://voicesofdemocracy.umd.edu/reagan-evil-empire-speech-text/.

109 Six months later: Thom Patterson, "The Downing of Flight 007: 30 Years Later, a Cold War Tragedy Still Seems Surreal," CNN, August 31, 2013, https://www.cnn.com/2013/08/31/us/kal-fight-007-anniversary/index.html.

109 *Parade* magazine invited: William L. Ury, "What We Can Do to Avert Nuclear War," *Parade*, March 25, 1984, 15–16.

110 The film, watched by: "All-Time 100 TV Shows," *Time*, https://time.com/collection/all-time-100-tv-shows/.

110 "It's very effective": "Diary Entry—Monday, October 10, 1983," Ronald Reagan Presidential Foundation & Institute, https://www.reaganfoundation.org/ronald-reagan/white-house-diaries/diary-entry-10101983/.

110 "A nuclear war cannot": "Joint Soviet–United States Statement on the Summit Meeting in Geneva," Ronald Reagan Presidential Library & Museum, November 21, 1985, https://www.reaganlibrary.gov/archives/speech/joint-soviet-united-states-statement-summit-meeting-geneva.

110 As I watched: You can read President Reagan and Minister Shevardnadze's statements here: "Remarks on Signing the Soviet–United States Nuclear Risk Reduction Centers Agreement," Ronald Reagan Presidential Library & Museum, September 15, 1987, https://www.reaganlibrary.gov/archives/speech/remarks

-signing-soviet-united-states-nuclear-risk-reduction-centers
-agreement.

112 Just imagine: To learn more about an innovative initiative on climate change, see the Climate Parliament, https://www.climate parl.net/.

115 "I never sought": Nelson Mandela, *Long Walk to Freedom* (New York: Little, Brown, 1994), 1132.

116 "We were expected": "Address by Nelson Mandela at Opening of Nobel Square, Cape Town," December 14, 2003, Nelson Rolihlahla Mandela, http://www.mandela.gov.za/mandela_speeches /2003/031214_nobelsquare.htm.

## SECOND VICTORY: BUILD A GOLDEN BRIDGE

119 "My right eye": The dialogue throughout this section is derived from Lawrence Wright, *Thirteen Days in September: The Dramatic Story of the Struggle for Peace* (New York: Alfred A. Knopf, 2014). This quote is on p. 312. Subsequent quotes from Wright's book are cited, and the remainder are reconstructed based on personal communications with participants.

120 "Never! If you do": Ibid., 155.

120 Like the rest: See "Camp David Accords and the Arab-Israeli Peace Process," Office of the Historian, United States Department of State, https://history.state.gov/milestones/1977-1980/camp-david.

122 "to form in the mind": "Devise Definition & Meaning," Merriam-Webster, https://www.merriam-webster.com/dictionary/devise.

126 "Mr. Prime Minister": Wright, *Thirteen Days in September*, 388.

126 "as stated by Ambassador Goldberg": See "President Carter to President Sadat," September 17, 1978, The Jimmy Carter Presidential Library and Museum, https://www.jimmycarterlibrary.gov/re search/camp_david_accords_related_correspondence.

127 "I will accept": Wright, *Thirteen Days in September*, 391.

129 In *The Art of War*: Sun Tzu, *The Art of War: Complete Texts and Commentaries*, translated by Thomas Cleary (Boston: Shambhala, 2003).

130 The setting was: Wright, *Thirteen Days in September*, 77.

## CHAPTER 6: LISTEN

133 *If we could read*: This quote is attributed to Henry Wadsworth Longfellow (quoted material extracted from a quote compendium). See Goodreads, https://www.goodreads.com/quotes/24180-if-we -could-read-the-secret-history-of-our-enemies.

134 The North Korean leader: Zachary Cohen, Ryan Browne, and Nicole Gaouette, "New Missile Test Shows North Korea Capable of Hitting All of US Mainland," CNN, November 30, 2017, https://www .cnn.com/2017/11/28/politics/north-korea-missile-launch/index .html.

134 A star of the world: Adam Kilgore, "Dennis Rodman's Strange, Naive Fascination with North Korea," *Washington Post*, June 23, 2017, https://www.washingtonpost.com/sports/wizards/dennis-rodmans -strange-naive-fascination-with-north-korea/2017/06/23/75e0787e -56aa-11e7-ba90-f5875b7d1876_story.html; Helena Andrews-Dyer, "A Brief Guide to Dennis Rodman's Long, Weird History with North Korea," *Washington Post*, June 12, 2018, https://www.washington post.com/news/reliable-source/wp/2018/06/12/a-brief-guide-to -dennis-rodmans-long-weird-history-with-north-korea/.

136 When Nelson Mandela: Nelson Mandela, *Long Walk to Freedom* (New York: Little, Brown, 1994), 1004.

142 Trump called Kim: Donald J. Trump (@realDonaldTrump), Twitter, September 23, 2017, https://twitter.com/realDonaldTrump /status/911789314169823232; Jacob Pramuk, "Trump Warns North Korea Threats 'Will Be Met with Fire and Fury,'" CNBC, August 8, 2017, https://www.cnbc.com/2017/08/08/trump-warns-north-korea -threats-will-be-met-with-fire-and-fury.html.

142 In return: Krishnadev Calamur, "Why Would North Korea Want to Drop a Hydrogen Bomb in the Ocean?," *The Atlantic*, September 22, 2017, https://www.theatlantic.com/international/arch ive/2017/09/trump-north-korea/540783/.

142 While the three: As noted in a report by the Wilson Center, the summit may not have resulted in the denuclearization of North Korea, but the "major outcome . . . was to change the psychology of the nuclear crisis with North Korea as the initiation of a diplomatic track pushed off consideration of a U.S. military option." See Robert S.

Litwak, *Preventing North Korea's Nuclear Breakout*, The Woodrow Wilson International Center for Scholars, February 2017, updated August 2018, https://www.wilsoncenter.org/sites/default/files/media /documents/book/preventing_north_korea_nuclear_breakout_up dated2018.pdf.

142 Trump was ridiculed: The term "love letters" was coined by the media after President Trump noted at a rally, "And then [Kim Jong Un and I] fell in love, okay? No, really—he wrote me beautiful letters, and they're great letters." See Roberta Rampton, "'We Fell in Love': Trump Swoons over Letters from North Korea's Kim," Reuters, September 30, 2018, https://www.reuters.com/article/us-northkorea -usa-trump/we-fell-in-love-trump-swoons-over-letters-from-north -koreas-kim-idUSKCN1MA03Q.

149 As part of the exercise: These interviews were done under the auspices of the Harvard-NUPI-Trinity Syria Research Project and compiled into a report entitled *Obstacles to a Resolution of the Syrian Conflict* by David W. Lesch with Frida Nome, George Saghir, William Ury, and Matthew Waldman (Oslo: Norwegian Institute of International Affairs, 2013), https://nupi.brage.unit .no/nupi-xmlui/bitstream/handle/11250/284440/NUPI%20rap port%202013-Nome.pdf?sequence=3&isAllowed=y.

154 "Let's start by getting": Personal communication with Father Luís Ugalde, October 2002.

## CHAPTER 7: CREATE

157 *We should never allow*: Mary Parker Follett, *Dynamic Administration: The Collected Papers of Mary Parker Follett*, edited by Henry Metcalf and Lyndall Urwick (London: Harper, 1942), 49.

157 That was the formidable: Andrés Bermúdez Liévano, ed., *La Fase Exploratoria del Proceso de Paz: Una Mirada desde Adentro*, Institute for Integrated Transitions, 2019, https://ifit-transitions.org/wp -content/uploads/2021/03/La-fase-exploratoria-del-proceso-de-paz .pdf, 58.

158 In those fifty years: "Víctimas del Conflicto Armado en Colombia Ya son ocho Millones." *El Tiempo*, April, 2016, https://www.el tiempo.com/archivo/documento/CMS-16565045.

159 The most recent one: "Previous Peace Negotiations Attempts with the FARC-EP," Open Library of the Colombian Peace Process, https://bapp.com.co/en/previous-peace-negotiations-attempts-with-the-farc-ep/.

165 But during the elections: "Colombia's Peace Process Through 2016," Congressional Research Service, December 31, 2016, https://crsreports.congress.gov/product/pdf/R/R42982/16; "Auto No. 075 de 2022," Jurisdicción Especial para la Paz, April 22, 2022, https://jurinfo.jep.gov.co/normograma/compilacion/docs/pdf/Auto_SRVR-075_07-abril-2022.pdf.

165 The previous attempt: Camilo González Posso, "El Caguán Irrepetible," Indepaz, July 2009, https://www.indepaz.org.co/wp-content/uploads/2012/03/721_EL-CAGUAN-IRREPETIBLE.pdf.

166 I was asking them: William Zartman and Maureen Berman, *The Practical Negotiator* (New Haven, CT: Yale University Press, 1982), 89.

167 The agenda turned: This framework agreement, called the General Accord to End the Conflict and Build a Stable, Enduring Peace, was signed on August 26, 2012. Read the agreement in both English and Spanish: "Acuerdo General para la Terminación del Conflicto y la Construcción de una Paz Estable y Duradera," United Nations Peacemaker, https://peacemaker.un.org/colombia-generalaccordendconflict2012.

168 "I am convinced that": "Alocución del Presidente Santos sobre el Acuerdo General para la Terminación del Conflicto," The Open Library of the Colombian Peace Process, September 4, 2012, https://www.bapp.com.co/documento/alocucion-del-presidente-santos-sobre-el-acuerdo-general-para-la-terminacion-del-conflicto-2/.

168 The result was: See "Final Agreement to End the Armed Conflict and Build a Stable and Lasting Peace," The Open Library of the Colombian Peace Process, November 24, 2016, https://bapp.com.co/en/final-agreement-to-end-the-armed-conflict-and-build-a-stable-and-lasting-peace/. For a summary, see "Summary of Colombia's Agreement to End Conflict and Build Peace," OCHA, September 30, 2016, https://reliefweb.int/attachments/bfc0aafb-a534-3c75-9c26-30e9b2c367c8/summary-of-colombias-peace-agreement.pdf.

176 Finding it challenging: Allison Sparks, *Tomorrow Is Another Coun-*

*try: The Inside Story of South Africa's Road to Change* (Chicago: University of Chicago Press, 1996), 4.

177 As my fellow anthropologist: I highly recommend Arrien's book *The Four-Fold Way: Walking the Paths of the Warrior, Teacher, Healer, and Visionary* (San Francisco: HarperSanFrancisco, 1993).

## CHAPTER 8: ATTRACT

179 *It always seems*: Quote attributed to Nelson Mandela (quoted material extracted from a quote compendium). See Goodreads, https://www.goodreads.com/quotes/36606-it-always-seems-impossible-until-it-s-done.

183 Step by step: William Ury, *Talk Out or Walk Out: The Role and Control of Conflict in a Kentucky Coal Mine*, Harvard University Graduate School of Arts and Sciences, July 22, 1982.

184 In my classes: You can read the full fable on the Library of Congress website at https://read.gov/aesop/143.html.

187 Without his ability: See "Security Council Resolution 242: The Situation in the Middle East," United Nations Peacemaker, https://peacemaker.un.org/middle-east-resolution242.

193 At the end of November: "Chronology of U.S.-North Korean Nuclear and Missile Diplomacy," Arms Control Association, April 2022, https://www.armscontrol.org/factsheets/dprkchron.

193 "What do you think": John Bolton, *The Room Where It Happened: A White House Memoir* (New York: Simon & Schuster, 2020), 56.

196 "A nuclear button": Bruce Harrison et al., "Kim Jong Un Highlights His 'Nuclear Button,' Offers Olympic Talks," NBC News, December 31, 2017, https://www.nbcnews.com/news/north-korea/kim-says-north-korea-s-nuclear-weapons-will-prevent-war-n833781.

197 "Will someone from his": Donald J. Trump (@realDonaldTrump), Twitter, January 2, 2018, https://twitter.com/realDonaldTrump/status/948355557022420992.

197 "And then": Roberta Rampton, "'We Fell in Love': Trump Swoons over Letters from North Korea's Kim," Reuters, September 30, 2018, https://www.reuters.com/article/us-northkorea-usa-trump/we-fell-in-love-trump-swoons-over-letters-from-north-koreas-kim-idUSKCN1MA03Q.

198 Trump praised Kim: David A. Graham, "Trump's Effusive, Unsettling Flattery of Kim Jong Un," *Atlantic*, June 12, 2018, https://www.theatlantic.com/politics/archive/2018/06/trumps-effusive-unsettling-flattery-of-kim-jong-un/562619/.

198 "The World has taken": Donald J. Trump (@realDonaldTrump), Twitter, June 13, 2018, https://twitter.com/realDonaldTrump/status/1006694541083021312.

198 Landing back: Donald J. Trump (@realDonaldTrump), Twitter, June 13, 2018, https://twitter.com/realDonaldTrump/status/1006837823469735936.

198 North Korean media: Justin McCurry, "Kim Jong-Un un Hailed Victor in 'Meeting of Century' by North Korean Media," *Guardian*, June 13, 2018, https://www.theguardian.com/world/2018/jun/13/kim-jong-un-north-korea-summit-trump-visit-kcna.

201 Two weeks later: "US–North Korea: Trump and Kim Hold Historic Meeting at DMZ," BBC, June 30, 2019, https://www.bbc.com/news/world-asia-48817898.

## THIRD VICTORY: ENGAGE THE THIRD SIDE

204 "This secret, swift": "Address During the Cuban Missile Crisis," October 22, 1962, John F. Kennedy Presidential Library and Museum, https://www.jfklibrary.org/archives/other-resources/john-f-kennedy-speeches/cuba-radio-and-television-report-19621022.

205 If that crisis: William Burr, "Cold War Estimates of Deaths in Nuclear Conflict," *Bulletin of the Atomic Scientists*, January 4, 2023, https://thebulletin.org/2023/01/cold-war-estimates-of-deaths-in-nuclear-conflict/.

205 Southern Florida looked like: Christopher Woody, "56 Years Ago, the Cuban Missile Crisis Took the World to the Brink of Nuclear War—Here's What It Looked Like from Sunny Florida Beaches," Business Insider, October 28, 2018, https://www.businessinsider.com/iconic-photos-of-the-cuban-missile-crisis-from-florida-beaches-2018-10.

206 What my American: Robert McNamara et al., *Argument Without End: In Search of Answers to the Vietnam Tragedy* (New York: Pub-

lic Affairs, 1999); "The Cuban Missile Crisis," Arms Control Association, https://www.armscontrol.org/act/2002-11/features/cuban-missile-crisis.

206 "Had a U.S. invasion": Martin Tolchin, "U.S. Underestimated Soviet Force in Cuba During '62 Missile Crisis," *New York Times*, January 15, 1992, https://www.nytimes.com/1992/01/15/world/us-underestimated-soviet-force-in-cuba-during-62-missile-crisis.html?.

206 He also knew: "The Cuban Missile Crisis, October 1962," Office of the Historian, United States Department of State, https://history.state.gov/milestones/1961-1968/cuban-missile-crisis.

207 I had the privilege: My interviews with the Kua took place in Bothapatiou, Botswana, in May 1989.

210 After decades of: For more information on the ANC, including eyewitness interviews, see "South Africa: Overcoming Apartheid, Building Democracy," Michigan State University, https://overcomingapartheid.msu.edu/multimedia.php?kid=163-582-27.

210 "Awful things were": "Tutus [*sic*] Message Forgiveness Peace," Crain's Grand Rapids Business, March 28, 2003, https://grbj.com/uncategorized/tutus-message-forgiveness-peace/.

210 "My best guess": Personal communication with Sir Robin Renwick, UK ambassador to South Africa, May 1989.

210 I had arranged: For a short biography of David Webster, see "David Joseph Webster," South African History Online, https://www.sahistory.org.za/people/david-joseph-webster.

211 "You must believe": I recall hearing Archbishop Tutu saying this in his speech in January 1995.

213 *Ubuntu* is the essence: In a 1997 lecture, Nelson Mandela explained the concept of *Ubuntu*: "The spirit of Ubuntu[—]that profound African sense that we are human only through the humanity of other human beings—is not a parochial phenomenon, but has added globally to our common search for a better world." See "Renewal and Renaissance—Towards a New World Order: Lecture by President Nelson Mandela at the Oxford Centre for Islamic Studies," Nelson Mandela Foundation, July 11, 1997, http://www.mandela.gov.za/mandela_speeches/1997/970711_oxford.htm.

213 "We have triumphed": Nelson Mandela, "Nelson Mandela's

Inaugural Speech—Pretoria, 10 May 1994," University of Pennsylvania, https://www.africa.upenn.edu/Articles_Gen/Inaugural_Speech _17984.html.

## CHAPTER 9: HOST

219 *He drew a circle*: The poem is entitled "Outwitted." You can read it, along with Edwin Markham's other poems, in *The Shoes of Happiness and Other Poems* (New York: The Century Company, 1913).

229 Taking care of another: To go more into depth on the philosophical concept of hosting, I recommend: Emmanuel Levinas, *Totality and Infinity: An Essay on Exteriority*, 4th ed., trans. Alphonso Lingis (Pittsburgh, PA: Springer Nature, 2011); David J. Gauthier, "Levinas and the Politics of Hospitality," *History of Political Thought* 28, no. 1 (spring 2007), Exeter, England: 158–80, https://www.jstor.org /stable/26222669.

232 Responding to the: To learn more about the Abraham Path Initiative, see www.abrahampath.org/.

233 Within a few short: Ben Lerwill, "10 of the Best New Walking Trails," *National Geographic*, April 8, 2019, https://www.national geographic.co.uk/travel/2019/04/10-best-new-walking-trails.

234 I am reminded: I first heard this story from Elias Amidon, but you can read the original story in Chrétien de Troyes, *Perceval: The Story of the Grail*, translated by Burton Raffel (New Haven, CT: Yale University Press, 1999).

236 Rather than wait: "Colombia Conflict Victims Join FARC Peace Talks in Cuba," BBC, August 17, 2014, https://www.bbc.com /news/world-latin-america-28822683.

237 It was the story: To learn more about Pastora Mira's story, see TEDx Talks, "Superando el Dolor: Reconciliación | Pastora Mira | TEDxBogotá," YouTube, September 23, 2019, https://www.youtube .com/watch?v=2SPaS_C1PXU.

240 I was reminded: Frans de Waal's research on primates is detailed in his book *Peacemaking Among Primates* (Cambridge, MA: Harvard University Press, 1990). Date per https://www.hup.harvard.edu /catalog.php?isbn=9780674659216.

## CHAPTER 10: HELP

245 *There is always*: Frances Perkins was the first woman to serve as a US cabinet secretary from 1933 to 1945. The text of the quote, along with more information about her life, can be found in "The Woman Behind the New Deal," Frances Perkins Center, https://francesperkinscenter.org/life-new/.

246 The peace talks: To learn more about the peace talks in Havana, I recommend this report: Andrés Bermúdez Liévano, ed., *Los Debates de la Habana, una Mirada desde Adentro*, Institute for Integrated Transitions, 2018, https://ifit-transitions.org/wp-content/uploads/2021/03/Los-debates-de-La-Habana-Una-mirada-desde-adentro.pdf.

246 There were more than: "Víctimas Conflicto Armado," Unidad para las Víctimas, https://www.unidadvictimas.gov.co/es/registro-unico-de-victimas-ruv/37394.

254 A terrible civil war: "Conflict Between Turkey and Armed Kurdish Groups," Center for Preventative Action, Council on Foreign Relations, April 25, 2023, https://www.cfr.org/global-conflict-tracker/conflict/conflict-between-turkey-and-armed-kurdish-groups.

## CHAPTER 11: SWARM

264 *When spider webs*: As I recall, the proverb is "halt a lion." Yet this proverb can be found in "Africa's Proverb of the Day," BBC, January 1, 2013, https://www.bbc.com/news/world-africa-20884831.

266 "In the tech world": To learn more about how "swarming" is used in the tech industry, see Marty Cagan, "Milestone Swarming," Silicon Valley Product Group, May 21, 2014, https://www.svpg.com/milestone-swarming/; Toby McClean, "The Collective Power of Swarm Intelligence in AI and Robotics," *Forbes*, May 13, 2021, https://www.forbes.com/sites/forbestechcouncil/2021/05/13/the-collective-power-of-swarm-intelligence-in-ai-and-robotics/?sh=266c2beb252f.

275 "I honestly believe": Personal communication, June 26, 2018.

281 A tragic example: Dave Davies, "30 Years After the Siege, 'Waco'

Examines What Led to the Catastrophe," NPR, January 25, 2023, https://www.npr.org/2023/01/25/1151283229/waco-branch-david ian-david-koresh-jeff-guinn. For an in-depth analysis of the negotiations, see Malcolm Gladwell, "Sacred and Profane," *New Yorker*, March 24, 2014, https://www.newyorker.com/magazine/2014/03/31 /sacred-and-profane-4.

281 "When I'm dealing with": Diane Coutu, "Negotiating Without a Net: A Conversation with the NYPD's Dominick J. Misino," *Harvard Business Review*, October 2002, https://hbr.org/2002/10/neg otiating-without-a-net-a-conversation-with-the-nypds-dominick-j -misino.

282 "Hostage situations can be": George Kohlrieser, "How to Manage Conflict: Six Essentials from Hostage Negotiations to the Boardroom," LinkedIn, April 26, 2018, https://www.linkedin.com/pulse /how-manage-conflict-six-essentials-from-hostage-george-kohl rieser.

282 He founded an organization: To learn more about Cure Violence Global, see www.cvg.org. I want to credit Dr. Gary Slutkin with introducing me to the concept of access, credibility, and trust.

283 I encouraged: You can watch the film, which aired on PBS on February 14, 2012, on the PBS website at https https://www.pbs .org/wgbh/frontline/documentary/interrupters/transcript/.

286 "Our conflict was so": President Santos made this remark upon receiving the Program on Negotiation (PON) Great Negotiator Award in 2017. Although there is no recording of the event, you can watch a similar roundtable here: "Advice for Peace: Ending Civil War in Colombia," Harvard Law School, October 11, 2012, https://www .pon.harvard.edu/daily/teaching-negotiation-daily/advice-for-peace -ending-civil-war-in-colombia/.

286 "De Waal was conducting": To learn more about the work of Frans de Waal, I recommend *Peacemaking Among Primates* (Cambridge, MA: Harvard University Press, 1990); *The Bonobo and the Atheist: In Search of Humanism Among the Primates* (New York: W. W. Norton, 2013); and *Mama's Last Hug: Animal Emotions and What They Tell Us About Ourselves* (New York: W. W. Norton, 2019). Date per https://www.hup.harvard.edu/catalog.php?isbn=9780674659216.

287 "Feelings of animosity: One of the biggest mobilizations in Co-

lombia's recent history occurred in 2008, when more than a million people marched against the FARC in Bogotá. See "Colombians in Huge FARC Protest," BBC, February 4, 2008, http://news.bbc.co .uk/2/hi/americas/7225824.stm.

288 The first surprising move: "Colombia and Venezuela Restore Diplomatic Relations," BBC, August 11, 2010, https://www.bbc.com /news/world-latin-america-10926003.

290 "Those who had met": For more about this event, see "Colombia Peace Deal: Historic Agreement Is Signed," BBC, September 27, 2016, https://www.bbc.com/news/world-latin-america-37477202.

291 Colombian citizens filled: "Thousands March in Support of Colombia Peace Deal," Deutsche Welle, October 13, 2016, https://www .dw.com/en/thousands-march-in-support-of-colombia-peace-deal/a -36028584.

292 "Six years ago": Juan Manuel Santos, Nobel Lecture, "Peace in Colombia: From the Impossible to the Possible," The Nobel Prize, December 10, 2016, https://www.nobelprize.org/prizes/peace/2016 /santos/lecture/.

## CONCLUSION: A WORLD OF POSSIBILITIES

295 Hope is not: Rebecca Solnit, Hope in the Dark: Untold Histories, Wild Possibilities (Edinburgh: Canongate Books, 2016). Available at: https://www.perlego.com/book/1456880/hope-in-the-dark-the -untold-history-of-people-power-pdf.

295 "Has anyone here": TEDx Talks, "What's Wrong with Me? Absolutely Nothing | Gabi Ury | TEDxSanDiago," YouTube, December 31, 2014, at https://www.youtube.com/watch?v=bDbN8R6Gb6Q.

305 Fifty years ago: Live, Learn, Evolve, "The Ancient Shambhala Warrior Prophecy," YouTube, May 9, 2020, https://www.youtube .com/watch?v=hWJWZd2UMKw.

306 So I ask you: Pirke Avot: The Sayings of the Jewish Fathers, trans. Joseph I. Gorfinkle, Project Gutenberg: 50, https://www.gutenberg .org/ebooks/8547.

# INDEX

# ABOUT THE AUTHOR

William Ury has been a student of human conflicts for almost half a century. As an anthropologist and negotiator, he has a passion for helping people, organizations, and societies get to yes, even when it may seem impossibly difficult.

The cofounder of Harvard's Program on Negotiation, he is the coauthor of *Getting to Yes*, the world's bestselling guide to negotiation, which has been translated into more than thirty-four languages. He is the author of many other award-winning and bestselling books on negotiation, including *Getting Past No*, *The Third Side*, *The Power of a Positive No*, and *Getting to Yes with Yourself*. Ury has taught negotiation to tens of thousands of leaders in business, government, and civil society. He has two popular TED Talks.

One of the world's best-known negotiation specialists, Ury has worked as a mediator and negotiation advisor in conflicts ranging from labor strikes and boardroom battles to political fights and wars around the world. During the 1980s, he helped the US and Soviet governments create nuclear risk reduction centers, designed to avert an accidental nuclear war. More recently, he served for seven years as a senior negotiation adviser to the president of Colombia to help bring an end to a fifty-year civil war.

Ury is founder of the Abraham Path, a long-distance walking route across the Middle East that seeks to inspire mutual understanding, respect, and hope. He is also the cofounder of the Climate Parliament, which offers legislative leaders and civil society around the world a problem-solving forum to accelerate solutions to the climate crisis.

Ury received his BA from Yale and his PhD from Harvard in social anthropology. He lives in Colorado, where he loves to walk in the mountains, his favorite balcony on the world.

For further information, please visit www.williamury.com.